A CODE TO KEEP

D0058784

Ernest C. Brace

Hellgate Press, Central Point, Oregon

A short portion of this account appeared, in slightly different form, in the November 1978 issue of the American Legion Magazine.

Originally published by St. Martin's Press.
Editor: Jared Kieling
Copyeditor: David Smith

ISBN: 1-55571-623-7

Library of Congress Cataloging-in-Publication Data

Brace, Ernest C.
  A Code to Keep / Ernest C. Brace.
    p. cm.
  Originally published: New York : St. Martin's Press, 1988.
  ISBN 1-55571-623-7 (paper)
    1. Brace, Ernest C. 2. Vietnamese Conflict, 1961-1975--Prisoners and prisons, North Vietnamese. 3. Vietnamese Conflict, 1961-1975--personal narratives, American. 4. Prisoners of war--United States--Biography. 5. Prisoners of war—Vietnam—Biography. I. Title.

DS559.4.B73 2001
959.704'37--dc21
[B]
                                   2001051669

*Nancy, without whom I would
have drifted back into the world
of never-never land and probably
never told my story.*

I am grateful to Charles Hood,
Dean of the University of Montana
School of Journalism,
for his assistance in the writing
of my story of survival
in the prison camps.

Foreword

In his book *Man's Search for Meaning*, Victor Frankl tells movingly of his captivity in Nazi Germany, and of man's ability to overcome evil and control his own destiny. He writes that under such conditions, "everything can be taken from a man but one thing: the last of human freedoms-to choose one's attitude in any given set of circumstances, to choose one's own way."

In October of 1968, I met a man who had chosen his own way. I had been a prisoner of war in Hanoi for almost a year, and again found myself in a prolonged period of solitary confinement. After hearing a commotion in the cell next door, I tapped on the wall to communicate, and thus began my friendship with a true American hero, Ernest Brace.

Ernie's imprisonment has no parallel in American history. A civilian pilot, Ernie was captured in May of 1965 at a small airstrip in Laos. After being marched to Dien Bien Phu, he was locked in a bamboo cage. The cage, three feet wide and four feet tall, was to be his home for the next forty months. Ernie's only extended periods of freedom came during three escape attempts, the last of which earned him a week buried up to his neck in a pit. To ensure that he did not again try to escape, he spent the next two years in the cage with his legs in stocks, leaving him unable to walk when he arrived in Hanoi.

His bravery and fortitude did not diminish when he joined the hundreds of military officers held prisoner in Hanoi. Offered an early release as a civilian, he declined, citing solidarity with fellow Americans who would accept release only in order of capture. Far from capitalizing on his status as a civilian, Ernie risked torture and possible death to become one of the prime links in the prison communications system that sustained us for many long years.

More than five hundred Americans were lost in Laos. Only nine survived and were released. Ernie's book is therefore a unique addition to existing accounts of the Vietnam POW experience, and to the literature on the war itself

His tale, however, has a more universal significance. One of the factors that enabled Americans to survive up to ten years of captivity in Vietnam was the faith and comradeship of our fellow countrymen.

For over three years, however, Ernie could rely only on his own boundless strength and faith to see him through. The account of courage contained in this book is timeless. I am proud to call Ernie Brace a friend.

Senator John McCain
Washington, D.C.
June 1987

1

My feet are in stocks, my neck's tied to a pole
What food I get is shoved in through a hole
At night I lie down and my hands are tied
And the rope is stretched to a post outside

I see a light coming toward the cage down the jungle path. It must be the sergeant doing his bedcheck. I slide down toward the leg stocks as far as possible. This puts a strain on my neck rope. When the soldier jerks the rope I let out a little cry to let him know I am still tied in securely. The sergeant says something to the guard in the lean-to, laughs at what he said, and starts back up the path that leads to their camp hidden in the jungle.

As soon as I know the guard has settled down in his thatch-covered shelter about fifteen feet from the side of my cage, I scoot back up to take the tension off my neck. I've given up untying my hands at night. There's no feeling below my wrists anyway. My sole purpose at this point is just to get as comfortable as possible and survive another night in this bamboo cage in the jungles of North Vietnam.

My clothes stink of urine and the results of diarrhea when I can't get my trousers down to shit through the slats of my bamboo bed. I'm cold, wet, and miserable. At times I want to die, and at other times I know I'll get out of this alive. Right now all I want to do is sleep, but it won't come easy.

Even in the dark I have a sense of being buried in a green mist. As I slip into a box I've created in my mind, another larger box takes shape around the first, and I can see the boxes advancing through the green haze to fit over each other.

I try to reverse the process and make the boxes get smaller rather than larger. The largest box develops into a building with large white columns, and the green becomes a lawn. I'm walking into the headquarters building of the Marine Corps School at Quantico, Virginia.

July 7, 1961, my son Patrick's birthday, and I'm going into the building to attend a general court-martial—mine! I hear a plane taking off and turn to look. I recognize it as a T-28. Fighting back a tear, I proceed into the building and head for the designated chamber where I know my career is coming to an end.

"Captain Ernest C. Brace, having been found guilty of deserting the scene of an aircraft accident, this court sentences you to be dismissed from the Naval Service." I looked at the officers who had sat on the board. Some of them I had known since the Korean War. I didn't blame them for what they had done. Based on what they knew, it was the only choice they had.

The tears burned, but I couldn't let them out. I did an about-face and went over to thank my legal counsel. I had to get out of there; I could find out later on what one had to do to check out of the service after he was dismissed. Fourteen years down the tubes, as we'd say in the Marines.

I left the building as I had entered, pausing to look over the vast expanse of green lawn that sloped down toward the Air Station. Green, green, everything was green.

The early sun is streaming through the bamboo canopy above my cage. The green leaves are casting green shadows across my green mosquito net. In about an hour, a guard dressed in a green uniform will come to untie my neck rope and put me in a sitting position with my feet still in the stocks.

Green has come to symbolize what I hate about this place— or is it this situation? My mind is going, and I have to slip into another world or I might start screaming.

Strange that I can feel this way about the jungle. I always hated the dry desert and loved the lush green of the jungle I flew over for so many months. One thing to look down at it, another to be immersed in it as I am.

I take myself back to my day of capture, and then back one more day, because that was when I set myself up for this experience. I seem to have developed a need to keep my emotional wounds open so I won't forget what being careless has cost me.

Despite the fact that I had the small windshield vent open, it was still hot in the cockpit of the small single-engine plane I was flying. I wiped my brow with the sleeve of my jungle suit and glanced at my Rolex. If I didn't find Terry's patrol soon, I'd have to head back to Boum Lao and report no luck. We were too close to the China border to use radios. I was relying on the patrol to use visual signals to indicate their position.

There was a flash of light off to my left. I banked steeply toward the flash and saw it again. It was a signal mirror; I'd found Terry's patrol.

Tony, my cargo kicker, was already getting set for the drop as I came around on a heading to pass over the clearing where I had seen the signal. I could now see the small orange and white signal cloth, they had laid out, so I knew it was our friendlies.

In this area you made only one pass, for several reasons. Everything had to go out in this one drop. If you stayed around too long, you pinpointed the position for the enemy, or you started to draw fire. Having dropped down to 300 feet I was set, and just before the signal cloth passed under my plane's nose I jerked the T-handle and let everything go. Dust swirled through the cabin and cockpit as the ammo boxes dropped from the aircraft. From this altitude you only got one swing of the parachute before the gear was on the ground.

I put the aircraft into a steep turn and glanced back at the clearing to see a group of men in jungle camouflage dragging the ammunition boxes and parachutes back into the jungle. Tony was already pulling the static lines back into the ship through the trapdoor. I rolled out on a heading to take us back to Boum Lao.

Looking back, I could no longer see the clearing. I marked my map where I thought it was located, so that Terry would have that information.

Tony closed and latched the drop door and then climbed up into the copilot's seat. Tony Alfonte was a Filipino mechanic who flew as kicker on these missions because he enjoyed the extra hazard pay. We were a team of two flying for USAID out of Chieng Mai, Thailand. I really think Tony would have flown without the extra pay because he liked to stay close to his Pilatus Turbo-Porter.

I was anticipating a promotion to major at the age of twenty-nine when in 1961 my charmed life came to an abrupt and sensational end. There were bizarre front-page news stories in the *Washington Post* about the Marine war hero who was accused of bailing out of a properly functioning aircraft in an effort to fake his own death and desert his wife and family. Then there was the highly publicized federal court trial, in which he was acquitted. Finally there was the court-martial followed by dismissal in disgrace from the Marine Corps. The Marines constituted the only life I had known since I had left home at the age of sixteen.

I managed to continue flying after I moved the family to California. Helicopter pilots were in demand. Over the next few years I flew forest fires, power line construction, and offshore oil jobs. In June 1964, through a past connection I had with the CIA, I was asked if I would be interested in a high-risk civilian flying job in Southeast Asia, a job that contributed directly to U.S. foreign policy objectives in that part of the world. I took the job immediately. It wasn't a return to the military, I knew, but it was probably the closest I would ever get again.

I had been flying out of a base in Chieng Mai, Thailand, when I made the late-afternoon ammunition drop to the Lao and Thai special forces troops. It had been the last chore of a routine day, noteworthy only because of what would happen the following morning.

Though I had led an eventful life until now, the real adventure lay ahead. I was about to begin what an intelligence document suggests was the most extraordinary POW tenure served by an American in the war in Southeast Asia, especially considering that that American was a civilian.

On this day before my capture, I was a relative newcomer to Indochina. I had joined Bird and Son the previous July, flying out of the large AID complex at Vientiane, the administrative capital of Laos. In November I was transferred to Chieng Mai, an ancient walled city surrounded by teak forests in the mountains of northern Thailand.

From Chieng Mai I flew daily missions "upcountry" in my single-engine Pilatus Turbo-Porter, a Swiss-made utility aircraft designed for mountain flying. Some days I took Thai Border Patrol Police on missions aimed at halting narcotics traffic across the Lao-Thai border.

I flew American AID officials to remote spots where no true airstrip yet existed. These areas were populated by hill tribesmen over whom the Thai and Laotian governments were trying to establish authority. I would land in the elephant grass on some mountain meadow, then hike with my passengers to possible sites for airstrips that could be slashed from the jungle and used for para-military special operations bases. If it was impossible to land in an area where they wanted an airstrip, an adviser would parachute in, along with some of the Thai Border Patrol Police. In about ten days they would have an acceptable strip built.

From such bases, Lao and Thai special forces soldiers operating as "civic action teams" would distribute photos of the appropriate king and royal family, establish schools and hospitals, introduce dried fish to the iodine-deficient diets of the tribesmen, and encourage the growing of alternative crops to replace the poppy fields that produced the region's sole cash crop, opium. An important goal of these American-advised teams was, of course, to enlist the support of the upcountry population in fighting the Communists.

On other days, such as this one, I flew supplies and people to airstrips that had already been established in northern Thailand and western Laos. Terry's troops, whom I had just resupplied with ammunition, were part of a civic action team based at Boum Lao, Laos. Terry was their American adviser.

A few minutes after the drop, I was back over Boum Lao, where my captivity would begin the next day. You wouldn't find this village on most maps. It's just a cluster of thatched huts on bamboo stilts, straddling a river at the southern end of a twisting mountain valley. Boum Lao wasn't the only airstrip I flew into regularly that was considered to be in territory claimed by the Neo Lao Hak Set, the Pathet Lao. Many of the civic action teams were working within Communist territory, and most had created small airstrips if they intended to remain in the area for any length of time.

The Communist guerrillas had renamed this area Udon Sai and had established a stronghold as close as Moung Sai, a village at the opposite end of the valley.

Right now the Pathet Lao were not the base's main concern. Intelligence reports placed units of the North Vietnamese Army in the area, and these big-brother allies of the ragtag Pathet Lao were disciplined, well equipped, and well led. They weren't supposed to be in Laos, of course. North Vietnam had never admitted that it had any troops within the borders of its smaller neighbor to the west; such an admission would have made it official that Hanoi was violating the provisions of the 1962 Geneva Accords, which had established Laos as a neutral country and forbade the presence of foreign troops and the interference of foreign nations.

Few Americans out here were disposed to make much of a fuss over the illegal presence of the NVA in Laos, however, because the United States itself was fudging on the Geneva agreements. Though no combat troops had been sent to this Idaho-sized kingdom of 2 million inhabitants, Americans like Terry advised paramilitary units; the CIA was footing the bill for a clandestine army and had sent agents to advise it; American F-105 fighter-bombers flew daily out of Thailand to hit Communist supply routes along the Ho Chi Minh Trail in the Laos panhandle; and civilians like me supplied Royal Lao forces with paramilitary assistance that included ferrying ammunition, soldiers, and Communist prisoners.

I was not alarmed by the intelligence about the North Vietnamese troops. The NVA spotted in Terry's area were well north of Boum Lao, and they seldom ventured any farther south. Moreover, Terry had sent out patrols, scouting to the northeast and northwest, and had received no reports of enemy contact.

By air, Boum Lao was only seventy-five miles northwest of Luang Prabang, the ancient capital of Laos where King Savang Vatthana and his royal family drank vintage wine and conversed in French learned in the colonial days before the fall of Dien Bien Phu. But those few miles might have been thousands, because the terrain surrounding the village was, like most of Laos, mountain-spined, jungle-choked, and roadless.

The isolated natives were still unfamiliar enough with twentieth-century technology to rush up the path from the village and gather along the edge of the runway when my silver plane with its black Laotian registration letters appeared overhead. I could see them today, in their black pajamas and coolie hats, as I guided the plane in on its final approach over the rice paddies and jungle that surrounded the strip.

The Turbo-Porter would be considered modern looking only in a place like this. Its high-set, strut-supported wings, boxy fuselage, and fixed landing gear were reminiscent of Lindbergh's Spirit of St. Louis, but the looks were deceptive. This Swiss airplane with the graceless square tail was the last word in STOL (Short Takeoff and Landing) aircraft design.

Its French turboprop engine would burn anything from stove oil to jet fuel and was fully reversible, enabling the plane to land with a full load on airstrips scarcely four hundred feet long. Its fifty-foot wingspan was just a yard longer than that of Lindbergh's Ryan, but the plane was big enough to carry half a ton of cargo and sturdy enough to take the punishment required of an upcountry airplane. Its reinforced tail-wheel strut was shielded by a makeshift cowcatcher device that fended off the stumps, snags, and boulders it encountered on newly hewn runways.

Boum Lao's airstrip, cut out of the jungle above the village only a few months before, was a luxurious six hundred feet long. It was what we called a one-way strip. You landed in one direction, turned around, and took off in the direction you had come from. I touched down and taxied toward the far end, where trenches had been dug along the jungle's edge. In the trees on the right, the south side, was the civic action team's command, bamboo-and-thatch huts clustered near the path that led from the runway down to the village.

The suntanned young American who came out to meet my plane spent most of his days alongside the soldiers he advised, blowing out stumps, falling trees, and doing the other jobs necessary to the mission of the civic action team.

Terry Burke looked fresh and clean now, having just emerged from a cold bath in the river below the runway. Shirtless, he wore khaki shorts, rubber shower thongs, and a Smith & Wesson .38-caliber pistol in a shoulder holster. I knew that Terry never went anywhere without that pistol. I had heard the Thai soldiers kid the young American about taking it with him even when he bathed.

Terry looked younger than his twenty-five or twenty-six years. Before coming to Southeast Asia, he had been a U.S. Marine Embassy Security Guard stationed with the State Department in Rome, and then a college student in Virginia. As a member of the U.S. Marine Guards, he told me, he had once served as a body-guard in Geneva for UN Secretary General Dag Hammarskjold. I first met him at Long Tieng, the headquarters of the Armee Clandestine, the CIA-financed force of Hmong tribesmen operating out of the mountains north of Vientiane.

I couldn't say whether Terry Burke worked for the CIA. It wasn't a question one asked out here, nor did it seem an unimportant one at the time. I knew that my friend was a "coordinator" assigned to the secret army, and that he often worked with Major General Vang Pao, the legendary Hmong leader who had been fighting the Communists for two decades. Terry had been working out of Boum Lao only a few weeks. My frequent supply visits from Chieng Mai had given us a chance to get to know each other a little better.

Terry was relieved to hear that his detachment had been found and that a successful drop had been made. The patrol had not reported in by radio for several days and he had been worried that it might have run into trouble.

The atmosphere around the airstrip was relaxed. The smoke wafting from the kitchen hut in the compound signaled the end of the working day and the approach of the evening meal. Thai and Lao soldiers in khaki fatigue pants and white T-shirts chatted together under the trees or headed down to the river to wash and fill their canteens.

Terry had been informed earlier in the day about enemy activity in Moung Hok. I knew that the village was a day's walk away and didn't pose much of a threat. To make sure, though, Terry talked with the Laotian lieutenant colonel, who had arrived recently from Vientiane, and suggested that a good perimeter defense be set up. Before I climbed back into the Turbo-Porter, I asked my American friend whether there was anything he needed the next day.

"The weekend's coming up," Terry said with a grin, "and we're completely out of beer."

2

Tony Alfonte and I took off for home, heading southwest toward Thailand with the sun low on the horizon ahead of us. Our route took us over John Milan, an American AID paramedic whom I had dropped off the previous day at his crude bamboo-and-thatch hospital at Huie Kan in the jungle along the Thai-Lao border.

A former Special Forces medic who left the Army after a tour in Vietnam, John lived with the natives, treating them for goiter and dysentery, doing dental work with a foot-powered drill, and digging bullets out of the victims of the intertribal gunfights that were commonplace in the area. Recently the American medic had extracted a cleaning rod from the chest of a villager who had been trying to clean an ancient rifle that turned out to be loaded.

I was John Milan's only link with civilization, and the paramedic liked it that way. This was the life he had chosen, ministering to people who were more accustomed to witch doctors' potions than to aspirin and antibiotics. When I was over John's hospital, I called him on the radio and asked him if there was anything he needed. There wasn't, and I promised to check in with him the following day.

I crossed over into Thailand, still flying a southwesterly heading toward Chieng Mai. The terrain hadn't changed. We still looked down on forested mountains and deep-cut valleys, but we were in friendlier country now.

This nation of 21 million, once known as Siam, was the United States' staunchest ally in Southeast Asia. Its military regime was fiercely anti-Communist and determined to thwart North Vietnamese and Pathet Lao efforts to extend their struggles across the border into Thailand. Only a few weeks before, Thailand's foreign minister had been in the United States strongly endorsing President Lyndon Johnson's Southeast Asia policy of "standing firm against aggression."

Soon we were over Chieng Mai, a picturesque city of 60,000 set in a wide green valley at the eastern foot of an imposing mountain called Doi Suthep. The travel writers called it "beautiful and exotic," and to an American pilot who had grown up in Redford, a Detroit suburb, the description seemed accurate.

Founded in 1296, Chieng Mai had been the capital of an independent kingdom for hundreds of years, and of a Siamese principality after that. The king of Thailand still used the city as his summer capital, retreating each year to the richly tiled palace on Doi Suthep to escape the heat of Bangkok.

Chieng Mai's medieval wall and moat still ringed the older part of the city, and its temples with their steeply canted roofs and spired domes housed images of Buddha that dated to the thirteenth century. The most famous of the temples, or wats, overlooked the city from the cliffs of Doi Suthep. From the balustrade of Wat Prabat Doi Suthep, one could see the shallow Nam Ping River twisting through the heart of the city; the red, green, and white splashes of color that would be the smaller wats; and the ancient wall, still well preserved, covered with ivy. Remains of the ancient moat, partially failed, were also visible.

Behind the hillside temple, farther up the mountain, were the Chin Dao caves, where orange-robed monks took visitors to see limestone formations sculpted hundreds of years ago into elephants and other sacred images.

It was dusk by the time I landed at the airport. I rode my motorcycle home through a city that was vastly different, both in size and atmosphere, from the Laotian capital where I previously had been stationed.

Vientiane was a fast-paced city of 150,000 and, as the center of government for a nation in the throes of civil war, was on a war footing. Soldiers and military vehicles were everywhere, and the presence of the enormous American AID mission gave the city an unmistakable Western flavor.

Chieng Mai, on the other hand, was half the size of Vientiane and was still relatively untouched by the war being fought in the jungle only a few hundred miles away. There were soldiers in the streets, to be sure, but not many. The American community, including the AID mission, was so small as to have hardly an impact on the city.

No external influence had been able to disturb the tranquil tempo and almost pastoral atmosphere of Chieng Mai. The ancient wall and moat that I drove by seemed to stand as evidence that here was one spot in volatile Southeast Asia not ruined by the ravages of time, war, and progress. It wasn't surprising that the city had become a haven for those who wanted to escape the frenetic pace of Bangkok.

We lived in a recently built Western-style home. The large lot with a lawn presented a dramatic contrast to the older residential sections, whose houses were built practically on top of each other in the old Thai style. This suburban area was the home of many members of the American community: the doctors who staffed the Chulongakom Medical University and McCormick Presbyterian Hospital; the teachers who taught at the Chieng Mai Co-educational Center, the missionary school my boys attended; the officers and men of the mission that advised the Thai army in this region; the AID people; and the diplomatic service personnel who staffed the U.S. Consulate.

Patricia and the four boys had left home in Los Angeles to join me in Chieng Mai, and they had settled comfortably into the social life of the American community. There were garden parties and bridge clubs. If the kids needed playmates, Patricia could have a party for the children who lived at the Presbyterian boarding school while their missionary parents were upcountry.

The boys, Ernest, eleven, Patrick, nine, Michael, seven, and Cary, three, had collected a small zoo of tropical pets. Parrots perched on bamboo sticks supplied with feeding cups. Monkeys climbed the furniture. An acrobatic white-faced gibbon zipped back and forth like a circus performer on a wire between the house and a front-yard tree. At night she curled up atop a bookcase in the front room. A docile Himalayan moon bear, which Patricia had bought from a passerby when it was a cub, happily prowled the yard like a dog, sleeping in a box in the garage before graduating to a tree by the river that passed behind the house. It didn't seem to mind the wide collar the family had given it, loved its daily meals of rice and sour milk, and showed no interest in leaving the yard. In a few months it had grown from a small ball of brown fur to the size of a full-grown German shepherd.

Wah Nee opened the gate as I drove in past the wrought-iron fence that closed off the front yard from the road. A villager from the north who had come to Chieng Mai to earn enough money to return home and buy the land he had been renting, Wah Nee did yard work and odd jobs, such as pumping the well water up to the large rooftop tank that held the household's water supply. He lived in the servants' quarters in back with his wife Tip, our housekeeper. She also fixed lunch each morning for the older Brace boys to take to school. Their three-year-old son, Kakouhee, was a playmate of Cary's.

I parked my Honda 250 outside a handsome two-story home whose stone-work had been tastefully blended with the landscape. Large windows looked out over a wide teak-decked porch to the tree-shaded front lawn beyond. The backyard sloped to the riverbank, where a willow draped its boughs over the water. Cradled in the branches was what the Thais called a *sala*; a bamboo deck with a thatched roof where the family could sit in the evenings and watch the river as it passed peacefully beneath us. The Nam Ping River probably would rise enough during the rainy season to wash away this little tree house, I had been told.

Patricia greeted me at the door, looking, as always, well groomed and fetching. We had met twelve years ago in Florida. I had been a young Marine aviator fresh from combat duty in Korea and she a nineteen-year-old University of Oklahoma coed.

Bored with college, she had jumped at the chance to deliver a pickup to Miami for her contractor father during an Easter break. She had been then, and still was, a beautiful woman. With her black hair, large eyes, full mouth, and fair complexion, she sometimes reminded people of Elizabeth Taylor in her movie heyday.

As with most marriages, ours had known some bad moments. Somehow we had survived the trauma of my dismissal and my first grim months as a civilian, when it had been tough to find a job. Next week we expected to be celebrating our twelfth anniversary.

After dinner I looked through the house for some beer for Terry Burke. I didn't find any but was able to borrow a case of Japanese Asahi from my next-door neighbor, Lou Allen, a retired U.S. Army colonel attached to the AID mission. I promised to replace the beer in the next few days.

By the time I had stowed the Asahi in the garage, it was dark. The patches of cumulus were gone, leaving an unobstructed view of the stars. Tomorrow would be perfect flying weather, and I could expect another long day in the cockpit. I went into the house.

3

As was his usual practice, Terry Burke had slept the night with his trousers and boots on and his weapons laid out on the mat next to him, so that he could reach them quickly if he needed them. It was just starting to become light out when he was awakened by an explosion and found that the bamboo wall of his hut had been blown away.

The compound was under heavy fire, most of it coming from the airstrip and from the riverbank near the village. Knowing he had little time, he grabbed his map, which had friendly and enemy positions in the area plotted on an acetate overlay, and began cutting it into pieces with his knife.

He had not completed the job when two green-uniformed soldiers burst into his hut, spraying it with submachine gun fire. Incredibly, they didn't see Terry immediately, who was slightly behind them, only a few feet away. He killed them both with his M-1 rifle, then looked outside to see more soldiers rushing up the hill toward the compound.

Carrying a wooden box with his papers under one arm and his M-1 under the other, the American ran out of the door, only to drop the box as he tripped and fell in front of the hut. The impact of the fall popped the ever-present revolver from the shoulder holster onto the ground. He rolled away as automatic weapons fire stitched the ground where he had fallen; then he scrambled to his feet and made his way into the brush between the huts and the airstrip.

Working his way toward the defensive positions he had dug at the wooded end of the strip, Terry came across some of the Thai special forces troops who were part of the team. Having found some of his men, Terry was organizing them for a counter-attack on the compound when the new colonel from Vientiane rashly charged the huts on his own. The Laotian officer was scarcely out of the brush before being stopped by a grenade *blast that tore away part of his hand. Swearing, Terry ran out, grabbed the wounded officer, and was pulling him back when he too was hit by a grenade fragment or rifle slug that creased his forehead. By this time the Lao contingent of the civic action team seemed to have deserted. Terry ordered what was left of his Thai team to fall back to the other side of the airstrip. He was not at all sure that they would make it.*

4

The rest of the household was still asleep. While, unknown to me, Terry Burke was under attack in the jungle, I climbed out of bed. The morning quiet was broken only by the calls of birds along the river and the whirring insects in the tamarinds and willows. I put on my green Dacron jungle uniform, a baggy-pocketed safari jacket, matching trousers, and flying boots.

I was finishing breakfast when I realized that I couldn't ride the Honda to work carrying Terry's case of beer. That meant waking Patricia and having her drive me to the airport in the Datsun. When Patricia took her time coming downstairs, I warned her that if she didn't hurry, I would have to take the car myself, leaving her with the motorcycle for transportation. That seemed to get results, and in a few minutes she was driving me out the gate and down the road.

It was not yet seven o'clock as we passed through downtown Chieng Mai, but a few shop owners already were opening their shutters. Soon the tourists would be spending their baht on the lacquerware, hammered silver, and carved teak for which the city was famous. The American, British, and German consulates would be hoisting their flags and opening their doors. Pilgrims would be visiting the wats, filling them with flowers and incense and plastering gold foil on the images of Buddha, and saffron-robed monks with shaven heads would be finishing their morning ritual of begging for food in the streets.

Noticing some Thai laborers loading ice at an icehouse, I had Patricia pull over and bought a twenty-five-pound block, which I muscled into the backseat beside the Asahi. Now I could surprise Terry in Boum Lao with a luxury practically unheard of in the jungle, cold beer.

At the airport, I left my wife with a short kiss and a perfunctory "See you tonight." I lugged the beer and ice out toward the parked Turbo-Porter. Having checked in with Cecil Cartwright, the AID administrator, the night before, I knew where I would be flying today. I was to take supplies and people to some "Tango" and "Lima" sites, phonetic alphabet designations for Thai and Laotian special operations airstrips that included Lima Site 174 at Boum Lao.

Already waiting in the damp grass next to the airplane were Tony Alfonte and a green-uniformed Thai border patrolman. The patrolman had several baskets of vegetables and sacks of dried fish stacked beside him. I was to fly the patrolman and the supplies to a Thai base along the Burmese border as my first job of the morning. Then we would cross over into Laos, touch down at the supply center at Xieng Lom, and go on to Boum Lao.

We climbed into a sky so clear and beautiful that it was easy to forget this was the beginning of the monsoon. The smoky season, when the hill tribesmen cut down and burned the jungle to make room for their crops, was over. Spring winds had swept the sky clear of the ash that hung in the air during the winter. For a few more days Chieng Mai residents could enjoy flying the colorful dragon kites they fashioned out of rice paper and bamboo. Soon the rain would fall. Intermittent daily thunder showers would come first, then the continuous downpour that would not stop until the end of October.

Below us, some of the best hardwood forests in Asia carpeted the landscape. Within the next several weeks, Thai loggers working in pairs would fell the teakwood trees with their handsaws. Trained elephants would then drag the logs to waterways where they would be floated southward toward Bangkok. There the timber would be exported or made into furniture and floors durable enough to last for centuries in the tropics. The hand-pegged teak floors and paneling in our home in Chieng Mai had come from these rain forests.

In less than half an hour we set down at a Tango site at the northern tip of the country, near the village of San Tan Dau. While helping to unload the vegetables and fish, a Thai army sergeant spotted the beer and asked hopefully if it was for him.

"No, it's for Terry," I told him. "I've got to take it over to Laos for Terry. "

"Next time you bring me beer. Okay?" said the sergeant in halting English.

"Sure," I assured him with a smile. "Next time I'll bring you beer."

Soon we were airborne again, this time flying east toward the Laotian border. We were passing over country that I knew well.

In the jungles below lived Nationalist Chinese, survivors of Chiang Kai-shek's Kuomintang. Instead of fleeing across the Formosa Strait to Taiwan in 1949 with the others, these people had come out the back door of China and settled in eastern Burma, western Laos, and northern Thailand. The Thai government knew that these refugees were responsible for much of the illegal drug traffic in the notorious Golden Triangle. This three-country border area was thought to be the source of 70 percent of the world's illicit opium.

I had frequently made bumpy landings in jungle clearings so that border patrolmen could question suspicious characters who looked as if they had just stepped out of "Terry and the Pirates." From the air we would search for the paths over which the mule trains carried the opium to heroin refineries. Ironically, high-level administrators in the Thai border patrol itself were at times implicated in the illegal narcotics traffic.

The Thais also were concerned about the continued association of the Chinese refugees with the Taiwan government. On a recent visit to the area, I had learned the refugees were being supplied with American M-1A1 carbines and ammunition dropped from Taipei-based C-46 transports. The Thai government seemed to be content to leave the Chinese alone for the time being, however, because the refugees constituted a buffer protecting Thailand from possible invasions by Burma or Laos. Border disputes among the three countries dated from the nineteenth century, when an Englishman had drawn the boundaries arbitrarily.

At Huie Kan, we circled John Milan's hospital long enough to learn that he didn't need anything, promised the medic we'd check again on the way home, and continued eastward into Laos.

On this heading, had we been high enough, warring Southeast Asia would have been laid out before us like a topographical map. To the right would be Vientiane, where Premier Souvanna Phouma, from his white mansion above the Mekong, was trying desperately to shore up the "coalition" government that had been disintegrating steadily since the Communists had left it more than two years before. To the left would be the northern Laotian provinces of Phong Saly and Sam Neua, Pathet Lao strongholds. Cave prisons were rumored to be located in that area. "Stay away from Phong Saly," an Air America pilot had told me a few months

before. "You go down there and you won't come out." Ahead of
the aircraft, beyond our immediate destination of Xieng Lom,
would be the Plain of Jars, where last spring General Kong Le's
Royal Lao forces had been routed by the Communists and forced
into the foothills of the Annamite Cordillera, General Vang Pao
covering their retreat. Beyond the Plain of Jars, spreading from
one wingtip to the other, would be the two Vietnams, whose
governments were fighting a war to which the United States was
just beginning to commit large numbers of troops.

In Hanoi, President Ho Chi Minh, still healthy and vigorous,
had celebrated his seventy-fifth birthday two days before. Last month
he had rejected President Johnson's proposal for a negotiated peace,
countering with his own peace plan, which called for immediate
withdrawal of American forces from the south.

Operation Rolling Thunder, the massive American bombing
campaign against the north, was in its fifth month. Some pilots
were already POWs somewhere up there.

In Saigon, the South Vietnamese government was near collapse,
and General William Westmoreland, the American commander,
was anxiously awaiting more troops. At this point he had 45,000,
most of them being used to build and defend American air bases
and to advise the Army of South Vietnam. But President Johnson,
his political hand strengthened by the Tonkin Gulf Resolution of
the previous August, had met last month in Honolulu with
General Westmoreland and South Vietnamese leaders and decided
that a much larger American military presence was required.

By July the number of American combat troops would reach
75,000, triple the number on hand at the beginning of the year.
And the troops would begin to be used on offensive search-and-
destroy missions. In the United States, "teach-ins" protesting
U.S. involvement in the war had begun in April.

We set down at Xieng Lom, whose 5,000-foot runway, designed
to accommodate C-47 transports and other multiengined aircraft,
dwarfed every other upcountry airstrip. At this supply pickup
point for the smaller bases in western Laos, we found five people
waiting for a ride to Boum Lao. Two were young Laotian soldiers—
an overweight fellow whose T-shirt bulged over the waist of his
olive drab fatigue pants, and a short, slightly built infantryman
carrying an American carbine and wearing full combat gear.

With the armed soldier were his young wife and their baby. I
had flown them out of Boum Lao several days earlier so that the

child could get medical attention from a missionary doctor. The barefoot native woman wore an ankle-length wrap-around skirt and a white muslin blouse. A cloth strap crossed over the baby in back so she could carry the child papoose-style. She asked through an interpreter for kerosene that she could take back to her village, and smiled her gratitude when Tony filled her bottle from a drum of JP-4 aircraft fuel, almost pure kerosene.

The fifth passenger was a twenty-four-year-old Thai special forces sergeant named Chai Cham Harnavee, who worked out of Xieng Lom as a field radio repairman. I had seen Harnavee occasionally as I flew in and out of bases in this area, but we had not met until now. He had been trained as a paratrooper, and he fit the stereotype. He was tall for a Thai, six feet, and powerfully built. Wide-set dark eyes looked confidently out of a face so square it could have been chiseled from teak. Because Harnavee could speak English and Lao as well as native Thai, I used him as an interpreter when I conversed with the other passengers.

His repair kit in hand, Harnavee was going to Boum Lao on the assumption that Terry's radio needed to be fixed. The base had not reported in to Lima Control, Xieng Lom's communications center, as usual that morning.

With the five passengers and the sacks of rice, salt, and dried fish they were now loading, the plane would be overweight, and I told Tony Alfonte he would have to stay behind. So the young Filipino stood on the runway and watched as Harnavee eased himself down beside me in the right-hand seat of the cockpit, and the other passengers climbed in on top of the rice bags in the cargo department.

I had known Tony as long as I had known anyone since I had come to Southeast Asia the year before. We had worked together in Vientiane and had come over to Chieng Mai together, arranging to have our families join us there. Now our parallel paths were diverging for good.

It was about eight-thirty when I took off, setting a northerly course that would take me over the Mekong River. The longest river in Southeast Asia, the Mekong rose in the Tibetan Highlands of China and flowed 2,600 miles south-ward, forming the Lao-Burmese and Lao-Thai borders, then wandering through Cambodia and South Vietnam before it spilled through the delta into the South China Sea. Flying at 5,000 feet, I would cross the river where it bolted the Lao-Thai boundary and flowed eastward into Laos on its way toward Luang Prabang and Vientiane.

As a kid during World War II, I had devoured every book I could find about the daring deeds of American aviators in this part of the world. I knew that just over the horizon, dead ahead, General Chennault's Flying Tigers had roamed the China skies, and that beyond the peaks to the left, Cochran's Air Commandos had helped fight the battle for Burma. But I also knew that such folklore belonged to a distant past. More relevant to the present political and military situation was the battleground that lay just beyond my right wingtip. There, in the valley of Dien Bien Phu, the Viet Minh had shocked the world by defeating a well-disciplined army of French paratroopers in 1954, signaling the end of France's Asian empire in Indochina. Soon the wide, muddy Mekong was below us. We crossed the last mountain range and then the last ridgeline. Now the terrain became the familiar Boum Lao valley with its river, rice paddies, village, and airstrip. I descended to 1,200 feet and made my usual pass over the field from the south. Everything looked okay. There on the edge of the runway was the large L made from parachute cloth, Terry's signal that it was safe to land.

I banked to the left, making the 270-degree turn that would put me on my final approach from the east. Cranking the flaps down, I eased the prop pitch back to slow us to our landing speed of forty-five to fifty knots. Now the plane was only a few hundred feet off the ground, and I could see its swiftly moving shadow ahead of us on the green jungle and brown rice fields.

The airstrip that only a few minutes before had looked so small and flat now dominated the view from the windshield and revealed its lumpy surface. Rocks, stump holes, and bumps came sharply into focus. Three hundred feet, the altimeter read. The slit trenches that Terry's men had dug a few weeks before were now clearly visible near the far end of the runway. Two hundred fifty... two hundred... I noted without alarm that the path leading from the village to the airstrip was empty.

Usually I could see a few villagers scampering up the trail to watch the landing. Perhaps Terry had everyone working this morning on some community project in the jungle. Or maybe the natives were simply getting over the novelty of seeing my silver flying machine descend from the heavens. Fifty feet, twenty-five, twenty... Now the trees and dirt and grass rushed alongside. There was a jolt as the wheels hit and the landing struts absorbed the shock. The plane bounced along the green-walled corridor that the soldiers had cleared from the jungle.

The engine noise swelled as I reversed the turboprop to slow the aircraft. For the first time I felt a twinge of uneasiness. Where was everybody? Not only were there no villagers among the trees, there was no sip of Terry or the civic action team.

The answer came immediately. Over the noise of the engine, gunfire crackled. It sounded distant and harmless, like firecrackers, but the illusion was shattered when the bullets struck the windshield, sending the Plexiglas flying. Rifle slugs whispered through the plane's aluminum skin, one of them finding the young woman, whose shrieks of surprise and pain filled the cargo department.

A few feet from the cockpit window, the JP-4 spewed from freshly made bullet holes in the wing fuel cells. Through the right rear windows I glimpsed kneeling soldiers firing at the plane from a path opening onto the runway. They were less than fifty feet away, close enough for me to see the weapons jump as the rounds were squeezed off. I could see spent shells kicking out of the chambers, and the brown faces snug against the rifle stocks. I pointed to the ambushers and gestured urgently to the armed Laotian soldier to fire back.

With the first rifle report, I had instantly released the brakes and accelerated, but I knew we were in desperate trouble. This was a one-way airstrip, and ahead of us a curtain of trees blocked our exit. Our only chance was to reach the end of the runway, wheel around, and take off in the opposite direction. We would then be heading into the rifle muzzles of our attackers, but there was no alternative.

Though it was closer than two hundred feet away, the turn-around seemed as distant as Detroit. The roar of the accelerating engine and the wind rushing in on my face through the broken Plexiglas told me we were picking up speed, but it seemed impossible that my scurrying little sandpiper of an aircraft was going to survive this dash for freedom. With each endless second the chances grew more likely that gunfire would disable the aircraft or slam into my unprotected back. I fought a moment of panic. "Cool it, Brace. Wonsan was worse than this. Clear your damn head."

With one hundred feet to go, the aircraft was rolling fast enough that the escaping fuel was running off the wings in flaxen sheets. Fifty feet... twenty-five... then I was pivoting the aircraft in front of the trenches, reducing the flap level to takeoff setting, and feeling a new glimmer of hope.

Though we were losing JP-4 in alarming amounts, the Porter still seemed flyable. Perhaps we could get back across the Mekong to a crash landing in the jungle, or even make it to Xieng Lom. I was completing my turnaround and was about to hit the maximum power button when two grenades exploded so close that the airframe shuddered violently from the concussions. Now I could see more green-uniformed troops out ahead of me in the trees on either side of the runway. Yet the soldier in back still had not fired his carbine. What in hell was he doing? We would never run this gauntlet unless we were shooting back. I knew the Laotian could not speak English, but there was not time to have Harnavee translate. I reached back and grabbed the soldier roughly by his fatigue shirt.

"God damn it, shoot!" I yelled, gesturing at the uniformed figures in the trees. I would never know whether it was fear or misconception that stared back at me from the beardless face. Whatever it was, in the next instant, the soldier flung open the large cargo door, jumped out, and dashed toward the trees, carrying his carbine as he ran. It was a fatal mistake. Almost immediately, the ugly and distinctive yammer of a machine gun sounded. The bullets struck the soldier in mid-stride and slammed him to the dirt, where he lay dying less than thirty feet from the aircraft's open door. His wounded wife was now hysterical.

When the Laotian had jumped out, the open door had locked against the wing strut and was now protruding from the fuselage at a right angle. Taking off in this condition would send us cartwheeling into the rice paddies. It was too late, I knew, to climb out and yank the door free. Our attackers, who were holding their fire, were too close for that, too close now even for me to pick up the radio's hand microphone and broadcast a distress signal. That would invite them to open fire again. Instead, I left the mike resting in its bracket below the instrument panel and keyed the transmit button.

"Mayday, Mayday," I said, trying to look as if I were talking to Harnavee. "I am under attack at Boum Lao. Mayday... Mayday..."

My voice trailed off when my eyes met those of the man who had just killed my passenger. Stepping out of the trees only a few feet from the left wingtip, the broad-shouldered enemy soldier held a machine gun with a drum magazine, a bipod fitted on the barrel. The weapon was trained on the cockpit, and there was nothing inscrutable about what his eyes were saying. I smiled and shut down the engine.

5

Beyond the jagged Plexiglas, the three-bladed propeller spun its last labored revolutions. I motioned the woman and the remaining Laotian soldier out of the plane, then told Sergeant Harnavee to follow them. "Walk, don't run," I advised the Thai.

Before climbing out myself, I grasped the canvas survival kit and put it under my arm. Inside, along with fishing line and emergency flares, was a nine-shot, .22-caliber pistol. To prevent pilfering, the kit's zipper was secured by a piece of soldered copper wire. If I could get to the weapon in time, we could break for the trees, work our way up to the trenches, and try to hold off the attackers until help came.

By the time I emerged from the cabin door, which was on the side away from the machine gunner, the heavy Laotian soldier had dashed into the bushes. Unarmed and overweight, he had little chance of getting away. The wounded, grieving young woman was hopping piteously around on one leg, trying not to look at the crumpled form of her husband in the dirt a few feet away. Whimpering, she pulled up her long skirt to expose a softball-sized black bruise where a rifle slug had lodged in the flesh of her upper thigh.

As we walked slowly away from the plane, I began working the wire that secured the survival kit. I felt the metal warm in my hand as I bent it back and forth. Just as the wire snapped, I felt Harnavee's elbow hard in my ribs.

"PL come," the Thai said urgently, looking over his shoulder. He meant the Pathet Lao.

The remark was punctuated with a burst of automatic weapons fire that tore savagely into the foliage above our heads. There was no chance of escaping now. My hand was on the pistol, but the weapon, intended for use as a survival gun, still had to be loaded. Keeping my back to the approaching enemy, I flung the pistol as inconspicuously as I could into the bushes. Then I dropped the kit at my feet and turned with the Thai to face the two soldiers running toward us, rifles at the ready.

If these were Pathet Lao, they were like none I had ever seen. The guerrilla prisoners I had occasionally airlifted toward POW camps wore the black pajamas of Southeast Asian peasants and were barefoot and bareheaded. The weapons they surrendered often were outdated French or German rifles or might even be handmade. But these soldiers were wearing green fatigues, canvas-and-rubber "jungle boots," and dungaree caps similar to those worn by American soldiers. Each carried a coiled rope on his belt and cradled a semiautomatic rifle that I recognized as a Russian-made AK-47.

The soldiers motioned us to put our hands on our heads, then frisked us from behind. A tug told me to put my arms behind my back. I felt a rope being cinched around my elbows, tight enough to hurt. Then it was looped expertly around my neck and brought down again to be tied behind my back. There was enough left over to provide a leash for my captors to hold on to.

I assumed the soldiers weren't interested in the woman, who watched with frenzied eyes from beneath the Porter's wingtip. There was nothing she could do for her husband now. "Go village, go village," I told her, motioning with my head toward the path leading off the runway. The soldiers did not attempt to stop her when she limped gingerly into the trees, her black-haired baby bouncing on her back.

Moments later the Laotian soldier, winded and woebegone, was brought in, his arms bound behind him in the same fashion as Harnavee's and mine. Then, with a soldier grasping each of our tethers, we were marched across the runway and onto the path that led downhill past Terry's compound.

Bodies of the civic action team lay scattered in the grass outside the huts. Most of the dead men were in their underwear, apparently having been surprised in their sleep and shot down as they ran. I could not make out Terry Burke's body among the dead, but we were pushed past the spot too quickly for me to get a good look. Below, on the path ahead of us, I could see the woman and her baby being helped toward the village by two other native women.

At the foot of the hill we followed a path bordering the rice paddies, crossed the narrow river over a footbridge near the village, and continued along the opposite bank. The villagers of

Boum Lao watched silently and impassively from their huts as we passed. No sign now of the shy smiles with which some of them had greeted me during my previous visits. Like it or not, the strange soldiers who had come at dawn were the new rulers of Boum Lao, at least temporarily. The villagers had survived this war long enough to know that one did not fraternize with "the enemy," whoever it happened to be at the moment.

After following the river a little farther, the soldiers took a path uphill into the trees and climbed for a few minutes before reaching a ray, a spot in the jungle where the brush had been cleared by the villagers for the purpose of growing vegetables and fruit. Hidden from the air by the forest canopy and offering a view of both the village and the airstrip below, the ray made an ideal base of operations for the enemy unit. Dozens of freshly dug one-man foxholes, each containing a green-capped soldier with an AK-47, pitted the sun-dappled slope. The soldiers looked at us prisoners with professional indifference and, in a few cases, amused smiles.

We were tied, standing up, to trees near a fourth prisoner, a frightened native boy of fourteen or fifteen. I had seen him working around the airstrip during my previous visits to Boum Lao. The youngster was wearing military fatigues that were much too large for him; probably the soldiers had given him captured clothing to put on.

An anthill rose only a few inches from my tree, and almost immediately I felt the colony's inhabitants crawling up my trouser legs and on the bare skin beneath my safari shirt. After a while they had become so numerous and bothersome that I was twisting in my ropes, stamping my feet, and trying to blow the insects away from my mouth, nose, and eyes. I attracted the attention of a soldier in a nearby foxhole, but the rifleman laughed at me and turned away. Finally, Harnavee appealed in Laotian to a passing officer, who sympathized with my predicament and had me moved to another tree.

The ray was alive with activity. Soldiers and guerrillas in native dress came and went, carrying captured supplies and equipment from the airstrip and stacking them in a pile that grew dramatically as the morning sun climbed. Most of the stuff was American-made. There were World War II-vintage M-1 rifles, a Browning light machine gun, crates of ammunition, rolled-up terrain maps, portable radios, U.S. Army C-rations, blue-and-white C&H sugar boxes, cartons of Camels and Lucky Strikes, and a variety of canned goods. A few feet away, wounded men writhed on litters beneath parachute cloth blankets. Terry did not appear to be among them, but it was clear that they were captured civic action team soldiers. When one of them cried out, a contemptuous enemy officer struck him hard with a bamboo walking stick.

The officer now strode toward us four tree-bound prisoners. Like the other soldiers, he wore no insignia. The unfaded patches on his cap and collar suggested that he had removed any devices indicating rank, unit, and nationality. His status as a leader was betrayed by his sidearm and by the two riflemen following him at a respectful distance. Judging from the captured equipment he was wearing, the officer was in command. Hanging from his shoulder, to my dismay, was my map case, which had been taken from the Porter's cockpit. The case contained the coordinates of every STOL airstrip in western Laos, information the enemy would be glad to have.

My hopes that Terry Burke might have escaped received a blow when I got a closer look at the officer's handgun. There, fitting snugly into the familiar leather holster, was Terry's Smith & Wesson revolver. Yesterday, the six-bullet elastic strap on the holster had been full. Now there were two bullets missing.

The officer stopped in front of me and, without a word, searched my pockets. After examining the ballpoint pen in my shirt pocket, he went through my wallet, unfolding the plastic ID card and photo folder. He paused to look at snapshots of my four boys.

"Could I keep those?"

The officer didn't understand English, but listened without expression as Harnavee translated the request into Lao. Then he turned to me and shook his head no. When he had finished examining the contents of the plastic folder, which included an identification card issued me by the Laotian government, the officer removed the three hundred baht from the billfold portion, stuffed the money, worth about fifteen American dollars, in my breast pocket, and placed the wallet in the map case. He pulled on my arm, which was tied behind me, to get a better look at my Rolex GMT watch, but didn't take it. Then he walked over to Harnavee and the Laotian soldier, questioning them both in Lao and conducting similar searches.

We had been tied up for about an hour when we heard the first airplane. I could see it through the trees, circling at high altitude, cautiously checking out the airstrip and village. It had been gone only a few minutes when a second plane appeared, this one a twin engine Caribou that may have been an Air America or Royal Lao aircraft out of Vientiane, or a U.S. Air Force plane out of Thailand. It also circled high, prompting me to worry that the body of the Lao soldier, dressed in a green uniform like mine, might be mistaken for me. At least I knew now that my Mayday had been heard.

About a half hour after the two planes had left, a pair of sleek American F-105s thundered into the valley and began strafing and bombing the abandoned aircraft, apparently trying to deny it to the enemy. They came in so low that from my elevated vantage point I could see the faces of the pilots, their eyes hidden by the dark visors on their brightly painted helmets.

Though we were two hundred feet above the runway, we felt the earth shudder as the bombs exploded below. The jets were followed by a flight of Royal Lao T-28s, propeller-driven close-support aircraft, that continued the attacks. I couldn't gauge their effectiveness because trees hid the end of the runway where the Porter sat crippled.

The last bomb had been dropped by the time the Bird and Son executive aircraft, a silver-and-blue twin engine Beechcraft Baron, arrived overhead for a look. It would not be long, I thought, before Patricia would be getting a phone call from the company or from Cecil Cartwright of the AID office.

Shortly before noon, the valley got its last airborne visit of the morning, this one from a plucky Air America helicopter crew. I first heard the distinctive engine noise that signaled the approach of one of the big Sikorskys, then saw the helo pass overhead. It was low enough that I could clearly see an American in a T-shirt and khaki pants in the open door, his eyes hidden by the snapped-down visor of his Air Force-type helmet. I had an impulse to yell, "Hey, Mac, down here!" but knew I could neither be seen nor heard from the air watched incredulously, dropped out of sight to a landing, apparently near the Porter. It was, I thought, a reckless but gutsy thing to do. The large, vulnerable Sikorsky would make an easy target for the enemy soldiers who undoubtedly were still around the runway. Sure enough, the helicopter had been down only a few seconds when the popping of the AK-47s could be heard over the idling rotors.

I waited anxious moments, then saw the aircraft appear again over the trees and head up the valley. I hoped the crewman in the doorway had had the time to jump out and check the identity of the dead soldier on the runway, and to note the absence of other bodies in and around the Porter. If he hadn't, we might be presumed dead and rescue efforts abandoned.

I had flown into Boum Lao perhaps fifteen or twenty times before today, but I had never seen the natives who were helping the soldiers in the ray. Obviously they were Pathet Lao, perhaps from some of the villages up the valley to the north, where Communist sympathy was known to be strong. Whoever they were, they seemed eager to learn how to use the captured weapons that were being turned over to them. Their uniformed friends were offering expert guidance. As the aircraft came and went in the morning, we prisoners watched the soldiers patiently instruct the natives in the use and maintenance of the M-1s. Though I couldn't understand much of the Lao being spoken, I could see that the soldiers were passing on useful jungle lore, such as how to keep dust and moisture out of the barrel by inserting a curled leaf that need not be removed before firing.

By midday, the stacked weapons and supplies had been turned over to the natives, who carried the materiel away, presumably toward more secure territory in the north. The guerrillas also took the wounded prisoners on litters. I was relieved that my passengers and I were not going with them. The discipline and self-restraint of the uniformed troops seemed prefer-able to the impulsiveness and inexperience that I associated with the Pathet Lao.

About noon, during a lull in the air activity, we four prisoners were untied and marched up the path that climbed into the jungle on the other side of the clearing. The trail took us over the ridgeline and into a ravine where another ray had been cleared. Hidden from the airstrip and Boum Lao, this small camp would be even less likely to be spotted from the air than would the foxholed area. Obviously our captors anticipated more air searches during the afternoon.

We had been retied to trees only a short time when a chubby, round-faced officer, accompanied by two riflemen, walked into the camp. He seemed surprised to see the prisoners, and his comment to the pair of soldiers guarding us produced a laughing rejoinder about "Americans." Removing his backpack, the officer spoke briskly to Harnavee in Lao. "He feed us," the Thai told me.

Dropping to one knee, the officer took four rice balls and a box of C&H sugar from the knapsack. He cuffed the balls expertly

with the heel of his hand, poured sugar into the clefts, and closed
them. When the guards had untied our hands, he gave the food
to us. We had to strain to get it to our mouths because our elbows
were still bound behind our backs. As we ate, the officer tried
unsuccessfully to communicate with me. He then interrogated
the Asian prisoners in Lao.

Harnavee seemed to be the only one who could make
himself understood. When we had been retied and left with our
guards, the Thai told me that he had been asked where our flight
had originated. He had feigned uncertainty, since he had been
picked up along the way. I decided then that when asked, I would
give Vientiane, not Chieng Mai, as my point of origin. It probably
didn't matter, but I was determined to yield as little accurate
information as possible, regardless of its importance. As a civilian
I was no longer bound by the Military Code of Conduct for Prisoners
of War. However, I had not forgotten that the code required
American military men to resist their captors, not cooperate with
them.

By this time I was sure I was a prisoner of North Vietnamese
Army regulars. They seemed everything their Pathet Lao allies
were not—well-trained, well-organized, and well-equipped. The
soldiers knew precisely how to take a prisoner, how to restrain
him efficiently and effectively, where and how to stand when on
guard duty.

Their Russian-made rifles and Chinese grenades were first-
rate, as was the rest of their equipment. They had good clips,
good leather, good sneakers. Guerrillas in this area might be
expected to inflict gratuitous violence on prisoners, sometimes
even killing them in the heat of the moment. These soldiers, with
the exception of the officer who had struck the wounded man on
the litter, had behaved with restraint. My rescue from the anthill
was a considerate act I would not have expected from the PL. Nor
would I have expected guerrillas to allow me to keep my wrist-
watch and money.

I was not surprised that so many of them spoke Lao. NVA
soldiers, I knew, were sent here for five or six years at a stretch.
They had ample time to pick up the language, which, owing to
cultural overlap, shared many words with Vietnamese.

We passed the rest of the afternoon watching the soldiers
come and go, some of them carrying boxes of captured supplies
on their shoulders. Once in a while, rifle shots echoed in the
valley, and several times aircraft engines throbbed overhead. I

felt reassured that friendly forces were still looking for us. At dusk we marched back to the ray overlooking the airstrip. We were allowed to sit on the bank of a dry irrigation channel while we ate a dinner of rice cooked with vegetables and pork chips.

The relatively relaxed atmosphere and the surprisingly good meal did not prepare us for what happened next. When we had finished eating, the Laotian boy was abruptly told to get to his feet, and soon he was stammering answers to the angry and rapid-fire questions of the soldiers who occasionally pointed with obvious hostility toward me and the Thai. None of the boy's responses seemed to satisfy his interrogators. They were unmoved when tears began to roll down the dirty face and his eyes pleaded for understanding. I looked at Harnavee, who was sitting next to me.

"They are going to punish him," the Thai explained in a whisper.

"What will they do?" I asked.

"I don't know," he replied.

They took the boy to the edge of the ray, where they tied a string to his little finger and placed his hand on a log. He was screaming now, and the soldiers shouted at him to be quiet. While one of them pulled the string to separate the finger from the rest of the hand, another took a machete from his belt and, holding it several inches above its target, lopped off the finger with a whack that reverberated off the trees.

A medic carrying a haversack marked with a large Red Cross insignia dressed the wound and bound the hand with a professional bandage. They then tied the sobbing boy and us three other prisoners to trees once again.

Harnavee, who was tied next to the boy, tried to comfort the youngster. After a while he stopped crying. They had a chance to converse quietly before the soldiers came over again, untied the boy, and sent him down the trail with a sack of food. They were letting him go!

'Will he report us?" I asked the Thai. "Yes. He will say he saw us."

The youngster's village was a day's walk away, the sergeant had learned. Probably attracted to the area by the airplanes, he had helped build the strip at Boum Lao several months ago. He was living with the civic action team, though he was not a soldier, when the compound was attacked. He probably had no idea of the politics of the war, and likely was paid for his work with fish and rice from the camp mess. Now he was being sent home with a stump where his finger had been. It was to warn his village of the consequences of cooperating with the enemy. Before he had been released, Harnavee had quietly given him our names. I hoped that friendly forces in the area would soon know we were alive.

Before dark, we three remaining prisoners were moved into the ditch, where we apparently were to spend the night. We were laid down in the dirt with our hands and elbows trussed behind our backs, and our ankles bound. A couple of riflemen sat on the grassy bank, keeping an eye on us as they pushed rice into their mouths from wooden bowls.

When darkness fell, it was decided that the captives should be tied to something. We were taken out of the ditch and bound sitting up to small trees along the bank. Ironically, the move gave me my first opportunity to escape. The soldier who had tied me up had not done a good job, and the darkness allowed me to work vigorously on the ropes that bound my arms behind the tree.

With the soldiers smoking and chatting quietly only a few feet away, I untied my hands and then the rope around my legs. I reasoned that the best time to slip away would be in the moments when the flash of one of the captured American cigarette lighters would temporarily hinder the guards' night vision. If I could make it to the jungle, I could hide out until daybreak, then signal an aircraft.

When the next lighter flared and went out, I made my move. I had crawled scarcely five feet when a flashlight flicked on, its beam finding me immediately. The soldiers grabbed me and threw me back hard against the tree. Their angry shouts aroused the camp. I expected to be slapped or slugged, but the abuse was limited to Vietnamese expletives delivered a few inches from my face.

This time the rope was replaced with field phone wire that was wrapped so tightly around my wrists that my hands were soon numb. I would have spent the rest of the night this way, had not an officer stopped to talk with the guards and shine his flashlight down onto my bleeding wrists. He ordered the wire removed, and the rope used once again. The rope was tied snugly, and burned where the wire had cut into my wrists.

Before falling into a fitful sleep, I spent hours staring into the darkness, wondering how Patricia and the boys were bearing up under the news, and tried to assess my chances of being rescued. This valley was considered to be Pathet Lao-controlled. It was within range of the tough, U.S.-supported Hmong tribesmen, who specialized in rescuing downed American fliers. Once our location was known, Vang Pao's helicopter-bome guerrillas might be able to surprise this isolated NVA unit. If I was lucky, I could be back in Chieng Mai with my family within hours after the rescue.

On the other hand, the NVA would not be waiting for Van Pao to come looking for them. Their surprise appearance in Boum Lao had demonstrated that they knew how to travel without being seen from the air. Also, I was well aware that other American pilots captured in Laos had simply disappeared into the jungle. Gene DeBruin, for example, had bailed out of a burning C-46 and dropped into the hands of the Pathet Lao in 1963. He had not been heard from since. There were other stories about downed contract pilots being shot and killed within sight of the rescue helicopters.

In a few hours, half a world away, American front pages would report that on this day, May 21, 1965, U.S. Navy and Air Force planes had bombed targets in North Vietnam that included barracks, a radar station, and naval craft; forty or fifty persons had been arrested in Saigon and accused of plotting to depose Premier Phan Huy Quat; American troops were wrapping up a sweep through the Mekong Delta in a search for Vietcong weapons caches; and Ambassador Maxwell Taylor's plane had been hit by ground fire as it flew over the site of a sprawling airstrip being built at Chu Lai, fifty miles south of Saigon. There would be no mention of one American pilot by the name of Ernest C. Brace disappearing into the jungles of Laos. Like the North Vietnamese, we weren't supposed to be here.

In the context of the escalating war in Vietnam, the disappearance of an American civilian in the jungles of western Laos did not seem significant, and even if the news media had known about it, my misfortune probably would have merited only a line or two. Ironically, a *New York Times* dispatch on the day before my capture reported a lull in the fighting in Laos. "This little kingdom, which has long been a center of inter-national crisis, is enjoying a breather," *Times* readers were told.

6

Dabbing his bleeding forehead as he ran, Terry Burke could tell his wound was not serious. He and the remaining members of the civic action team were crashing through the underbrush between the huts and the airstrip, trying to make it to the other side of the runway.

When they reached the airstrip, a machine gun opened up on the other side, pinning them down on the dirt bank until the American tossed a couple of grenades. Motioning his men to move laterally toward a burned-off knoll at the end of the runway, Terry yelled for cover fire from the mortar and recoilless-rifle team that was supposed to be positioned atop the knoll. He could have saved his breath—the Laotians had panicked and fled.

The American adviser was climbing the knoll when the Vietnamese moved onto the airstrip in a disciplined attack. His Thai team leader, Juk, fell from a rifle slug in the foot, and two other soldiers were hit less seriously.

Ordering a pullback into the jungle, Terry had the wounded team leader carried from the hill while he and another Thai held off the enemy. Some of the enemy were already at the foot of the slope.

Terry would have used his pistol now, but he had lost it when he slipped and fell outside his hut. Instead, he emptied his M-1 and threw his last grenades. Then he and his comrade dashed after the other.

There were no more than half a dozen of the friendlies left now. Terry ordered them to move deeper into the jungle.

Carrying the Thai team leader and the wounded Laotian colonel whom they had picked up along the way, they made slow progress, but fortunately their pursuers were distracted by a helicopter that appeared over the airstrip, apparently about to land. The enemy opened fire before the aircraft reached the ground, and the helo was able to pull away in time. Terry

assumed it was an Air America craft, perhaps from Cheng
Kong. He hoped the pilot would radio a warning to Xieng Lom
that the strip had been overrun.

The American adviser and his men were about three hundred
yards east of the airstrip when, some time later, they heard
Ernie Brace's Turbo-Porter overhead. It seemed to be descending.

"My God, he's going to land, " Terry Burke said to himself.
Perhaps the Pathet Lao knew about the landing signal and had
set up an ambush. He heard the engine noise fade as the plane
set down. Gunfire opened up, the engine revved to full pitch as
the pilot tried to escape, then there were grenade explosions and
machine-gun fire. Feeling utterly helpless, Terry heard the
engine shut down.

A return to the airstrip was impossible at this point. The
few Laos who remained with him during the fight had taken off
on their own and the Thai team was scattered, some of its
members dead. Terry was now left with his Thai interpreter, the
two wounded men, and a former Pathet Lao prisoner who had
joined the civic action team some weeks back

They headed south through the jungle, following a natural
drainage. After traveling for some hours, Terry was able to
attract the attention of a helicopter with his signal mirror.

Picked up with the wounded, he was flown to Xieng Lom
where a rescue operation for the American pilot and his passengers
was already being organized. When Terry arrived, the F-105s
were already over Boum Lao. He radioed them directions to hit
the ammunition storage area near the compound, as well as
Ernie's captured aircraft

One of the pilots reported that he thought he might have
seen the pilot still in the Porter's cockpit. Terry was determined
to take a look for himself. With a Thai captain named Dakar,
who also knew Ernie, Terry flew back to Boum Lao in a
helicopter. They landed on the airstrip while a flight of T-28s
strafed the surrounding jungle. (It was this helicopter that
Ernie had seen from the ray, and Terry Burke may have been
the American peeping down at the jungle from the helo's open
door.)

With the Thai officer covering him, Terry dashed out on the
runway past the slain Laotian soldier and found the Porter's
cockpit empty. He was afraid to yank open the cargo door for
fear it might be booby-trapped. Automatic weapons fire from

the trees forced him to retreat to the helicopter. He left the airstrip reasonably assured that his American friend, Ernie Brace, had not been killed at the scene of his capture.

During the next two days, Saturday and Sunday, Terry Burke searched the area by air. He guided Air America T-28s in on strikes of suspected positions around the airstrip. The pilots dropped leaflets announcing a reward for the release of the American pilot and his passenger.

On the ground, at a Lima site known as 20 Alternate, commando units were standing by, awaiting orders that would launch their rescue mission. But until someone found out where Ernie Brace was, they would be going nowhere.

7

I heard and sometimes saw the aircraft that searched for us over the weekend. We prisoners had remained tied in the ray overlooking the airstrip both Saturday and Sunday. We slept in the ditch at night. As a captured pilot, I hadn't expected to remain here this long. The planes must have been expanding their search radii on the assumption we were being taken out of the area.

On Monday morning we were awakened early, fed rice balls with sugar, and prepared for travel. For traveling, a rope bound each prisoner's elbows in back, climbed to make a neck loop, then formed a tether for a guard to hold. Like the soldiers, each of the captives was given a long blue cloth tube filled with rice. The ends were tied, forming a loop, and it was carried as a shoulder sling. The troops stuck branches into our ropes. The wide leaves draped over our heads and served as camouflage. The NVA soldiers covered themselves by inserting boughs in their backpack straps.

I estimated that the twelve enlisted men and one officer that were now taking us down the trail toward the village constituted no more than one-fifth of the troops involved in the Boum Lao raid. That meant our rescue chances might be improved by our departure from the area.

We passed through the village and crossed over the airstrip. A cardboard sign on bamboo poles warned natives in the area of the price they would pay for cooperating with the Americans and the Vientiane government. Over the Lao writing was a crudely outlined hand, a large drop of blood falling from its severed finger.

At the end of the runway rested the forlorn Porter, its bullet-freckled fuselage down on the side where the landing gear had been blown off. After all the bombing, strafing, and rifle fire, I was surprised the plane hadn't been damaged more. Had the jet fuel ignited, the Porter would have burned like a torch.

The path we followed on the other side of the airstrip cut over to the river. We snaked north up the valley toward the Pathet Lao stronghold of Moung Sai, which I knew was several days' walk. Beyond Moung Sai were the northern provinces of Phong Saly and Sam Neua. There, other captured American pilots were rumored to be held. Beyond lay China's Yunnan province.

We walked in broad daylight on paths without jungle cover, sometimes passing rice fields and small villages. Huts rose on bamboo stilts along the stream. Two shots from lookouts posted along the valley appeared to mean aircraft were heard. The column then simply stepped under trees or squatted in the bushes, which were usually no more than a few feet away. When the jungle was too distant to reach quickly, we would sit down in the tall green grass along the trail.

Some of the villagers greeted the troops as guests. They gave them, and their prisoners, rice balls and water. Sometimes we were even given cooked meat. Obviously out to make a good impression, the soldiers were courteous and appreciative, and chatted in Lao with the natives as they passed their huts.

It was nearly two o'clock when we reached Moung Hoc. A good-sized village of some thirty huts, it had been the site of a French army camp during the years before Dien Bien Phu. Across the stream from the village, rows of wooden barracks, windows broken and paint peeling, overlooked a parade ground. The drill field had long since been reclaimed by the waving elephant grass. A short distance downstream lay the airfield, its runway scored by Communist-dug ditches designed to make it unusable.

I knew Terry Burke had received reports of enemy activity in Moung Hoc. It was apparent that the troops were acquainted with this area. While the prisoners waited under guard in the grass along the airstrip, the soldiers rendezvoused a few hundred feet away with a twenty-five-man NVA unit that came down out of the hills. Then, apparently deciding to stay in the area for a while, the smaller detachment marched its captives into the village. We were instructed to sit down in the shade beneath a stilted hut.

The occupant of the hut was an old man who, surprisingly, treated the soldiers coolly and the prisoners sympathetically. He scurried about, looking for something that we could sit on, but was told brusquely that the prisoners were to sit on the ground. Unintimidated, the Lao quickly gathered some leaves and spread them on the dirt for us.

We passed the afternoon under the hut, watching natives come and go from the village. The old man's daughter, apparently retarded, did chores around the hut. The soldiers did not ingratiate themselves with the elderly Lao when they laughed at the young woman's pathetic attempts to feed the pigs from a rice bowl she couldn't keep from spilling.

When the Laotian prisoner had jumped out of the Porter at Boum Lao, he had been doused with jet fuel that was escaping from bullet holes in the wings overhead. His kerosene-soaked T-shirt had produced boils and welts on his back. By the time we reached Moung Hoc, the soldier was in considerable pain. His condition seemed to worsen as the sun dropped behind the trees. Noticing his suffering, one of the guards walked over and pulled up the Lao's T-shirt, exposing massive boils excreting blood and mucus.

Appalled by the sight, the old man appealed to the soldiers to get medical help. They waved him away with a warning to behave himself. The medic who had bandaged the native boy's mutilated hand after his punishment in the ray had not accompanied this unit. None of the troops seemed inclined to get near the prisoner's ugly sores, much less treat them.

I knew the soldier must be in agony. I had been splashed with some of the JP-4 myself, and was already sore from a boil that was developing under my arm. The old man, in defiance of the soldiers' instructions to stay away, came over and pleaded with me to do something. He turned to our captors and asked them to untie my hands. They simply laughed.

The old man was not to be deterred. Disappearing up the stairs of his hut, he returned a few moments later with an ancient canvas medical kit. Dark brown, bearing a faded red cross, it had probably been left behind by the French. Opening it carefully with his wrinkled brown hands, he produced several penicillin vials. He then made signs indicating that I should apply the medication directly to the man's infected back.

Using Harnavee to translate, I explained that the medicine must be administered with a syringe. Simply dabbing it on the open sores would do little if any good. Though the old Lao could find no syringe in the medical kit, he did produce a needle that could be used to drain the boils.

When a soldier began rummaging through the medical kit, more out of curiosity than concern for the patient, the old man snatched it away. For an instant it seemed that the grizzled Asian in his ill-fitting black pajamas had worn out the patience of the Vietnamese. Then the guard shrugged, untied my hands, and sat down with the others. They watched in silence as I dipped the needle in the penicillin, pricked the boils, and drained them.

When I was through, the man's back was a mess of blood and pus. The Lao soldier smiled his thanks. He seemed to be relieved by the drainage. As they retied me, the old man washed the Laotian soldier's back with a clean wet rag.

Before dark, our Laotian host climbed to his fields and returned with vegetables. He boiled the vegetables over an open fire. Each of the prisoners was given a steaming bowlful. The Lao offered nothing to the soldiers, nor did they attempt to take any. The soldiers gathered greens on the edge of the jungle and boiled them with some of their rice.

At nightfall we were taken across the stream to one of the old French barracks. We found the wooden floor less comfortable for sleeping than the ground had been the three nights before. We remained tied, and our footwear was removed and placed outside the door. I spent the moments before sleep thinking about the compassionate, plucky old man and his moldering medical kit. I hoped the old-timer's defiance would not get him into trouble with the Communist leadership of the village. The Pathet Lao might be less indulgent than the NVA.

8

It was Monday evening, and I lay tied on the floor of an old French barracks, listening to the jungle sounds coming through the humid night. I reflected at length and for perhaps the thousandth time on the crisis four years earlier that had ended my life as a Marine officer. What crossroad had I taken that had led to the end of my career?

When I met Patricia Lou Emmons in 1953, things were about to blow up in my face, literally. Just back from combat duty in Korea, I had moved into an off-base residence with several other single Marine aviators. We were all assigned to a squadron based at Opa Locka Marine Air Station outside Miami. For a monthly rent of only seventy-five dollars apiece we had found a dream pad. It was a veritable mansion on Collins Avenue in Miami Beach. The owner was willing to rent it for the time being for the cost of his taxes.

Overlooking a private beach on the ocean, the house had seven spacious bedrooms, each with its own bath, a kitchen large enough to feed a squad of Marines, and a dining room with wormwood ceilings and a long table whose place settings had individual buzzers to signal the kitchen. The master bedroom had a Roman-style bath.

I had just moved in and was helping a fellow Marine move his gear into the mansion when I met Patricia. Her father had loaned us his pickup to use during the move. A dark-haired beauty with a soft Oklahoma drawl, she delivered the pickup to the mansion. I had learned not to drag my feet on such occasions, and asked her out for the same evening.

The hot-water heater serving the house had not yet been lit. Anxious to get a shower before I picked up my date, I went down to the basement to light it. When I put the match into the opening at the bottom of the huge heater, the gas exploded, knocking me backward and burning my face severely. My God, I thought, I've burned my eyes.

My buddies took me to the base, where I was treated in the emergency room and admitted to the hospital. My eyes were still bandaged the next day when Patricia came to see me, bringing fruit and offering sympathy. She came again a few days later. After the doctors had removed my bandages, they found that though my forehead was badly burned, there was no permanent damage to my eyes. I was released to duty after three days in the hospital.

Patricia stayed on in Miami rather than going back to school, and soon we were seeing each other virtually every day. Her mother owned a small self-service laundry near the beach. Patricia and I would meet for breakfast at a nearby cafe and then I would go to the base. She worked for her mother during the day. After spending my day at the air base, I would pick her up at work and we would go out to the house on the beach. We had met on March 28, 1953. In early May I asked Patricia to be my wife.

When we were married on May 28, exactly two months from the day we met, we seemed to be the perfect couple. I was a young fighter pilot with an impressive combat record and a good Marine Corps future. She had a charming little-girl manner and an appetite for excitement.

It was a colorful military wedding. Marines in full dress whites raised swords in salute as we hurried out the doors of the air base chapel. A squadron formation of F4U Corsair fighters thundered overhead in our honor during the reception at the house on the beach.

We had been married only a few weeks when my Corsair squadron flew aboard a Navy carrier for a five-week trip to Nova Scotia. The deployment would be the first of many!

Our marriage was happy for several years and produced three boys. The transient military life took us from Miami to California, Hawaii, Texas, North Carolina, and Virginia over the next seven years. The separations on cruises and the household moves were placing severe strains on our relationship, however, by the end of the fifties.

Once when I returned with my helicopter squadron to the base at New River, North Carolina, following a Caribbean deployment in 1959, hints were dropped by friends that Patricia had been seeing other men. This was not the first time I had heard these rumors. Friends had dropped hints before when I had come home from off-base assignments, but I had not wanted to believe them then, and I didn't want to now.

By the time we were transferred to Quantico, Virginia, the following year, it was apparent the marriage was in serious trouble. The crisis at home couldn't have come at a worse time in my career. I was enrolled in Amphibious Warfare School, a rigorous program in strategy and tactics required of all regular Marine Corps officers. "Junior School," as it was called, required eight hours a day in the classroom or the field. Night work included writing assignments and tactical problems.

Trying to patch up my disintegrating relationship with my wife, I began falling behind in my studies. By the time the school recessed for the Christmas holidays, I was under tremendous strain, not only from our relationship, but also from a financial debt load. Neither Patricia nor I had learned to control our desires for things we couldn't afford. More than once I had considered leaving my wife.

It was in this state of mind that I took off in a single-engine T-28 on a proficiency flight from the Marine Air Station at Quantico on January 3, 1961. School was still closed for the holidays.

I put on a leather flight jacket and a one-piece flying suit over my civilian clothes before climbing into the trainer to pick up the hours in the air I needed to maintain my proficiency pay. It was late afternoon, and I figured I could also get in a few hours of night flying. Ten were required each year.

As I climbed into the air and headed northeast past Washington, D.C., I didn't realize I was only a few minutes away from an emergency, and an irrational act.

The heater in the T-28's unpressurized cockpit was not very efficient, and I shivered in the January cold as I started some air work. I did some lazy-eights and tight turns, not the full aerobatics variety, but maneuvers that killed the boredom and kept the blood circulating. I was over the river and delta area of eastern Maryland when I developed what at first appeared to be engine trouble.

It turned out to be a runaway propeller—a malfunction that flattens out pitch and causes the propeller to speed up out of control and lose thrust. I tried to remedy the problem by pulling the nose up to place a load on the propeller, but when the engine continued to race wildly, I shut it down. I called "Mayday" several times over the emergency channel, and received a response from some Navy base in the area. I told them I was going to have to bail out, because I couldn't hold my altitude.

I searched through the dusk for a place to set down, but I couldn't find a spot I thought I could reach. The plane was losing altitude so fast that it would be a matter of seconds before it was too low for me to bail out safely. I threw open the canopy, unbuckled my seat harness, and jumped.

The chute opened completely, and as I floated down through the cold evening air I saw the T-28 crash and burn in one of the rolling fields below. A few seconds later I landed hard in a field, not far from a river in rural Maryland. Later I would learn it was the Choptank River. I got to my feet and stared in a daze at the airplane that was burning fiercely in the darkness about a mile away.

The notion came to me suddenly that I could walk off from here, and people would think I was dead, that I had parachuted in the darkness into the river and drowned. I could leave my old life, a life that had grown unbearable, and some-how start again. Later it would seem crazy, illogical thinking, but now it seemed that fate had presented the opportunity to sweep away my troubles overnight.

I threw the parachute in the river, then walked along the bank toward the highway, where I could see the blur of head-lights in the distance. Along the way I took off my flight suit and hid it under a large wooden spool that had once been used to transport transmission line cable. I was now in my civilian clothes. I had less than a hundred dollars in my wallet and no idea what I was going to do. Across the fields I could hear sirens sounding as the fire tmcks headed for the crash site.

I hitched a ride into Baltimore, which was just across Chesa-peake Bay, and checked into a motel. I thought I'd stay here while I tried to get my bearings and decide what I wanted to do with my fife. The newspaper the next morning reported the crash and noted that the missing pilot might have drowned in the river.

I was already having misgivings about what I had done. I had left the scene of an aircraft accident and had, in effect, deserted the Marine Corps. Yet I had taken this step, and now I didn't know how to turn back.

Guilt-stricken, I phoned Patricia and told her where I was. I was still confused about what I should do about my predicament. She promised me she would not say anything for the time being.

For the next several days I wandered around Baltimore, badly troubled and confused. I called Patricia again and asked her to send some money. It was about a week after the crash that a newspaper reported my flight suit had been found. By that time I had decided it was no use. I phoned the FBI office in Baltimore and turned myself in.

Taken back to Quantico, I was held in the bachelor officers' quarters for a day before being allowed to join my wife at home. I was told to consider myself under arrest. I had been at home only a few days when I was indicted by the FBI for deliberate destruction of government property.

Taken before a federal marshal in Alexandria, Virginia, I was given a pretrial hearing. The law firm of Sperling and Dragon agreed to represent me, and Ed Dragon accompanied me to the hearing. Though the FBI wanted a large bail set, the marshal released me on my own recognizance. Reporters were waiting outside to snap my picture as I left the federal building.

I could hardly blame the government attorneys and the Marine Corps for suspecting that I had planned the whole thing, faking my death in an effort to establish a new identity. However, the runaway engine had been real, and the decision to leave the scene of the accident unpremeditated.

Things were going to be tense for a few months, so we took the boys to Oklahoma for the time being, to live with their grandparents. Patricia remained with me through the difficult months that followed. The jury trial, which took place in June in federal court in Baltimore, was a nightmare. Testimony about our private lives enlivened the pages of newspapers in Baltimore and Washington, D.C.

When all the evidence was in, I was acquitted, primarily on the strength of testimony given by Master Sergeant Rusty Arcuni, a Marine aircraft mechanic who had worked extensively on T-28 propellers. He confirmed the runaway propeller from the physical evidence of the teardown and inspection of the wreckage.

Though immensely relieved, I still faced a Marine Corps general court-martial on charges of leaving the scene of an aircraft accident. It was an offense qualifying as "conduct unbecoming to an officer"—not as serious as desertion, but it would certainly put me out of the service. This was not an accusation I disputed. I knew before the first day of the military tribunal that my career in the Corps was finished.

On the advice of my attorneys, I pleaded not guilty to the Marine Corps charge. But I knew that whatever the extenuating circumstances, I could not, and should not, escape responsibility for what I had done.

On July 7, 1961, before a stern-looking assembly of high-ranking officers, I was found guilty and dismissed from the Marine Corps.

It had not been an easy thing to walk into that crowded military courtroom and be dismissed from the outfit that I had joined at sixteen and had served in for fourteen years, four as an enlisted and ten as an officer. I had decided I would exit like a Marine, with my uniform cleaned and pressed, my captain's bars gleaming, my shoes spit-shined, my Air Medal with four stars and my Distinguished Flying Cross pinned proudly on my chest.

The Corps is a relatively small fraternity, and I knew personally every member of the five-officer military court that faced me from behind a long table on that sunny summer morning in Quantico. I accepted their dismissal decision with a salute and a crisp about-face, and strode out of the room promising myself the world had not heard the last of Ernie Brace.

Now here I was, less than four years later, a prisoner of war, tied hand and foot, lying on the wooden floor of an old French barracks in what had been called Indochina. Perhaps there really were no ex-Marines, and this was my destiny, to go on in life as if I had never left the Corps. I wondered if civilians were bound by the Code of Conduct; somehow I knew in my heart that I was.

My mind wandered on to my family. Had my three oldest boys gone to school as usual in Chieng Mai that day? It must have been a long weekend of waiting for word about their father. My three-year-old son, Cary, wouldn't understand what had happened. I knew Patricia would stand up under the strain. Suddenly alone with four children in a strange country, she might be confused and afraid, but our friends in Bird and Son, and in the agency, would help and advise, I was sure. The possibility of my capture, and what she should do if that happened, were subjects so unpalatable that I had never discussed them in any detail with my wife. Now I wished that we had taken the time to talk about the subject.

Money shouldn't be a problem for my family. Civilian aviators working in Southeast Asia under contract to the U.S. government were covered by insurance that provided monthly payments to their families should something happen to them. I was optimistic that Patricia would never have to seek those payments, however.

It was a long way from Moung Hoc to Moung Sai, and Vang Pao's men would be setting up a rescue operation. I knew that I would have to be mentally and physically ready for ambushes along the trail.

In any event, I did not intend to pass up any opportunities to escape on my own. The farther north this column moved, I knew, the worse my prospects for freedom became.

The next day we left the village and continued down the trail for only about thirty minutes. It confused me when the soldiers bivouacked in a small clearing that was pretty well concealed from the air. It seemed we should spend the day walking. Apparently this was a small move on their part to throw off any pursuers. We spent another day tied to trees.

For a few minutes around suppertime, we were released to help in the preparation of the greens that the soldiers had picked in the jungle. Even when not tied to the trees, our elbows were still tied behind our backs and the ropes looped around our necks.

I was already familiar with the routine for preparing the evening meal, the only hot food of the day. Each blue tube carried enough rice to feed a man for a week. Everyone contributed one-seventh of his ration per day to a communal pot for cooking.

The soldiers, obviously familiar with all kinds of edible vegetation in the jungle, picked it along the trail as we traveled, or found it a short distance from their campsites. I recognized some of the vegetables from an old Navy publication I'd read as part of a Marine survival course.

The Vietnamese soldiers were experts in jungle lore. Anybody who lived in it continuously as they did would have had to become an expert. When they realized the prisoners needed to carry some water, they fashioned ingenious canteens from sections of thick bamboo.

With the steaming bowls of rice in their laps, the soldiers sprinkled it with kiki, a seasoning that looked like fine gravel but was a concoction of seeds, pepper, and salt.

When everyone had been served, the leftover rice was made into balls about the size of a softball and tied into a rag. This was then carried tied to one's belt and would be eaten for breakfast and lunch the next day. We prisoners carried the same rations.

Before turning in, some of the soldiers washed in the stream, using a weed found on the bank that, when wetted down and rubbed together, produced a soapy lather. They also carried water back to the camp, boiled it for drinking, and filled everyone's bamboo tubes.

The column that moved out the next morning beneath threatening thunderclouds now included eighteen soldiers, five more than before. We had been on the trail less than an hour when the rain came, at first in a mist and then in a downpour that battered the broad-leafed jungle foliage and drowned out all but shouted conversations.

Though Communist sympathy was strong in this province, it was by no means universal. After a long day of hiking in the rain, the troops stopped before a village whose headman was decidedly unfriendly. He met them on the trail and quickly got into an argument with the officer about where the soldiers and captives should sleep. Gesturing at the soaked, bedraggled prisoners, the Lao seemed to argue that the three men should sleep in the communal hut. He apparently did not want the soldiers sleeping in the hut, however. The officer said no, we could not sleep anywhere unless the soldiers were with us. Finally the headman and the officer agreed to allow the prisoners to sleep tied under a covered porch.

At last the column entered the village, and we were taken out of the rain. The villagers built a fire on the ground under the porch, removed the captives' clothes, and dried them. Later they brought food to the prisoners, but never offered any to the soldiers, who prepared their own.

Watching the soldiers preparing their meal, I could not help admiring their discipline. My experiences with the Thai Border Patrol Police, Vang Pao's hill tribesmen, and the Chinese Nationalists in Thailand had given me the impression that Asiatic troops generally took what they wanted from the public. The NVA never seemed to take anything from a village unless they paid for it. As I ate my dinner I watched the Vietnamese officer haggle with a villager over the price of some bananas, buy them, and record the purchase in a book he kept for the purpose. Then he distributed several of the bananas to each soldier, and gave one to each prisoner.

Yet, if the soldiers were disciplined, I had not forgotten that a few days before they had maimed a fifteen-year-old native boy who had done little more than wield a shovel for the civic action team. Should I try to escape again, and be caught, I was sure that the soldiers would punish me, and it would be more than a slap on the wrist.

The next day we were on the trail early, climbing into higher country through monsoon rains that I knew would curtail the air searches. I had not been permitted to remove my wet boots the night before, and my feet were grimy and sore by the end of the day. My expensive U.S.-made flying boots were falling apart. The zippers, which allowed swift egress should a pilot crash in the water, had already jammed and become unusable. The soles flapped as the stitching disintegrated from the moisture. I was chagrined at how much more serviceable were Harnavee's seventy-nine-cent shower shoes, which seemed to wear forever. They permitted his feet to dry off only minutes after the rain stopped falling or we came out of a streambed. Even if we were marched all the way to China, I thought, Harnavee would still be flip-flopping along in his damned rubber thongs.

We finally stopped in a village large enough to have its own wat. The prisoners slept in a crudely fashioned bamboo temple whose interior was draped with string on which money was hung to encourage Buddha to bless the crops.

I recognized this observance of the planting season as an opportunity to get my name to the outside world. Untied to eat my dinner, I took a one-hundred-baht note from my shirt pocket, wrote my name and the date on the face of the bill, folded it in half, and, when the guard wasn't looking, placed it on one of the strings. I hoped the note would turn up later in a friendly area, and that word would eventually get back to Patricia that I was alive.

This celebration of the growing season, I knew, corresponded to Songkran, the Thai water festival marking the beginning of the monsoon. My family and I had been looking forward to enjoying our first Songkran in Chieng Mai. The Thais devoted days to merrymaking that included free-for-all water fights in the crowded streets. Armed with plastic squirt bottles sold by vendors, young men by the hundreds would chase laughing girls through the downtown traffic, drenching their long black tresses and white cotton shifts. No one, not even the smartly uniformed policemen directing traffic from parasoled pedestals, would be safe from the exuberant squirt-bottle attacks.

A few days ago I would not have guessed that my first celebration of Songkran would take place in a remote jungle wat, or that my first contribution to a Buddhist good-fortune string would be under such deadly serious circumstances.

Another rain-plagued hike the next day brought us to the largest village in the valley, and the center of Pathet Lao activity in the province the Communists called Udon Sai.

Moung Sai sat at the northern end of the Boum Lao valley. Its dozens of wood-frame buildings were a legacy of French colonial rule. An old fort dating from the turn of the century commanded a hill bracketed by the two rivers that ran through the village.

As we approached, I could almost picture the tricolor fluttering above the old fortress and blue-kepied Legionnaires patrolling the stone-and-mortar ramparts. The airfield, disabled by ditches, was large enough for C-47s.

Terry Burke's intelligence had indicated the fort was now being used by the Pathet Lao. I could see communications antennae bristling from bunkers built into the base of the hill just below the bomb-damaged walls. As we walked past the abandoned French runway and into the village, I noticed fresh bomb craters along the trail.

We were placed in the entrance hall of a dilapidated wooden schoolhouse near the center of the village, and were told to sit on the floor opposite a door leading into the building's single classroom. Our arrival obviously had created some excitement in the community, and curious villagers peered at us through cracks in the walls.

It was after dark when a visitor came in with a flashlight. I recognized the shaven head and saffron robes of a Buddhist monk, and sensed somehow that the man was a Thai. The flashlight stopped when it reached my face.

"How are you?" came the quiet greeting in perfect English.

"*Sa bai,*" I responded, testing my hunch.

"Oh, you speak Thai?"

"No, I know only a few words."

The priest knelt down on one knee, and I got a better look at the handsome, intelligent face with its searching eyes. I was certain I had seen that face on a wanted poster circulated by the Thai Border Patrol Police. A leader of the militant Buddhist sect called the Cao Dai, the monk was wanted for antigovernment political activity.

"Where is your home in America?" the monk asked in a voice that betrayed a British accent.

"Michigan," I replied.

"Oh, yes, the University of Michigan at Ann Arbor. Its campus is very beautiful."

"Have you been there?" I asked.

A smile appeared, then vanished. "Why did you bomb our wat?"

"I didn't," I replied.

The monk's words were measured, but tinged with anger. "Two days ago you bombed our wat."

I explained that I had been captured a week ago, but I knew what the Buddhist was talking about. On the way into the village, I had noticed that the large temple with its graceful tiled roof and colorful decorative trim had been damaged by what appeared to be a direct bomb hit. Apparently Royal Laotian or Air America T-28s had been bombing the fort and had accidentally hit the wat situated just below. What a time to arrive in Moung Sai, I thought grimly, two days after my buddies bomb a church.

I was astonished to hear the monk accuse me of flying missions into China in support of the Koumintang soldiers along the Thai border. My denial produced a sigh of disbelief.

"I know that you do," the Buddhist said. "You fly a special airplane. We call it the whisper aircraft because it is very quiet."

"I fly an aircraft that is made in Switzerland and can be bought by anybody," I replied. "You could buy it. There's nothing special about it."

Obviously skeptical, the priest abandoned that line of questioning and began asking about the civic action team projects. It was a subject he already knew a lot about, and the interrogation soon turned into an attack on American aid.

"The Lao do not need your hospitals and aid programs," he told me acidly. "You are corrupting the values of a four-thousand-year-old civilization with your technology and machines."

I pointed out, without rancor, that the priest was carrying a flashlight in one hand and a transistor radio in the other. Both were products of American ingenuity developed within the last hundred years. The monk laughed and dismissed them as luxuries. Besides, he added in apparent earnestness, the Russians had invented those items first.

The Buddhist had moved over to Harnavee and was inter-rogating him in Thai when several young guerrillas carrying rifles came in and chatted with the NVA guards. When the monk was finished, he addressed the uniformed soldiers in Lao, and they turned over the prisoners' neck ropes to the guerrillas. In English, he told me, "We will make you comfortable for the night." In a moment the NVA soldiers were gone.

Our new guards took us outside and led us toward the hill. The walls of the fortress loomed above us in the darkness. We crossed a stream at the foot of the slope and walked past several huts and a bunker that appeared to be a communications center.

Stopping at a long thatch-roofed building that rose on stilts near the path leading up to the fort, we climbed the stairs and entered one of the large rooms that opened onto the porch. When we had been fed some rice, we were left for the night, with our new guards posted outside the door.

I lay in the darkness, listening to the hum of the insects and the barking of village dogs in the distance. I felt more appre-hensive about my future than I had felt since the first day of my capture. What I had feared most had just taken place. We had been turned over to the Pathet Lao.

9

In the morning we were taken down to the stream and allowed to wash for the first time since we had been captured eight days before. A T-28 had evidently crashed somewhere near here. One wing was being used as a platform on the edge of the fast-moving mountain stream. The rest of the aircraft was not in sight. Some women washing clothes on the wing moved over to make room for the three captives. We were given a small piece of what looked like homemade brown soap to use.

While we were washing, a large patrol came out of the jungle on the other side of the stream and crossed at a ford near us. They were curious as they passed, but made no threatening moves toward us. Their arms appeared to be mainly captured American weapons.

At first I thought we would have to put our wet clothes back on, but a soldier came up with some black pajama-like tops and bottoms for all three of us. Sergeant Harnavee and the Lao soldier could have passed for Pathet Lao in the black pajamas, except for the fact that the garments were about three sizes too small and came to just below their knees. Mine didn't fit any better.

After we had returned to our room, the Buddhist arrived and took me down the wide porch to another room, several doors away. A lean-faced Pathet Lao guerrilla in his early thirties, wearing a pistol on his belt, was waiting by the desk and chair that constituted the room's only furniture. He said something in Lao to the Buddhist. His eyes stayed on the American in the week-old beard who stood before him.

"This is the commander of the Neo Lao Hak Set," the monk announced.

"The Pathet Lao," I said bluntly.

The priest looked annoyed. "The correct name," he said, "is Neo Lao Hak Set."

The Buddhist listened to the officer's rapid-fire Laotian, then translated.

"We know you are a spy pilot who works for the Central Intelligence Agency," he said. "We know your rank is colonel, that you are based at Chieng Mai, Thailand, and that you fly a special aircraft into China."

Before I could dispute these charges, the officer began his interrogation, using the Buddhist to translate.

"Where are you based?"

"Vientiane," I replied.

"You are based in Chieng Mai!"

"My family lives there, but my company is based in Vientiane."

The officer picked up a bamboo cane from his desk and began tapping it in the palm of his hand. "Whom do you work with?"

"Lao soldiers," I said.

The answer wasn't satisfactory. "You work for the Vientiane government!" the interrogator shot back, glaring at me as his words were translated.

My answers to the subsequent questions brought increase-ingly irritated responses. When I refused to confess that I was a "CIA spy pilot," the guerrilla leader came angrily around the desk, brandishing the cane. He warned me I would be punished if I didn't start answering the questions "sincerely." He then ordered me to my knees and had me place my fingertips on the edge of the desk.

As the officer continued the interrogation from behind me, I could hear the angry cane whistling through the air. I flinched as he whipped it back and forth around my head.

What did I know about Terry, the American at Boum Lao? What was the nature of the young adviser's authority? What projects had Terry planned for the civic action team? The Communist officer was obviously familiar with the daily routine of the special operations base, indicating that the camp had been studied closely before the attack.

The questions about Terry made me wonder whether my friend might have escaped after all. I had no chance to ponder the possibility, as the cane crashed down on the desk or the floor each time one of my answers wasn't "satisfactory."

"Why do you fly the whisper aircraft?"

"There is no whisper aircraft," I said.

The cane came down hard only a few inches from my fingers, making a sound like a pistol shot. I jumped involuntarily. "You are to be tried by the people's court," the guerrilla leader told me savagely through the monk. "And you are going to be punished."

I tried not to appear shaken as I was taken from the room, but there was cold sweat on the small of my back. It was possible, I thought, that this was the standard interrogation procedure, and the threats were only that. But I had heard enough about the Pathet Lao to know that their threats were not always just theatrics. If the "people's court" decided I was some kind of a war criminal, there was no telling what the guerrillas would do.

After the hostility of the PL commander, I was surprised that the next stop along the porch was a doctor's office. There, a gray-haired French-speaking doctor, who appeared to have Western as well as Oriental blood, asked me if I had any injuries. Soon the physician was examining the large boil that had developed under my arm. His hands and arms were dyed red to the elbows with merthiolate. I guessed the doctor must have been working recently on personnel wounded at Boum Lao or perhaps in the bombing raid, and that the merthiolate served as his disinfectant. The doctor lanced the boil and bandaged the shoulder and armpit with professional skill.

The rest of the day passed quietly in the room I had slept in the night before. Harnavee and the Lao soldier were taken, one at a time, through the same procedure I had just finished. After they had finished their sessions with the interrogator and the doctor, we were left alone. Late in the afternoon we were brought our evening meal, a surprisingly appetizing dish of sticky rice and pork chips served with a spinach-type vegetable. Then we were taken outside to use a latrine. We slept our second night in a row without being tied. I fell asleep thinking that perhaps my fears about the Pathet Lao had been groundless.

The next morning in the predawn darkness, the guards shook me awake roughly and tied my elbows behind me. They led me by the neck rope along the porch and into a room where the Buddhist monk was waiting. The kerosene lantern cast eerie shadows about the room. The monk was very grave, and without his usual smile.

"The people's court has met," he told me, "and you are in very much trouble. You must follow me now."

Escorted by the guards, I followed the monk down the stairs and along a path under the stilted building. Next to the several underground bunkers that had been built into the base of the hill waited the Pathet Lao commander. A ragtag detail of young guerrillas carrying M-1 rifles and with grenades hanging from their belts stood off to the side. They were kids, I thought, no more than fifteen or sixteen.

The Buddhist climbed onto the dirt-covered logs that formed the roof of a bunker, and ordered me to follow. When I was on the bunker, looking slightly down at the guerrillas, the monk motioned for the armed kids to form a line facing us. He then pulled a piece of paper from his flowing sleeve. The writing was in English, done in beautiful script with purple ink.

"The people's court of the Neo Lao Hak Set has found you guilty of being a spy pilot, and you are therefore to be shot!" the Buddhist announced.

Though I had half expected such a verdict, I couldn't stop the tears from welling up in my eyes. The guard who had been holding my neck leash dropped it and moved away from me. The Buddhist moved down off the bunker.

I thought of making a run for it, but I knew I wouldn't get more than a few steps. The Pathet Lao commander spoke to the priest. He came back up on the bunker and showed me the paper with the purple ink, explaining it was a confession of my crime. There was enough morning light now to read the short script easily. If I would sign it, the monk said, "the people's court might show leniency."

I tried to collect my thoughts. It would make no sense to sign a confession. My signing it would give me no guarantee that they wouldn't shoot me and publish the confession anyway. Moreover, by admitting I was a spy, I would lose my status as a civilian contract pilot and thus any protection under the Geneva Convention. When I told the Buddhist as much, the priest talked with the officer, then turned back to me.

"You will not confess?"

"No, I'm not confessing to this. I'm an AID pilot. I was carrying a woman and child and supplies for a civic action team."

"Then you must be shot." The Buddhist left the bunker and said something to the commander.

The officer barked an order. The young guerrillas loaded rounds into their rifles in a manner so unmilitary that I guessed they had been pressed into service only days before. The next command caused the rifles to be raised to their shoulders.

Was this how it would end, with a ragged volley fired by youngsters in a place few Americans had ever heard of?

Looking at these kids committed to war, I thought about my own four boys in Chieng Mai. They had looked up to me and counted on me. I wondered what would happen to them now.

Though I couldn't keep my eyes from misting up, I'd be damned if I would die in a way that would make those boys think less of me. I remembered the awful moment when, standing at attention before a court-martial, I had been dismissed from the Marine Corps that had been my life for fourteen years. I had told myself to stand tall then, and the advice had strengthened me. I tried to summon that same strength now. I shivered, even though it wasn't cold.

Out over the heads of the firing squad, I could see the sun coming up through the trees. The haze with the greenish gold glow was more from my misty eyes than from the early-morning steam rising from the jungle.

10

Before the firing squad was given the final order, the Pathet Lao officer and the monk exchanged words again. Then the Buddhist pulled another piece of paper from his robe and handed it to me.

"You have one more chance," he said. "If you answer these questions, we will not shoot you."

Looking over the questions, I could scarcely believe my eyes. The first required me to compare President Johnson's foreign policy with that of President Kennedy. The second asked whether the Peace Corps was a division of the Central Intelligence Agency. The third and fourth inquired about my educational background and asked why my family was living in Thailand. Under the circumstances, the questions were utterly absurd. Yet I could tell that my captors did not consider them a joke, and I was not about to ruin this opportunity by ridiculing them. I studied the questions soberly.

"Okay," I said. "I'll answer these."

My hands were untied and I was taken beneath the long building on stilts and seated at a picnic table. Using a fountain pen with purple ink provided me by the monk, I wrote a paragraph on each question. My answers were as innocuous as the questions, and the Buddhist didn't find them satisfactory, but he told me they would not shoot me now.

In a few minutes the two other prisoners were brought under the building and seated on a bench next to me. We were told to turn over all our personal possessions, which in my case meant my watch, pen, and wedding ring. Before the items were tied up in a rag and placed in a knapsack, the monk wrote out a formal receipt, which was signed by him, the officer, the doctor who had treated the prisoners the day before, and then by me.

We were then taken up the path toward the fort. We walked along solid gray walls some fifteen feet high before reaching the crumbling gate that led into a cobble stoned courtyard. We stepped over charred timber and fallen stone to get into a tiny cell with a barred window and a bricked-over fireplace. We waited while the guards brought in three pairs of leg stocks, which appeared to have been made especially for us.

The room was so small that we could have reached over and pulled the pins securing each other's stocks. If we were left this way for the night, I felt we might have a chance to escape.

About mid-afternoon the Buddhist monk arrived. He gave each prisoner a blanket and a large square of black cloth designed to carry personal belongings. Then, accompanied by guards, we were marched out of the fort and down the hill to bathe in the river. The cold stream water was invigorating, and in spite of everything, I enjoyed my few minutes in the sunlight. As we scrubbed ourselves, several well-equipped guerrilla patrols forded the river, stopping to stare at the white-skinned prisoner and to chat with the guards. After we finished, we were taken back to the fort.

Despite the bomb damage and the fort's rundown condition, I could see that it was being used extensively. Perhaps twenty people were working on the other side of the courtyard in an armory that had the capability of repairing weapons. A foot-powered lathe whined along a wall where captured American rifles stood. Two 57mm recoilless rifles rested on tripods, apparently ready for service. Some guerrillas worked on getting an 81mm recoilless back into operation.

Returned to the cell and stocks for the night, I considered an escape try after dark, and discussed the matter with Harnavee and the Lao, one of whom would have to reach over and remove the pin from my stocks. Every time I sat up in the darkness, the guard was there, silhouetted in the doorway with his AK-47.

Even if we could make it to the courtyard, there was still the problem of getting out the gate and through a hostile village. I decided to await a better opportunity. If this was the place where we were to be held for the duration of the war, I would have time to plan an escape that had a better chance of succeeding.

The stay in the fort lasted only a night for Harnavee and me. Before dawn the next day, we were taken out of our stocks and advised that we were leaving. We put our extra clothing into the large black cloth squares the Buddhist had given us, tied them, and slung them over our shoulders.

The Laotian soldier had worried that his nationality might single him out for special punishment from his Pathet Lao countrymen. When he saw he was being left behind, he began to cry pitifully. The Thai spoke to him comfortingly, and I leaned down and gave the young man's shoulder a squeeze.

We walked into the courtyard to find the same North Vietnamese soldiers that had turned us over to the guerrillas two days before. I never thought I would be relieved to see a squad of NVA regulars waiting to take custody of me, but I felt that way now.

A few of the familiar faces ventured smiles as we were bound in the usual fashion and given our blue rice sacks and bamboo-tube canteens. Morning light was streaking the eastern sky when the column filed out of the old fort, the prisoners in tow on neck ropes. I would never see the Lao prisoner again.

We headed north into the jungle again, and I guessed we were on our way to Phong Saly and the caves where American pilots were supposedly held. Having flown over this area on numerous occasions, I knew exactly where I was, and I could tell that my captors weren't aware of that. Other prisoners had been taken through the jungle blindfolded in an effort to confuse them as to their where-abouts, but the NVA obviously didn't consider such a precaution necessary for me. Their ignorance of my knowledge, I knew, might cause them to slacken their vigilance and afford me an opportunity to escape.

The prospect of an airborne rescue seemed diminished. We were not so far north yet that I couldn't make my way to Vang Pao's supporters if I could just get away. I had been told as a youth that I had something approaching a photo-graphic memory. The location of a Vang Pao camp at Cheng Kong, a few days' walk from here, had been etched in my memory ever since I had noticed it on a map many months ago. In the next few days, I decided, I would be as friendly to my captors as possible in an effort to get them to relax their guard.

A day's travel brought us to a checkpoint near a river junction. An NVA soldier stopped the column and examined the squad leader's papers. The guard waved them onto a trail leading around a village and into a large army camp in a clearing protected from air surveillance by the jungle canopy. Green-uniformed sentries patrolled the perimeter of a compound that included dozens of huts and a variety of solidly built bunkers and revetments.

A well-equipped field hospital operated at one end of the camp, and I noticed that the medics in surgical whites had arms dyed red in the same manner as the doctor in Moung Sai. The squad stopped here for the night. Before darkness, I had counted more than 150 uniformed troops coming and going on patrols. I concluded that this was a major base camp, probably run by the North Vietnamese but also used extensively by the Pathet Lao.

The next morning we continued hiking north for about an hour, then left the valley and began climbing east up into the mountains. For the first time, I began to question my assumption that we were headed for Pathet Lao headquarters in Phong Saly. The soldiers, believing me to be totally lost, repeatedly told me that we were now in China. I knew exactly where we were, and we would not reach either Phong Saly or China by heading east.

Wherever we were headed, it was rougher going now. We followed mountain trails that alternately climbed and descended so steeply that frequent rest stops were required.

During the next several days of traveling, I worked hard to cultivate friend-ships with my captors and to appear as if I had no intention of attempting an escape. Soon I was being offered the special seasoning the troops carried for their rice. A soldier offered me a Gillette razor that he had undoubtedly picked up at Boum Lao. I passed up the offer because I had no water at the time, and a two-week beard would be difficult to shave. Another soldier entertained us with a sleight-of-hand act.

A few of the troops were familiar enough with me to show me the North Vietnamese insignia and identification cards they carried in their shirt pockets. The insignia were kept in a plastic folder, and the ID cards were hidden in the false back of the small signal mirror each soldier carried.

After supper at one overnight stop, a soldier asked me to translate a letter in English purporting to be written by an American girl. The letter, which was undated, unsigned, and had no envelope, began, "My Dear Boy, I am an American college girl and am so proud of what you're doing in your country towards freedom and happiness." I summarized the contents and relayed them to the soldier through Harnavee. I was convinced that the letter had been prepared in North Vietnam as part of the Communist propaganda effort.

I knew the time was getting ripe for an escape try when the column made a rest stop in a small village and several of the soldiers laid their weapons within easy reach. My elbow ropes had been loosened enough so that I could drink. At one point I had to reach around a rifle leaning against a tree in order to get to the bamboo water jug. I knew it would be foolish to try something in broad daylight with so many people awake. I hoped my apparent indifference to the rifle would convince the soldiers that I had no intention of trying to escape.

On June 6, the column stopped for the night at a small village whose inhabitants were quite friendly to Harnavee and me. As I ate my hot meal outside the communal hut, curious children gathered, fascinated by my unshaven face. It was entirely possible, I thought, that I was the first American they had ever seen. When Harnavee and I had finished eating, we were placed in the communal hut. Our neck ropes were tied to the bamboo supports in the thatched walls.

I went to sleep thinking of Patricia and the kids. I had been keeping track of the date in my head, and knew that I had been gone now for sixteen days. If she didn't hear from me soon, she would have to consider taking the boys back to California to wait there.

I awoke about four o'clock in the morning, feeling the gas pains that accompanied the diarrhea I had experienced in the last few days. I needed to get outside to relieve myself.

The fire in the sandbox near the center of the hut was still sending smoke up through the thatch ceiling. Harnavee and the soldiers were fast asleep. The guards had not tied me carefully the night before, and I was able to work my hands and feet free. I stood, untied my neck rope, and tiptoed to the door and out onto the porch, where I expected to find a guard. Finding none, I stood for a few moments in the gray predawn light, listening and looking. My boots had been left on the porch the night before. After putting them on, I walked off the porch. I peered down the side of the hut and spotted a guard a few hundred feet away.

I turned the other way and walked into the bushes to relieve myself. When I finished, it was still clear, so I started to walk quietly down the path leading out of the village and back the way we had come.

I walked slowly, not wishing to startle a sleeping dog that might awaken the village with his barking. I listened for sounds coming from the huts on either side of me. The only noises, other than the thumping of my heart, came from the jungle. The occasional call of a bird and the incessant hum of the insects were common noises.

I was passing the last hut when the door opened and a sleepy-eyed villager peered out at me. The startled native immediately motioned me to return to the communal hut. I was not about to turn back now. I broke into a run. My adrenaline was pumping and my heart was pounding in my head. Behind me, I could hear the screams of the villager waking up the soldiers. The reports of an AK-47 on automatic sounded the alarm.

11

The path dipped and climbed like a roller coaster. After just a few minutes I was getting winded. The smacking of the soldiers' tennis shoes on the path behind me kept me going for a while. I knew I couldn't stop to rest on the trail. Gasping for breath, I dove off the side of the path into the elephant grass. Scrambling and falling down the Mountainside, I rolled into a heavily foliaged ravine about thirty or forty feet below the ridgeline trail. Then I climbed under the overhang of the closest bank, and pulled the grass and other vegetation down over me.

In a few moments I heard the soldiers above me, yelling to one another as they spilled onto the Mountainside from the direction of the village. I remained crouched in my hiding place, trying to correct my thoughts about what to do next.

With all the activity on the trail, it would be unwise to try to move now. It seemed unlikely they would find me unless they came down the ravine itself. My best bet was to wait until nightfall, then make my way south. I knew we were on a series of mountains and ridgelines stretching from the Moung Sai Valley to the Nam Ou River. Vang Pao's guerrillas occupied some of this territory, including a base probably not more than fifteen miles away. If I could not make it to that camp, I could try my luck in one of the mountain villages nearby.

Some of the villages we had passed through during the past few days had been decidedly cool toward the soldiers. I knew that Vang Pao's name carried enormous weight among many hill tribesmen. Perhaps some young native, acting out of loyalty to the Hmong leader or hoping to collect the reward money offered for downed American flyers, might take me to safety.

I had been in my hiding place for about an hour and a half when I heard two soldiers leave the trail and begin walking downhill through the ravine. One of them nearly stepped on me as they made their way through the narrow, brush-choked gully

64 Ernest C. Brace

and continued downhill. If they came back the same way, they would be looking uphill and would be sure to spot me. A move now seemed too risky, and I reasoned that the soldiers would not return over a route they had already searched.

I was wrong. About an hour later I heard the pair of returning soldiers climbing uphill. They were apparently following the bank of the ravine. My heart sank and I gulped for air as I realized one of them had spotted me. They fired a burst into the bushes above me, and yelled something in Vietnamese or Lao that needed no translation. I climbed out of my hiding place.

There was no easy familiarity now. The soldiers struck me repeatedly with the bamboo poles they carried for walking sticks as they pushed me roughly up the hill. When we reached the path, several more soldiers were waiting. One of them fired two shots in the air, paused, and fired two more, the signal that the prisoner had been captured. Then they tied my elbows tight behind me, and pushed and kicked me back down the trail toward the village.

When we reached the village, a crowd of soldiers and natives was waiting outside the communal hut. I was tied standing up to a post in the center of the village. Women and children stood wide-eyed nearby, fear showing in their faces. It was a reflection of the fear I felt myself

The squad leader was brought out on a litter, with both feet bandaged. At the first sound of the alarm, he had apparently rushed out in the semidarkness and had run barefooted into bamboo defense stakes planted by the villagers between the huts. One of the sharpened stakes had gone all the way through his foot, I would learn later. It was clear he blamed me for his wounds.

The soldier couldn't stand, but he was helped to his knees, and from there he fired questions at me that were translated by Sergeant Harnavee. "Why did you try to escape?"

"I wanted to go home."

"Where were you going?"

"Chuck Chung."

The answer was scarcely out of my mouth before I realized I had betrayed my familiarity with the area. Chuck Chung was the Vang Pao base I knew was just about fifteen miles to the south. These soldiers thought I believed I was in China. The squad leader himself had not heard of the base, and had to ask the village headman where it was.

"Do you know the name of the village you are in?"

"No," I answered, telling the truth.

"They are going to punish you," Harnavee told me.

The squad leader slapped me hard with his open hand. He closed his fist when he saw he had not inflicted enough damage. As the blows struck my face, the village headman, much more hostile than he had seemed when we arrived the night before, held a bolt-action rifle a few inches from my temple. Occasionally he poked me in the head with the muzzle. A few of the other soldiers joined in, kicking me in the thighs or throwing punches.

I was getting numb until one of the harder blows split my nose. The sharp crack of bone breaking, which I heard as well as felt, aroused me to a level where everything seemed to be happening in slow motion. I sensed that I was going to die tied to that pole. My mouth was swollen, and several teeth had been knocked loose. The bridgework in my upper jaw was broken; I could feel the rough edge of the metal brace cutting my lip.

Knowing I was bleeding from the nose and mouth, I slumped in my ropes, feigning unconsciousness.

It worked. The squad leader turned his attention to Harnavee. He slapped him a few times, apparently as a warning, and had the Thai returned to the communal hut. I was left tied to the post.

After several hours had passed, a soldier untied me. The villagers gave me some water to drink and wash with. I was then taken back into the hut from which I had escaped. Harnavee and I were fed, then tied up tightly for the rest of the day. I had a hard time eating anything, with my mouth in its present condition. I managed to pry the metal brace of my permanent bridge back almost into place. Before dark, the squad leader came in again to berate me for having delayed the column's progress by a full day. They would now be late in arriving at their destination, I was told through Harnavee.

Though my escape try had meant Harnavee too was bound much more tightly and uncomfortably, the Thai showed no resentment toward his fellow prisoner. A Buddhist, he seemed to be ready to accept the difficulties we had endured since our capture. I appreciated this tolerance and patience, though I couldn't espouse that attitude myself. More than once, when we were talking quietly in the night, with the fire in a sandbox glowing softly in the thatch hut, the Thai would dismiss our troubles with a remark uttered with such serenity that it sounded like a benediction. "Buddha will provide," he would say. "Buddha will provide."

12

I awoke the next morning swollen-faced and very sore. When the Thai and I were taken outside, the soldiers were already forming up. A few were lifting the squad leader onto a stretcher that was to be carried by villagers. In a few minutes we were off, walking toward the sunrise at a brisk pace that indicated we were, indeed, late for a rendezvous somewhere down the trail.

The next several days of walking were particularly difficult ones for me. I was wracked by diarrhea that diminished my appetite at a time when I needed all the energy I could get. The soreness from my beating made walking an effort. The soles had come loose from my deteriorating boots and were flopping as I took each step. Soon I would be walking barefoot if we had much farther to go to our destination.

The large black leeches constituted the worst problem. Nearly two inches long, the slimy things sat on the leaves or twigs of bushes, expertly camouflaged. They had the ability to cling to you as you brushed by them along the trail. They anesthetized the skin so a person couldn't feel the wound they made, or the blood being sucked out.

Worse than the blood loss was the one-inch long anticoagulant slug the leeches injected into the wound to prevent clotting. After the insects had sucked their fill, they dropped off. The slug was left to decompose and after a few hours produced an ulcerated sore about the size of a quarter. Both Harnavee and I developed numerous such sores on our feet and lower legs as our journey continued. The local people and our escort all had scars from these leeches on their lower legs. The soldiers showed me how to get the slug of slime out of my leg by scraping the wound with the sharp edge of a piece of split bamboo. Usually you didn't know a leech had been on you, however, until you took your boots off, or rolled up your trousers, and found a trail of blood.

We were perhaps two days out of the village from which I had escaped when we came upon an albino native boy walking slowly on the trail, hungry and alone. I had occasionally come upon albinos among the hill tribesmen, but the effect of the white-skinned, white-haired, pink-eyed twelve-year-old in a jungle setting was startling. Obviously an outcast, the boy needed food, but the soldiers, repelled by his appearance, laughed at him and kept their distance.

It was at moments like this, and the time the soldiers had laughed at the retarded girl in Moung Hoc, that I was reminded of how young some of my captors were, despite their jungle savvy and military discipline. Harnavee gave the boy some of his rice and I handed him an entire rice ball, my ration until evening. I had little appetite anyway, because of my intestinal disorder and sore mouth.

Near sunset a few days later, the column left the ridgeline and moved down into a valley to a river that I knew must be the Nam Ou. The squad leader was no longer with us. He had ordered the troops to leave him and the fitter bearers behind so that the squad might make its rendezvous on time.

When I saw the recently bombed French fort on the hillside above the village, I knew we had reached Moung Kheo, another Pathet Lao stronghold. The fort was one in a series of French strongholds that had fallen during the early 1950s. The stone bastion appeared to have been abandoned because of the bombing. The camp was situated about a half-mile away in a clearing hidden from the air by the jungle canopy. When we walked into the camp to spend the night, I saw large quantities of supplies stacked among the huts and bunkers, and guessed this was a major distribution point.

After turning our blue-cloth rice tubes over to a man that looked to be of some authority, we were escorted to the river to wash. I noticed the Nam Ou was high and fast-moving, almost at flood stage, and my pulse quickened at this new opportunity for escape. Years of skin diving had made me a strong-lunged swimmer, and this swiftly flowing river would take me south to friendly forces. But the guards proved too attentive for me to make a break. Two were right with us, and a third stood farther downstream along the gravel bank, watching closely. Anyway, I reasoned, I was exhausted from a day's walk. Assuming they continued east the following morning, they would have to ford the river, and I would look for an opportunity then.

We had been returned to a hut for only a short time before I heard a soft female voice asking, "*Parlez-vous Français?*" I looked up at a young military nurse in green fatigues and uttered a surprised "No." Our communication problem didn't matter when she spotted the ulcerated sores on my feet.

She expertly treated the infections from a Chinese first-aid kit and chattered with a guard in what seemed fluent French. I concluded that she must be Vietnamese; her features were too sharp for a Lao woman. Her black hair was rolled neatly on the side of her head in the Chinese fashion. I could picture the pretty young woman in a bao dai, turning men's heads on the streets of Hanoi, or even Chieng Mai. But she was all business now, and after bandaging my sores she moved over to Harnavee and treated his infections.

The unexpected appearance of the attractive young woman brought all the pleasant images of my life before captivity rushing into my head, images that belonged to another world. I went to sleep thinking of Patricia, the boys, and Chieng Mai, and was more determined than ever somehow to get back home.

My hopes for a river escape were dashed the following morning when the column, which now included the nurse, began fording the Nam Ou. I reasoned that the soldiers would have to untie me during the crossing, since the river was too deep to walk across. The soldiers were taking no chances now, and kept neck ropes on the prisoners as they were ferried one at a time across the river on a raft.

I thought of the puzzle of the boy trying to get a fox and some geese across a river. These guys apparently knew the story. Three went across the river first, paying out a long rope as they went. One came back with the raft and picked me up. The neck rope was tied to the rope that the soldier on the other bank was holding. Another rope was paid out as a soldier and I crossed. The procedure was repeated with Harnavee, troops on one side paying out a neck rope, those on the other gathering it in.

The crossing must have taken at least two hours. I kept hoping for an aircraft to come by, but none appeared. When we were all across, we started up a steep trail that required some of the most arduous climbing of the trip. The rain started down worse than I had seen it since we had started walking. I knew now I was getting out of Vang Pao's country into mountains I was not familiar with. We would be crossing Laos far north of the

Plain of Jars. In fact, we were far enough north that we would probably be in Vietnam soon.

The walking was very strenuous, and I had little time to worry about the problem of escaping. The air grew thinner, and the rain fell often enough that we were given plastic shawls to throw over our shoulders, but the plastic made me sweat so profusely that I was soaked anyway.

I guessed now we must be heading toward Dien Bien Phu, which lay just beyond the Laotian border. Never having seen the place, I didn't know what to expect. I amused myself by picturing a massive French fortress or a Tibetan-style monastery waiting around each bend on the trail. We were walking above some of the lower clouds, and the scenery was what the Tarzan jungle stories were made of. It was easy to fantasize.

We made camp that night alongside the jungle path. It was the first night we had slept out. It was interesting to watch the soldiers set up their plastic sheets to keep them out of the rain. When I thought of my boot camp days in the Marine Corps and the heavy pup tent sections each man carried, I knew we Americans had a lot to learn about existing in the jungle.

A day and a half out of Moung Kheo, the path curved down into a valley and broadened into a road that was almost wide enough to accommodate motor vehicles. I spotted surveyors' stakes and old geology cuts designed to test ground load capability, and guessed the road was to be extended west through the jungle toward the Nam Ou. When I kicked up one of the stakes, one of the soldiers gave me a harsh upbraiding, then shoved the stake back into the hole it had come out of.

We had been on the road only a few minutes before we arrived at a good-sized village. The surrounding hills were sprinkled with caves that I guessed contained Pathet Lao or NVA supplies. I learned later that we were in Moung Lao, a Laotian community on the North Vietnam border and the western terminus of the road to Hanoi. Under the trees were parked some green-painted army trucks, the first motor vehicles I had seen since leaving Chieng Mai more than three weeks before.

Harnavee and I were placed in separate cells of a jail consisting of a log-covered slit trench hidden from the air by a thatched roof on stilts. I spent an uncomfortable night in a malodorous, dirt-walled cell about two and one-half feet wide, seven feet long, and five feet high. At one end was a hand-dug hole from which the smell of urine came. We were the only occupants of the dugout jail, whose eight cells branched off four to a side from a central corridor.

Moung Lao was apparently the soldiers' rendezvous point. After we had been taken from our cells and fed the next morning, another NVA unit arrived, wearing their rank and insignia. In a formal ceremony, the new outfit took custody of the prisoners, and the eighteen-soldier guard detail would now, presumably, head back into the Laotian jungles.

We couldn't help getting to know the soldiers during our three-week journey through the jungle, and I found myself sorry to see them go. I didn't resent the beating they had given me. It was punishment I knew would come if I tried to escape. To do their job, I knew, they had to discourage such escape tries. I also knew that I must not let such punishment discourage me from trying again. It was a game we were playing—a deadly one, to be sure, but all the same a game. Each side observed its own rules.

Any animosity the soldiers felt toward us seemed to fade. They had done their job. The captives were delivered safely. When they took back the rice tubes, the bamboo canteens, and the plastic rain covers, the soldiers clapped Harnavee and me on the back and wished us well. I felt they meant it.

The new unit took us east along a dusty road that I assumed would eventually take us to Hanoi and its POW prisons. I wasn't upset at the prospect. At least we seemed to be leaving the jurisdiction of the unpredictable Pathet Lao.

Perhaps I would be imprisoned with the American military pilots who were being shot down over North Vietnam as the war there heated up. I knew that two of the earliest shootdowns, Navy pilots Ev Alvarez and Bob Shumaker, were reported to be held in Hanoi, and there might be others. Alvarez, the first American aviator to become a POW in North Vietnam, had been shot down the previous August, and Shumaker in February.

Trucks loaded with green bamboo passed us in both directions as the sun climbed in the sky, but the soldiers had no interest in hitching a ride. The military checkpoints were more frequent now. I guessed that one of them, whose sentries inspected our papers in front of a log barricade, might have marked the North Vietnamese border. After walking for about half a day, the column waded across a small river. We walked a few hundred yards on past some small bomb-shelter dugouts and a camou-flaged tracked vehicle that could have been a tank.

A little farther down the road, the soldiers rendezvoused with a pair of trucks hidden from the air by the trees. We were placed in the back of one, beneath the canvas canopy. Though I had seen no bomb craters along the road, I guessed the drivers were concerned about enemy aircraft, because they waited until darkness before moving out on the road.

With the soldiers bouncing around in back alongside the prisoners, the trucks rolled eastward for several hours. We were stopped at checkpoints where an officer in the cab patiently produced the necessary papers. I could not see much in the darkness outside the back of the truck, but I could tell we had moved into a large valley scattered with small villages.

About midnight, the truck turned right off the road into a smaller valley and drove a short distance before pulling off the road. I wondered why we were stopping in the middle of the night. If they continued down the road, they might be able to reach Hanoi by morning. Harnavee was taken out first and led off around the side of a limestone cliff.

I was told to get out and was taken up a hill and put in a bamboo cage that was barely long enough for me to stretch out and not high enough for me to stand up in. As I lay on my back on the dirt floor, the soldiers tied my ankles and secured my foot ropes to the rear of the cage. My neck rope was run through the bamboo bars and tied, with no slack, to a stake in front of the cage. The soldiers threw a blanket over me and tied the cage door shut behind them as they left. Two guards kept watch on me from a lean-to about a dozen feet away. It was not the most comfortable way to spend the night. I knew I could manage until morning, when I guessed we would be on our way again, toward the French-built prisons of Hanoi.

It was a few days before I realized that my journey had ended. This was to be my prison.

13

In the morning the soldiers untied my hands and feet and gave me some slack in my neck rope. This allowed me to sit up and move around somewhat. The daylight gave me a better look at my new place of confinement.

I was in a cage about three feet wide and seven feet long. The five-foot-high entrance in front slanted down toward a rear wall no more than thirty inches from the ground. The entire cage was constructed of bamboo poles tied firmly together with water-soaked bamboo strips. Its thick ground-anchored corner posts supported smaller vertical and horizontal crossbars about the diameter of broom handles. The top, rear, and two long sides were covered with thatch that kept out the sunlight and the rain. The front of the cage faced the guards' lean-to across a narrow dry streambed. It was left open to permit the soldiers to watch me.

Hidden from the air by one of the numerous bamboo thickets in the area, the cage and sentry lean-to were surrounded by waist-high elephant grass that obscured my view but offered almost immediate concealment for an escape. Beyond the lean-to, perhaps no more than a hundred yards away, I heard the voices and sounds of what I guessed was an army camp. Peering through the thatch at the rear of the cage, I saw the foot of a limestone cliff that presumably rose above the vegetation and seemed to block escape in that direction.

I spent the next few days digging the rocks out of the dirt floor so that I could sleep more comfortably at night. I did a lot of resting in an effort to build my strength after my forced march. I guessed that I had lost more than thirty pounds because of the diarrhea and the arduous walk. My six-foot frame now carried no more than 150 pounds. My captors had confiscated my belt as a security precaution during the trip. By the last few days I had lost enough weight that I was having difficulty keeping my pants up.

Though there were no immediate escape opportunities, I began right away to keep track of the guards' movements and habits and to learn the camp routine. The schedule followed during my first full day in the cage became a pattern. They usually consisted of sticky rice and bamboo shoots. Once in a while some pork, chicken, salt fish, or dog meat was included.

Twice a day, usually after a meal, I was taken out of the cage for a few minutes to use a latrine. A hole had been dug nearby and framed with a bamboo platform to squat on. From my squatting position I could see Harnavee's cage a few hundred yards away. Except for my visit to the latrine, when the guard hit a bamboo gong to summon help from the camp, I was watched by a single rifleman relieved at two-hour intervals. The soldiers coming on duty were careful not to tramp down a trail in the elephant grass that could be seen from the air.

At nightfall a second soldier was added. The two guards tied me hand and foot and pulled the neck rope taut to the stake outside. They hung a kerosene lantern stamped MADE IN POLAND on the front of the cage to illuminate the inside.

I learned quickly that the attitudes of my guards varied from friendliness to open hospitality. Some of them seemed to enjoy yanking on my neck rope at the least excuse and tied me down at night so tightly that I couldn't move. Others were thoughtful enough to bring a bamboo water tube with them when they reported for duty. They would pour it on my neck, head, and hands so that I could wash myself after being untied in the morning.

None of them spoke English, but I soon established a rapport with two of the young guards and gave them nicknames. "Toothpicks" passed his guard duty carving his namesakes from bamboo, and occasionally gave a handful to me. "Needles," who often spent his two hours mending his uniforms, lent me a needle and thread, which I used to repair my clothing. Through the two guards, I picked up hundreds of Vietnamese words.

My boots had been confiscated, but I still had my black pajamas and the and the contents of the black bundle I had carried with me from Moung Sai. The jungle uniform I was captured in was now full of holes, and the pants were much too large around the waist. My T-shirt and undershorts were little more than rags. The pair of socks I was wearing when captured no longer had any bottoms. Though I had never done much mending, I learned quickly now. During the hours when Needles was on duty, I used the patch pockets of my jungle jacket to repair holes in my trousers and jacket. Twisting the rags of my T-shirt into long strips, I wove them into the bottoms of my socks.

From the first night, mosquitoes were a vexing problem. The soldiers stood their night watches under the protection of mosquito nets. I had not been given one. Large and fearless, the buzzing insects tormented me every night, and bit me so often I was sure I would get malaria. With my hands tied and then stretched down to my waist by a lead rope tied to the bottom of the cage, it was difficult to swat at the damned things.

I had been in the cage only a few weeks before I dubbed the site of my imprisonment with the Laotian name I thought appropriate. I knew I was being held in a canyon that snaked into the mountains from the large, lush valley of Dien Bien Phu. The Vietnamese undoubtedly had their own name for the place, but I called it Doi Sai, "Mosquito Mountain."

While I was adjusting to my place of imprisonment, Terry Burke was getting ready to return to the United States. He had spent a good part of late May and early June trying to track me down. He seemed on the verge of finding me on a couple of occasions, only to be disappointed. His intelligence on the prisoners' movement in the Moung Sai valley had been accurate, but was always received late.

Only after the American had been moved to another spot would Terry learn where he had been. Terry heard that I had been taken to Moung Sai and treated badly, and then taken east through the mountains toward Dien Bien Phu. At that point Terry lost track of the prisoners. His Southeast Asian assignment was up, and there was nothing he could do now but hope Ernie would survive.

In Chieng Mai, Patricia and the boys were still waiting and hoping. In Superior, Arizona, where my parents now lived, Cary and Ruth Brace were checking their mailbox each day for news about their son's whereabouts. They had received other disturbing news about their aviator son over the years. I had been forced to bail out of a burning plane over Hawaii, and I had been shot down in Korea. Those telegrams had always assured them their son was all right. This one was different.

The State Department wire informed my parents that I had been captured by "military forces presumed to be Pathet Lao." Boum Lao had been reoccupied by Royal Lao forces, the telegram continued, but the enemy had withdrawn with their prisoners, and had headed north toward a village used as Pathet Lao head-quarters. The Braces were assured that the American embassy in Vientiane, working with the Laotian government and the International Red Cross, was seeking to learn the whereabouts and physical condition of their son. They would try to establish contact with his captors, for the purpose of negotiating his release.

The State Department did not know, or did not choose to reveal, that I had been captured by North Vietnamese regulars. Though North Vietnam was not reluctant to identify the American flyers shot down over its own territory, and to reap the propaganda benefits therefrom, it was another thing to acknowledge that NVA soldiers had captured a civilian American in Laos, a country where foreign troops were forbidden under an international agreement that North Vietnam had signed.

Even if the State Department had been positive that Ernie Brace's captors were NVA troops, it might have been reluctant to say so for fear of provoking a controversy in which the military roles of the United States and Thailand in the Laos war would be brought into question.

I was the victim of these circumstances. Unlike the vast majority of American POWs in Southeast Asia, I would never appear on a POW list released by the Communists to the outside world. I was to be held in secret, but I didn't have to be there in the first place. It was hard to feel sorry for myself as long as I was still alive.

14

About three weeks after I had arrived in North Vietnam, an interrogator arrived and moved into an old U.S. Army tent pitched uphill from the camp just beyond Harnavee's cage. Late in the evening I was taken through the elephant grass and ushered into the tent, where I found an elderly white-haired civilian and an aide sitting at a table.

I was seated on a log near a small fire designed to take the chill off the night air. The soldiers tied my neck rope to a second log. It was a weird scene, with the campfire throwing shadows about the old tent. Some tears in the canvas were flapping in the wind, adding to the spookiness of the moment. The young aide began the questioning in broken English.

"State your name."

"Ernest Cary Brace," I replied.

"Your age."

"Thirty-three."

"Where were you captured?"

"Boum Lao, Laos."

"Were you captured in a liberated area?"

"No, at a government outpost."

"How many Americans were there?"

"I was alone."

"Do you know of Alvarez?"

"Yes. I know he was captured in August 1964."

"Shumaker?"

"Yes, I've heard of him."

"Bloot?"

"No."

"Vohden?"

"No."

"Storz?"

"No."

These were no local officials, I thought. Their manner, their appearance, and especially the nature of their questions suggested they were intelligence officers from Hanoi. I had not heard of Bloot, Vohden, and Storz, but I assumed that, like Alvarez and Shumaker, they were other Americans shot down in Southeast Asia.

The interrogators were working from notes, and I soon learned that the Buddhist in Moung Sai had sent along a report. "You fly a special aircraft?"

I sighed. "I fly an aircraft anyone can buy. They are made in Switzerland."

"No," the aide responded sharply, "it is a special aircraft."

I suppressed an urge to raise my voice. "I fly an aircraft anyone can buy," I repeated evenly. "They are made in Switzerland."

The answer brought a mocking smile from the older man, but I said nothing. When the aide advised me acidly, "You are not welcome in Laos," I could not resist pointing out that we were not in Laos. The answer produced a frown.

"How do you know you are not in Laos?" he asked.

"The road we came in here on does not extend into Laos," I replied.

Again the old man smiled. He listened for a few more minutes while I answered the aide's questions about my work and background in a manner that was deliberately vague. Then the old man spoke in fluent English.

"You think you are very smart," he told me. "You think you are carefully evading the questions."

I had told Harnavee on the trail that I had once been a Marine captain. The Thai, interrogated earlier in the day, apparently had mentioned that fact. Now the old man used it as evidence in support of the Pathet Lao's assertion that I was a colonel in the CIA. Warning me that I had better answer his questions truthfully, the white-haired official began an interrogation that I would record in my mind virtually word for word.

"Who do you work for?"

"Bird and Sons," I replied.

"What do you do?"

"Build runways and fly supplies in Southeast Asia."

"Do you fly to Vietnam?"

"No!"

"Do you fly to China?"

"No, I fly to Thailand and Laos."

"Now," said the old man, spreading a map on the table. "I show you a map of Laos. You show me where you fly."

I knew that the soldiers had taken my STOL map from the Porter. It had almost every government airstrip in Laos and Thailand marked clearly on it. Since they already had the information, I decided to comply with the request. I marked the locations of about twenty of the well-known airstrips in Laos, put down the pencil, and said, "This is where I fly."

"How many missions do you fly?"

"We don't call them 'missions,'" I said. "Maybe a thousand trips."

"Where do you get supplies?" The answer to that was common knowledge among my captors, I knew, and I saw no purpose in trying to mislead them.

"You know that the USAID distribution point for this area is Xieng Lom," I said.

For the next hour I received a lecture on how the Vietnamese had defeated the French. The old man launched into a lengthy dissertation that would have done any professor of history credit. A couple of words he used made me think he had visited Texas at some time. When I asked, he smiled and told me he had learned his English from an American who came from the Western United States.

The old man seemed satisfied for the time being, and abruptly changed the subject. "Are you worried about your family?"

"Yes, I would like to write to my family."

"Are you comfortable?"

"I need a mosquito net and a bed board."

"I will see that you get a net," he said.

When the old man turned me over to the soldiers, he gestured toward my six-week-old beard and my filthy, disheveled appearance, and ordered me cleaned up.

That night-I figured it was the Fourth of July—I slept for the first time with a mosquito net, celebrating my independence from the mosquitoes.

The next morning the old man came to the cage and allowed me to write a letter to my wife. I was surprised and elated. Patricia would now know for certain that I was alive. When I indicated that my wife was in Thailand, however, the Vietnamese told me that getting mail through Laos to Thailand was difficult. I thought my family might already be heading back to the States anyway, so I addressed the letter to Patricia's mother in Oklahoma. This confused the old man, who asked if I had two wives. He folded the letter and put it in his pocket. It would be many years before I learned that the letter never reached Oklahoma.

Before the old man left, I asked to be put with other prisoners, like Shumaker or Alvarez. The answer provided one of the first indications from my captors that I was not to be treated like other American POWs.

"That is impossible," he said. "Your situation is different." But he promised to pass the request on to his superiors.

He did offer one ray of hope. "We may try to make a deal with you as we did with Klusman, you know Klusman?"

I recognized the name. Klusman was a Navy pilot shot down in Laos in March of 1964. He had been walked out of Pathet Lao territory by defectors in November of that year.

"Yes," I said. "He escaped."

"He did not escape," the Vietnamese said. "We let him go."

"Maybe you could exchange me for some rice."

"We do not need anything you Americans have."

The Vietnamese didn't indicate what kind of a deal could be struck, but I was glad to hear that negotiations for my release were at least not out of the question.

The old man left me with a warning: "I have instructed the guards to shoot you if you attempt to escape." He disappeared into the elephant grass, and a few minutes later I heard a truck rumble down the road toward the large valley and, presumably, Hanoi. In the months and years to come, I would repeat in my mind the conversations I had with the interrogator. The old man was the last English-speaking person I saw for more than three years.

15

The monsoon months passed without an opportunity to escape. My guards seemed forever alert and not in the least overworked. I had deduced that this was a rest-and-recreation camp for NVA combat units in Laos. We two prisoners appeared to be their only responsibility. The two-hour guard shifts made it unlikely that their attention would lapse while on duty.

About every six weeks, the personnel in the camp changed completely. The clean, rested troops would be replaced by tired, dirty, unkempt infantrymen fresh from combat duty. I could sometimes hear the formal turnover ceremony in the camp. It would be confirmed by the appearance of new guards who enjoyed showing me the plunder they had collected from their American-supplied enemy.

They flaunted Japanese radios, which they tuned to Chinese and North Vietnamese stations. American cigarettes and parachute cloth were shown to me with pride. Among the most prized possessions seemed to be the aluminum combs and other implements they claimed were made out of American aircraft they had shot down. One soldier proudly produced a bomb shackle from a World War 11 bomber—a B-24 or B-25, I guessed—and insisted it came from an American Phantom jet he had shot down with his rifle.

Harnavee and I were seldom allowed to bathe and never permitted to exercise. Though I would have been happy to work around my cage if it meant stretching my arms and legs, my latrine trips were the only chance I had to stand upright each day. I was occasionally allowed to wash with water from a bamboo tube, but bathing and washing my clothes were allowed only once every six weeks. My cage soon stank.

On bath day, I was taken to the ten-foot-wide stream that ran beside the army camp and permitted to sit in running cold water, scrubbing myself and my clothes with a porous piece of brown soap.

The bathing trips gave me a chance to get a look at the army camp. It appeared to be a former French installation whose wooden buildings stood on concrete blocks under the protection of the jungle canopy. I noticed carefully sorted and piled rocks in the area, indicating that the place had once been a quarry.

Taken past one of the barracks buildings, I noticed a newspaper article posted near a louvered door showing American jets in various diving positions with appropriately placed gunsight aiming points. In nearby trees the soldiers had hung models of planes at various angles, so they could practice snapping their rifles at them.

Though I was given meat only once every few months, my portions at mealtime were nearly always plentiful. Often there was too much rice to eat, but rather than return it uneaten, I fed the extra rice to the chickens and dogs that wandered up from the camp. The lack of protein resulting from a forty-five-day diet of only rice and bamboo shoots in midsummer gave me mouth ulcers and fading eyesight.

I became an expert on bamboo shoots. They came out of the ground shaped like an inverted cone. Some were pink in color after the outer skin was stripped off, and some were a yellowish white. The pink bamboo shoots were the best. They were slightly sweet.

Keeping the date became a game. Sundays were easy to tell because the soldiers were extremely quiet. I didn't need to scratch dates off as you see in prison movies. Not having to make decisions about any facet of life in the cage, it was easy to concentrate on the only thing that mattered—the passage of time.

By the end of the summer I suffered from intestinal disorders probably caused by parasites. I could see wiggling white worms in my stool in the hole. After I showed the guards my stool, they gave me a couple of white tablets, but the problem persisted into the fall.

Large red ants became a problem at the hole. I would have to take a stick with leaves on it and sweep them away from the platform to keep from being bitten. They would actually rise up on their rear legs and wave their pincers at me as I swept them off. The bites raised large red welts.

Ringworm showed up on my arms first, and then my groin area. My captors treated it in the Vietnamese fashion of applying iodine directly on the open sores after I had scraped them with the edge of a piece of split bamboo. That medication, and an all-purpose cream the soldiers provided me, cleaned up the sores. Bamboo figured in all aspects of jungle life.

The animal and insect life that entered my cage was a constant irritant and sometimes worse. The rats that nested in the thatch of my cage were getting big and fearless. They would start squealing and running back and forth through the rustling thatch at night. I could only cringe, knowing what was going to happen next. They came out searching for food at night, and crept under the mosquito net, running over my body as I lay pinioned to the ground. When I felt them on my legs, I would lie as still as possible, praying they would find their way out before they bit me. I was bitten repeatedly on my ankles and feet, which were uncovered. More than once I was sprayed with urine from a rat in the thatch overhead. I had to lie in disgust, unable to wipe my face.

The worst experience of the summer was the visit of a large snake to the cage. The snakes were attracted to the cage by the increasing rat population. In July, the guards and I noticed a twenty-foot rock python slithering among the boulders at the foot of the cliff. It made me uneasy to think of the reptile hunting at night so close to my cage.

Tied down on my back as usual one night, I awoke feeling a heavy weight on my feet. I knew instantly what it was, and hoped a light movement might urge the visitor to leave the cage. When I moved my foot, I felt the snake crawl alongside me, circling back across my arms and chest. I instinctively lifted my arms, which were tied by the wrists, in an effort to push the snake away. The movement only alarmed the reptile, which became entangled in the mosquito netting and flailed violently in an attempt to get free.

"*Gunzun! Gunzun!*" I cried, using the Vietnamese word for snake. The guards rushed to the cage just in time to see the reptile free itself and slip away into the darkness. It had been after the rats in the thatch. Though the snake had been as frightened as I was, there was no guarantee that it, or another one, would not be back. I didn't sleep well for several nights. To make matters worse, the thrashing snake had ripped the mosquito net badly. Once again I was at the mercy of the mosquitoes, leeches, ticks, and scorpions that came in the night.

To pass the time during the day, I sharpened a piece of bamboo on a rock and began carving figures out of the small sandstone rocks I found near the cage. I had never worked a lot with my hands, but I found the pastime relaxing. By the end of the summer my small people, animals, and other images were good enough that the guards began stealing them from my cage while I used the latrine. Seeing their larceny as an opportunity, I began scratching my name and the date on the bottom of each figure, hoping that if the soldiers were captured or killed, friendly forces might find the carvings.

With fall came cool weather, and I spent miserable nights shivering in forty-degree temperatures in my flimsy clothing. Although I would see the guards come on duty with blankets wrapped around them, they never offered me one. I had used what was left of my T-shirt and undershorts to patch my pants and shirts. The humidity in the summer months, combined with my sweat and occasional urine, had rotted new holes in the clothing and there was nothing to cover them.

The guards usually had fires near the lean-to. Some of them occasionally stuck a glowing log in the cage at night in an attempt to keep me warm. As I lay shivering uncontrollably, I swore to myself that when I got out of this situation I'd never be cold again.

Though I was occasionally treated roughly by the guards, I never lost my temper until an incident late in the year. It involved a troublesome guard who habitually wore a hand-kerchief over his face when he entered my cage. I had pains-takingly woven a facsimile of a wedding ring from bamboo strips, and had worn it for months as a reminder of my wife and boys.

One morning the guard I called "the Bandit" stopped me on my return from the latrine and demanded to see the ring. He examined it closely and then contemptuously threw it to the ground. When I leaned over to pick it up, the guard pushed me and my temper flared. I lunged at the Bandit, landing a blow to his ribs that put him on his back in the grass. Quickly jumped by the other soldiers, I was put back in the cage with my neck rope drawn very tight. I waited apprehensively for the punishment I expected would be forthcoming.

Soon an officer arrived to see what the commotion was about. He questioned several of the guards, and then ordered them to loosen my neck rope. The Bandit was relieved on the spot, and though he stood guard duty again, he was never allowed to take me from the cage. At first I thought of the incident as a victory. As I began to consider seriously the possibility of escape, I realized that my momentary loss of control had worked to my disadvantage. Hostile guards were likely to be the most attentive. I could forget about escape opportunities when the Bandit was on duty.

Though the cage and lean-to were surrounded by elephant grass and bamboo thickets, there was one opening in the undergrowth that allowed me to look south down a rugged, steep-sided valley. I decided the valley would be my escape route. If I followed it far enough, it would surely take me to Laos.

Except for that one view of the outside world, I had to rely on my sense of hearing to determine what was going on around me. My ears told me that American air activity must be stepping up in the area; virtually every night now I could hear the "talkers" in nearby antiaircraft emplacements repeating bearings and distances of American aircraft. My ears also told me that a truck-repair facility must be in the area. The revving of engines and the clanking of tools could be heard down the valley almost every night. In the early evenings I heard the soldiers in the camp below singing. At times I could hear them enjoying a game of volleyball, playing table tennis, or preparing dinner in the mess kitchen.

Two or three times a month, a political indoctrinator would come to camp, I knew, because I could hear the visitor lecturing to the soldiers and teaching them chants and songs. The next day the guards would appear with little red books containing the wisdom of Ho Chi Minh.

One day, near the end of the year, a few days after a political indoctrinator had left, a camp guard who spoke no English came to the cage and handed me a note in English.

"This," said the note, "is the week of solidarity of the Vietnamese people with the American people."

When he saw that I understood, the guard smiled and handed me a single banana through the bars. It was a little thing, but it was a gesture that I would never forget. After unbroken months of tedium, loneliness, and discomfort, the soldier's act had renewed my faith that the war would not last forever.

16

Scarcely a day passed when I did not devote some time to the prospect of escaping. Studying the construction of my cage, I discovered that as the bamboo strips tying the poles together dried out, they became brittle and eventually broke. When the guards weren't watching, I helped the process along by twisting or rotating the bars. Every few weeks a soldier with a handful of water-soaked bamboo strips replaced the old bindings. Wrapping each critical joint, the guard twisted the two ends tightly, then tucked the twist underneath to make sure it would not come undone. As they dried they tightened. I made a game of trying to remove or break the dozens of bindings before the guard came to replace them.

The rear of the cage, I decided, was the most vulnerable part. It was the darkest, least-inspected section, and the most distant from the lean-to. If I was to try an escape, it would be through the rear, at night.

Though escape was on my mind, my thinking was tempered somewhat by the increased air activity that came at the end of the summer, as the monsoon rains eased. I could hear the jets coming overhead, presumably on their way to Hanoi, and wondered how long this little country would be able to take the punishment. Perhaps the war would soon be over and I would be going home anyway. Under the circumstances, I decided, I would not hurry an escape try. I would make sure that when I made my break I would have a reasonable chance of getting away. I had not forgotten the beating I had taken after my escape on the trail, and I did not want to undergo similar punishment unless my chances of making it home were good.

That rationale, as sensible as it seemed on the face of it, raised nagging doubts. Though I was a civilian, and not bound by the Code of Military Conduct for Prisoners of War, I still thought of myself as a Marine. The remarkable memory that had startled my high school teachers back in Michigan unfailingly recreated the salient portions of the code. A POW was to "continue to resist by all means available," and to "make every effort to escape."

Some soul-searching during the long nights in the cage convinced me that my go-slow reasoning was merely an excuse for not really wanting to escape. Whatever its discomforts, the cage had become a kind of womb. Inside was shelter and food. The predictable behavior of the guards told me that they would not mistreat me. Outside was coldness, uncertainty, and a North Vietnamese jungle whose villages would be hostile.

It was perfectly natural, I knew, this mental aversion to escape. I sensed that the worst error I could make would be to accept my present condition, and I told myself repeatedly that I must always think of my captivity as temporary.

It was late in the year when I was ready to make my move. I had spent my days surreptitiously fashioning small bamboo picks that I could use to undo the ropes on my hands and feet. The bamboo ties at the rear of the cage had been loosened so that the top could be opened enough for me to climb out. I planned to slip into the elephant grass and make my way down the valley I had seen to the south.

Tied rather loosely one evening by a guard, I decided that this was the time. It was an excellent opportunity; the lantern that usually hung on the front of the cage had been broken, and no light illuminated me. Moreover, the second guard had not yet arrived for the night, and the one on duty was the densest one in camp.

I managed to pull the bamboo picks from their hiding place in the thatch, then used them to undo the ropes on my feet and hands. I untied my neck rope, crawled to the rear of the cage, and pushed up the top. All I had to do was crawl out. The guard had not noticed anything, and there was still no sign of the second guard.

I couldn't make myself go! *This is so stupid*, I thought, listening to my own excited breathing. *Damn it, Brace, you're ten feet tall, get out of here.* The guard was only fifteen feet away; I felt he would be sure to hear or see me lifting myself out of the cage. I had been warned that the guards had orders to shoot. After a moment I quietly put the thatch back in place, crawled miserably under my mosquito net, and tied myself back up. I cried in my disappointment with myself.

The next morning I was so disgusted that I immediately began devising a plan to overcome my hesitation about making a break. *If you need a kick in the ass, I told myself, I'll give you one.* I committed myself to a twenty-point plan that would, by my own rules, force me to make an escape attempt once the twenty points were achieved. The plan, entirely in my head, assigned a certain number of points for each of several categories.

Five points each were awarded for such conditions as an inattentive guard, a dark night, strong winds, or a heavy rain. The jungle rain provided enough racket to cover the noise of an escaping prisoner. Each piece of helpful equipment I managed to steal or make contributed a point. From then on, I spent a few moments of every evening adding up the points, but though I came close on several occasions, the conditions during the next few months never came together to produce a twenty-point night.

Christmas came, accompanied by the ache of loneliness and concern for Patricia and the boys. I was sure they must now be back in the States. New Year's Day arrived, and it was 1966.

The truck-repair facility a short distance up the valley had been an occasional target of American warplanes ever since the monsoon rains had let up the previous October. By late February of 1966, the facility was being bombed every two or three days. The explosions were close enough to rock the earth. On a few occasions the bomb fragments fell on the cage and the guards' lean-to. The guards showed me fragments of shrapnel they picked up around the area.

Twice, as the bombs fell around us, they moved me out of the cage and into a cave formed by large pieces of the limestone karst that had fallen in the past. Several days of steady bombardment in the area convinced the NVA that I must be moved to a safer spot.

During the first week of March, a work detail appeared at my cage. I was tied to the guards' lean-to while about fifteen soldiers dug around the six main posts of the cage, trying to work it free from the ground. When the legs were loose in the soil, they lifted the cage carefully and began walking it very slowly down the path toward the camp.

What followed gave me my first good laugh since being captured nearly ten months before. As they stumbled downhill with their awkward load, the soldiers on the right got out of step with those on the left. This caused the cage to twist and sway precariously. As the alarmed soldiers yelled urgent instructions at each other, I watched the stays break and the thatch begin sliding off the roof. Then the whole cage disintegrated into a pile of bamboo and sections of thatch.

For a moment the soldiers stood in a silent circle around the wreckage, a few of them still holding corner-poles. Then everyone began to laugh. Some of the men grinned sheepishly at me, as if embarrassed that they had destroyed my residence. I knew they would reconstruct the cage at its new location, but there was something about seeing it as a heap that lifted my spirits.

The soldiers dismantled what remained of the cage and took it in pieces down through the army camp and up the opposite slope. I watched them reconstruct it among some large rocks that offered some protection from the bombs. They positioned it directly under a large rock overhang that would hide it from the air. Harnavee's cage, apparently not endangered, was left in its original spot.

When I was put in my new cage, it had a welcome addition. The bed board I had requested of the interrogator some nine months before had been added. It was no more than three wooden planks nailed together by crossbeams on the bottom. Worn smooth by years of use in someone's hut, it would keep me off the ground.

The most important discovery concerning the new cage was that it had been reconstructed shoddily. Uncharacteristically, the guards had been careless; they hadn't properly spaced the bamboo poles. The bottom bar on the rear wall was now high enough off the ground that I thought I might be able to slip under it if the ties were loosened enough. Conveniently, the soldiers had offset the rear center post, making the hole in back even bigger.

Knowing that the noisy monsoon rains would be coming in late April, I began preparing for my escape in a variety of ways. I had been able to get a pretty good look at the area around the camp when the guards took me to the cave during the intensifying bombing attacks. I was evaluating possible escape routes. I couldn't go south down the valley any longer, since I was now just north of the guards' huts.

I found a suitable route about mid-April. Hearing a noise behind my cage one day, I peeked through a hole in the thatch. I saw a soldier coming down a ravine that climbed to the top of a ridge above the cage. Here was an escape route practically in my backyard. The discovery stimulated me to step up my preparations.

Every opportunity I got, I worked on the poles in the rear of the cage, twisting them in an effort to weaken the stays. The guard lean-to, as before, was situated scarcely more than a dozen feet away, so I could work only during moments when the guard was distracted or had walked out of my line of sight temporarily. After several weeks of surreptitious work, I had weakened the rear of the cage enough so that I thought I could slip through the hole near the ground. I lived in dread of a soldier arriving with the familiar water-soaked bamboo strips to refasten the poles of the cage.

I also worked hard to be ready for the time when I would be in the jungle on my own. Though my boots had been confiscated, the guards had given me several pairs of worn-out tennis shoes. With a borrowed needle and thread, I patched the least-worn pair with pieces from the others. Using my sandstone and some quartz, I produced sharp sticks to dig with and to help me untie myself when the time came, and hid them in the thatch.

On one of my washdays, I found a small piece of aluminum and smuggled it back to the cage. I polished it to produce a reflective surface for signaling friendly aircraft, and sharpened one side on a rock so it could be used for a knife. My escape tools were beginning to fill the thatch walls and ceiling. The implements were nearly discovered on several occasions when the guards inspected the cage. Fortunately, their shakedowns were never thorough enough.

As the monsoon season approached, I began watching the skies for the late-afternoon storm clouds that would bring showers in the evening.

When the rain began falling just before sunset on a day in late April, I began tallying my escape points. If the rain continued after dark, I decided, this would qualify as a twenty-point night. When the guards attached a thatch rain shield covering the lower half of the front bars and partially hiding me, I was further encouraged.

After I had been tied for the night in the darkness, with the rain still coming down, I freed myself with the help of my bamboo picks, rolled off my bed board, and tried to slip out the hole in the rear of the cage. Though I could get my head and part of my body through, the opening wasn't quite big enough. I lay in the darkness twisting the bars, trying desperately to get the few more inches I needed to make it through the hole. Soon the rain began to let up, preventing me from making any noisy adjustments. I abandoned the escape try, and tied myself up again.

Though I was disgusted and angry at myself for having underestimated the size of the hole I needed, I knew the rainy season would afford more opportunities. A few days later I discovered a hole near the roof bars that offered an even better chance to get out than the one on the bottom. The mosquito net hanging from the ceiling over my bed board would make it more difficult for the guards to see my movements.

There wasn't much question that I could get out of the roof hole. I began the process of twisting and bending the thatch over the opening. I could push it aside as noiselessly as possible when the time came. During the days that followed, I repeatedly went over my recent aborted escape attempt, trying to analyze my behavior in the light of cold reason.

My calculation about the size of the hole was a mistake that could have been corrected. I concluded that I had been too quick to abort the attempt. I had rationalized myself back onto the bed board. If I was to make it out of the cage, I must make myself go when the next opportunity came. No excuses, no justifications —the next time there must be no turning back.

One night as I lay half-awake, an instance to spur me, or anyone else, to get out of that cage occurred. The rock python had been seen around the area again, and the guards delighted in telling me how big he was by sign language. The night was fairly quiet and I could hear the rats rustling around in the thatch. Slowly a bump in my mosquito net started growing. It looked as if someone was pushing a stick in from the side toward the rocks. I watched, fascinated, as the stick started moving from side to side just above my chest. Then it let out a hiss that must have started right down near its tail. If I hadn't been tied down, I would have risen right through the roof of that cage. It was the most awful sound imaginable. I started yelling

"*Gunzunl Gunzun!*" The guards got excited and started beating on the cage with sticks. The snake backed off and disappeared in the rocks before the guards could get him.

I had to wait only a few days for another twenty-point night. On April 17, rolling thunderclouds moved across the late-afternoon sky, and soon the rain was falling in torrents. High winds buffeted the cage, and I could hear dead limbs cracking and falling down in the valley.

When darkness fell, the guard tied me for the night. After attaching the thatch rain cover on the front bars, he retreated to his lean-to and wrapped himself in a plastic tarp. He had a lantern in the lean-to, which, I reasoned, would destroy his night vision. The second guard, probably waiting for the rain to let up, had not yet arrived from the camp below. *This is the moment, Ernie Brace*, I told myself

I untied my hands and feet, then my neck rope, which I attached to the cage so that if the guard pulled on it from the stake, he might think I was still inside. I put on my tennis shoes, double-tying the knots. Following my plan, I wrapped a piece of black cloth around the metal canteen I had been allowed to keep in my cage. I did not want it clanging against a bamboo pole when I removed it from the cage. I coiled the fifteen-foot rope that had bound me, and placed it and the canteen in the rear of the cage, near the bars. Then, with my aluminum reflector and other implements in my pockets, I pushed my blanket through the thatch, making the hole through which I would crawl. With the ram still hammering down hard outside, I took a deep breath and pushed my head and shoulders through the hole, and then my chest and waist. Bending at the waist, I felt for the ground, then putting my weight on my arms, I pulled my feet out and slid quietly to the ground at the rear of the cage. The guard, wrapped in his plastic cocoon, had not noticed.

I reached back through the bars for the rope and the canteen. Then I slid cautiously into the shallow ravine behind the cage, which led to the path up to the ridge. With the guard still no more than a few dozen feet away, I lay in the elephant grass, allowing my racing heartbeat to slow and the surging adrenaline to subside. I began climbing, with no idea of what I would find at the top of the ridge. Above me, forked lightning lit up the night sky. The rain and wind continued to make noise.

17

At the top of the ridge I found a plateau covered with chest-high elephant grass, sloping upward toward mountains black in the distance. As a lightning flash lit up the landscape, I arbitrarily picked out a landmark to the south and set out for it, heading directly across the plateau. The going was tough, the tall grass interwoven with thorn patches so thick as to be virtually impassable. Detouring around the thorny areas was time-consuming, and even though the plateau was no more than several miles across, nearly two hours had passed by the time I reached the embankment of a road. I hid in the underbrush to let trucks roll by through the rain, then crossed the road and found a trail leading south through the valley.

I had not gone far on the path before seeing flashlights and hearing a dog barking in the distance. Dashing for cover across a small stream, I hid about ten feet from the path, behind a large rock. A few minutes later, three men and a dog passed by and disappeared into the darkness. I would have to travel south for several days and reach Laos, I thought, before I dared reveal myself to any natives. I was going to have to take some of their food, since that was one item I had not been able to bring with me.

The rain had subsided. I heard voices and dogs barking in the distance. There was a village upstream, and though my Marine survival training had told me to stay away from them, I knew that this might be my best, and perhaps last, chance to get food for the journey ahead. Most small villages had a communal kitchen situated along the stream, away from the other huts. When the residents had gone to bed, I could raid the kitchen for some food and perhaps pick up a knife or digging tool to help me get food along the trail. No one yet knew a prisoner of war was loose in the area. If I was going to do this, I thought, I should do it tonight.

Leaving my hiding place, I walked in the stream beside the path, so as not to make footprints in the mud and to avoid people who might be on the trail. This way, too, I would come upon the village at the nearest point to the kitchen.

In the darkness I had trouble keeping my footing, and my worn out tennis shoes provided little traction on the slippery rocks. Ten months without exercise had left my legs uncertain, and I spent practically as much time crawling through the shallow stream as I did walking.

I had hoped to find a small, quiet village whose inhabitants had retired for the night. When the huts began to take shape out of the darkness, I saw that this was a relatively large community. Perhaps it was a base camp where an NVA unit kept its families. Huts were clustered on both sides of the stream, not just one, and the communal kitchen was in such a large hut that I decided not to enter it for fear of finding someone there.

I couldn't continue walking upstream through the village. The lightning was continuing to illuminate the jungle, and my chances of making it through a community this size were minimal. I turned around and retraced my route downstream, looking for a way to get around the village. I found a narrow path leading uphill, and followed it to a grove of banana trees that may have been part of the village's ray. I considered picking some bananas, but abandoned the idea because I knew that the missing fruit would signal my presence to the natives.

I continued up the steep trail, stopping to rest at frequent intervals. Finally the trail leveled off on a ridge. I stood gasping for breath and trying to get my bearings. In the lightning flashes I could make out the stream below, twisting through the jungle, but there was no sign of the village. Apparently the path I was on had taken me above the community and beyond it. I headed down the mountain again to find the continuation of the path that would take me south alongside the stream.

When I reached the valley floor, I encountered jungle foliage so heavy that I could not find the path I knew must be there. By this time I had been in flight for more than four hours and was exhausted. I continued to push through the tangled undergrowth in search of the path. Hoping the trail was on the other side of a steep embankment, I climbed uphill through brush so thick that I was forced to tunnel through it on my hands and knees. When I reached the top, scratched and mud-caked, the path was nowhere in sight. A half-hour of such fruitless searching left me gasping and on the verge of panic, and I knew enough not to continue the search in such a condition. If I was to make good my escape, I told myself, I would have to have rest as well as my wits about me. Totally lost, but assuming I was in undergrowth that would hide me in the morning, I spread my blanket on the jungle floor and slept the rest of the night, soaked to the skin.

I awoke shortly after daybreak to hear Vietnamese voices on the path, which, to my disgust, was only ten feet from where I lay. When the voices faded, I withdrew several more feet from the trail to a more secure hiding place in the undergrowth. In the morning quiet, I heard voices from the village I had walked around the night before, and I guessed that it was no more than five hundred yards back down the trail. The rain had stopped during the night, and the sun had been up for about two hours when I heard horns blowing in the distance and men yelling in the village. My escape was now general knowledge. I guessed there must be quite a commotion at Doi Sai.

Within half an hour, troops ran by on the path, heading in the same direction I had intended to travel. By midmorning they returned the same way, in no hurry and apparently satisfied that I hadn't come that way. I remained hidden all day, hearing the natives on the trail.

The path was old and well-traveled, and I guessed it might be part of an ancient route south that I had read about in a history book. The Thai and Lao tribes, including Vang Pao's Hmong, had migrated south from China on a network of trails that historians called "the Ancient Road," part of which snaked through the jungle from Dien Bien Phu toward Sam Neua. If I was right about the path, it would take me from this spot on the southern perimeter of the Dien Bien Phu valley directly south into Laos. I would again be in familiar territory. The locations of all the Lima sites, the special operations airstrips in Laos, were firmly established in my mind, and I would make my way to the closest one.

By dusk, I was anxious to begin my journey. The trail traffic had died down, and I knew the tribesmen in the villages along the path would now be eating their evening meal. I climbed from my hiding place and made my way to the trail, carefully replacing the vegetation I had disturbed. I began to walk, but had been on the path for only a few minutes before I heard someone coming toward me, whistling. I dashed into the underbrush and waited, my pulse racing, while a native man passed. I was shaken by the incident, and cursed myself for having been in such a hurry to move on. If the man had not been whistling, we would have run into each other in the twilight, and my location would have been reported immediately. I remained in the underbrush for about an hour, until darkness had fallen. Then, my ears pricked for sounds on the trail ahead of me, I set out again.

This time there was no one on the path, and I walked for about an hour and a half before I saw the ceremonial gate of a village looming before me. The huts were barely visible beyond it. The gate, which stood astride the path, ushered visitors directly into the village, and I knew I would have to find a way around the community. The surrounding vegetation was too thick for me to leave the trail, and I began to realize that the numerous villages along the path were going to constitute significant obstacles as I made my way south.

Backtracking, I looked for a trail that, like the one the night be-fore, would take me up the mountain and past the village. I found one a short distance down the main path, and had been climbing a tortuous trail for only a few minutes before it began to rain again.

After I had climbed for some distance along the steep and increasingly muddy path, the trail showed no tendency to level off and crossover above the village. My sense of smell, sharpened by more than twenty-four hours without food, told me I was passing near the village's orchards. The pungent odor of citrus fruit, mingled with the fresh smell of the rain, was intoxicating. I left the trail to search for the fruit trees, but was frustrated by the rain, the darkness, and the undergrowth. The tantalizing smell of fresh fruit was all around me, yet eluding me. After a while I gave up.

The rain was continuing to pour down, and it seemed unwise to continue climbing uphill until I got a better idea of where the path was taking me. Certainly there was no sense in retracing my steps downhill to the village, and besides, I was not anxious to leave the area where I knew fruit was available. Finding a spot a few dozen feet off the trail, I crawled under some elephant grass in an effort to get out of the rain, but the foliage provided little protection from the downpour. As I dozed off, I could feel the persistent raindrops hammering a drumbeat on my back.

I awoke shortly after daylight to find myself on a sunny mountainside whose jungle vegetation was much thinner than that in the valley below. The path I had been following climbed through high elephant-grass meadows and occasional orchards and patches of jungle.

I could see now that my journey up the mountain had damaged the grass growing in the path, leaving an obvious trail. There was no turning back now, I concluded, and I continued up the trail in broad daylight, knowing that there would be few, if any, people at this elevation. This time I avoided disturbing the grass growing on the little-used path, staying to the sides and crossing the trail occasionally, in hopes of confusing anyone tracking me.

I had not gone far before I found a pomelo tree, which bore fruit similar to a grapefruit. Using a weathered pole I found near the foot of the tree, I snapped off six pomelos from several inconspicuous places and took them into the brush to have breakfast. It was the pomelos I had smelled the night before. Using my aluminum reflector-knife to cut through the thick skin, I found a small amount of fruit so bitter to the taste that I preferred the thick pulp to the fruit itself. I forced myself to eat all of one pomelo, put the others in my blanket, and set out again up the trail.

I had not been climbing long before the sound of voices from below chased me to a hiding place in the elephant grass. In a moment I saw two teenaged Hmong girls with baskets coming up another trail, chatting and giggling as they gathered vegetation. No doubt it was for the communal rice pots of some village in the valley. I looked at them enviously. They seemed not to have a care in the world.

When the girls had gone, I took to the trail again, climbing ever farther up the mountain, whose peak seemed forever obscured by the ridge fine directly above me. An hour of hiking brought me to a long-deserted village, whose dilapidated huts leaned forlornly on their bamboo foundations. Searching the area for useful implements, I stumbled on some wild tomatoes and strawberries, a discovery that lifted my spirits as well as assuaging the hunger pangs that were unsatisfied by the pomelo.

I resumed my climb with no apprehension about being discovered. The almost-obscure trail was now bordered on each side by high grass and other vegetation. The area was so high, and so far within the Communist-controlled area, that I was certain I would not come upon any military checkpoints. I could tell by the condition of the grass on the path that no one had preceded me in a long time. The trail was taking me toward the mountaintop. Though that had not been my original plan, I knew my new destination would afford me the opportunity to signal one of the friendly aircraft I had heard when I was in the cage.

This area was close enough to the Laos border that a chopper crew could fly in and pick me up off some mountain meadow. The question was whether I could get the attention of a plane before I ran out of water. My canteen was small, and water wasn't plentiful now at the higher elevations. In a few weeks the monsoon rains would begin to fill the mountain streams, but right now many of the stream-beds were dry, and the sun was beating down on the exposed mountaintops. If I was going to attract the attention of an aircraft up here, I would have to abandon the shade offered by the scattered trees.

The higher I climbed, the steeper the trail became, and by mid-afternoon I was stopping often to rest. Upon reaching a small plateau, I found an old bamboo water pipe in an abandoned grass hut, and took the implement with me for the purpose of carrying additional water.

Above the old hut, the trail was heavily overgrown, and I had to struggle to reach another grassy plateau. In the distance I could see a road leading up the mountain to three antiaircraft gun emplacements. I kept low in the grass, knowing that the soldiers could see me through the binoculars they were sure to have. Looking back down the mountain, I found that I was high enough to get a panoramic view of the terrain I had covered since my escape.

There were the villages along the stream, the road I had crossed, and the plain of elephant grass and thorns I had struggled through during my first hours of freedom. Only the cage itself was hidden from view, behind the ridgeline.

Staying out of the line of sight of the soldiers in the gun emplacements, I skirted the plateau and found another old path, so overgrown I suspected that it hadn't been used in years. An hour's climbing took me to a grassy slope from which neither the gun emplacement nor the road could be seen. When I could see no prominent higher point on the horizon, I dropped to the ground, exhausted. This would be the spot from which I would signal the aircraft. Tamping down a place in the tall grass, I lay down on my blanket and was asleep before the sun went down.

In the morning I began stamping down the elephant grass around my blanket. The exercise was tiring, especially after I'd spent the last ten months doing nothing more strenuous than carving sandstone. By noon I was bathed in sweat, and my hands were bleeding from the razor-sharp grass blades. I had cleared out a twenty-foot square.

Finding a nearby banana tree that had gone to seed, I picked some of the bright yellow leaves and laid them in the square to form a large K, a distress signal that American aviators would recognize. Having done that, I sat down in the corner of the square and waited for the sound of a plane. I was ready with my aluminum mirror. Above me, a hot sun burned as yellow as the banana leaves, but a thunderhead in the distance promised more rain.

18

No plane appeared during my first full day on the mountain-top, or the next. For hour after tedious hour, I strained my eyes for specks in the sky and my ears for the murmur of a piston engine or the whine of a jet. The only thing in the sky was the persistent sun, blotted out occasionally by the monsoon clouds, and the only sounds were the rustling of the elephant grass and the chattering of small animals in the brush.

By the second full day of waiting, I had grown weak for lack of proper food and had run out of water. I had been free nearly five days, and aside from the few tomatoes and strawberries I had found on the way up the mountain, my intake had been limited to the unpalatable pomelos. The strictly acid diet had created sores in my mouth and caused my tongue to swell so badly that I could not make myself eat the remaining fruit. The water was a worse problem. Though I had seen a stream partway down the mountain, I was hesitant to leave the slope for fear a plane might come by. I had become so weak that I was afraid if I went down-hill I wouldn't have the strength to get back up to my plateau.

By evening of the second full day on the hill, I had decided to abandon the aircraft watch. Even the planes that had bombed the truck-repair facility at Doi Sai had done so from high altitude. The possibility of a plane passing over this mountain and seeing my signal seemed too remote to justify waiting here any longer without food or water. I decided to trace my steps downhill to the stream I had seen. Then I would bear south as I continued my descent, so as to join the main valley path on the other side of the village I had tried to avoid a few nights before.

Weak and lighthearted, I stumbled down the mountain at dusk, and abandoned the trail in search of the stream. After a while I found myself on a steep slope, up to my chest in thick elephant grass intertwined with a thorny dry brush that reminded me of the mesquite I had seen in Texas. Every step was a struggle. At times I was virtually locked into the brush, unable to make any progress. I had gone too far downhill, and was too fatigued, to retreat back up the slope. I pressed on through the fading sunlight, stumbling, sliding, and gasping for breath.

What I had expected would be a quick downhill walk through the grass to the banks of a cool mountain stream turned into a desperate foray through brambles that ripped my clothing and scratched my hands, legs, and face raw.

When my legs became too rubbery to keep me upright, I tried crawling through the tangled underbrush, and soon was tasting the blood trickling down from cuts on my forehead, cheeks, and nose. Tears came, and I knew I was starting to panic when I heard myself cry out, "God help me."

By crawling, falling, and rolling through the brush, I somehow managed to make some progress downhill. It was almost dark by the time I finally reached the stream I had been looking for. The cold water quenched my thirst, soothed the swelling and sores in my mouth, and stopped the bleeding on my hands and face.

After resting a while to build up my strength and to calm my nerves, I followed the stream downhill, hoping it would take me beyond the village that had stopped my progress a few nights ago. But I had not walked long before I found myself back at the pomelo tree from which I had picked fruit on the way uphill. I was in no better position now to get around the village than I had been before. In my weakened condition, the discovery was a devastating blow. Not since I had escaped several days before had I felt so discouraged.

Knowing the pomelos would only further aggravate my mouth, I left the tree untouched and began walking down the path toward the village. If I could steal some food, I told myself, I could gain back the strength I needed for the journey south.

Had I been thinking more clearly, I would not have taken such a risk. My survival training and natural instincts told me that villages should be avoided, especially now that my escape was known. I rationalized my fears by recalling that the hill tribesmen usually shut their doors at dark and would not open them till morning, even if someone knocked or if their dogs began barking in alarm. The villagers believed, I had been told, that dogs barking at night were scaring off evil spirits, and should be left alone to do their jobs.

Soon I could see the familiar ceremonial gate in the darkness, and walked round it so that I would not enter the village the way a visitor might be expected to. The huts that loomed ahead were not on stilts, indicating that this was an Akai village, rather than a Meo or Lehu community. The village was quiet, the only signs of life being a few reclining dogs that looked up curiously at the intruder without barking. When I approached a hut, looking for the corn and other vegetables that the natives often tied under the eaves, the door opened and a woman looked out.

Startled, I spoke quickly, trying to suppress what I feared would be an immediate call for help. "Food," I blurted in English, rubbing my stomach. The woman seemed neither alarmed nor unfriendly and called to someone in the hut next door. It was a North Vietnamese soldier, who hastily grabbed his weapon and trained it on me. I was too exhausted to care. I just sat down.

As the other villagers spilled out of their huts to get a look at me, I saw the irony of what had just happened. There did not seem to be another soldier, not even another young man, in the community. The male faces that encircled me were either very young or very old, and the only teenagers or young adults were women. The soldier who had captured me was obviously home for a few days of leave. Had he not been there no one could have captured me, even in my debilitated condition.

While the soldier put on his uniform, the elderly headman of the village kept me under guard. Wide-eyed children who seemed never to have seen an American offered me food, but the soldier came in and prevented it. He consulted a small notebook that apparently contained some English expressions, and came up with the one-word order that seemed to fit the situation. "Go," he told me. Escorted by the soldier and the village chief, I was marched down the path leading back the way I had come.

After an hour or so of walking, with few stops to allow me to rest, we reached the large village whose communal kitchen I had tried to raid on the night of my escape. Noticing that the community was full of soldiers, I guessed there was an NVA camp nearby. I could make out in the darkness a cage similar to my own, with a lantern hung on the door. As soon as our presence was recognized, my young captor fell into a tough-guy role. He started treating me in a rough manner apparently designed to impress his fellow soldiers.

Placed under a stilted hut, I was given a canteen of hot tea and a bowl of rice and pork bits. I noticed that the soldiers who

fed me wore red patches on their shoulder straps, indicating they
were not from the same unit as my guards, who wore green
patches. Seemingly pleased that I had been found in their area,
they watched proprietorially as their thin, bedraggled prisoner
with the brown beard skillfully manipulated the chopsticks to
wolf down his first hot food in days.

After the meal I was allowed to sleep, without being tied.
When I was kicked awake only a short time later, I looked up to
see a familiar face. It was "Old Dad," the oldest of the soldiers
who guarded my cage, and it was clear that neither he nor the
two other guards accompanying him were in a mood to wait.
Without so much as a word, they pulled me roughly to my feet,
tied my arms tightly behind me, and replaced my neck rope.

Standing nearby with large smiles and taunting remarks were
the soldiers with red shoulder boards. I could see that the Doi Sai
guards were furious. Not only had they lost face by letting their
prisoner escape, but they were now forced to endure the ridicule
of the outfit that had captured me. They shoved me harshly down
the path leading from the village, leaving behind a chorus of
laughter in the darkness.

A grueling two-hour march with no rest stops brought us
back to the cage, where I was tied down tightly and watched closely
by two guards. In the morning I woke to find that my cage had
been wrapped in barbed wire. Escape now would be a more
complicated task. I had been awake only a few minutes before
the guards took me out of the cage and tied me, spread-eagled,
against the wire. Using five-foot bamboo poles whose ends had
been split to produce efficient flogging instruments, the guards
began raining blows on my back and legs, from my neck down to
my ankles.

They worked in pairs, taking turns administering the punishment, which produced an involuntary outcry from me virtually
every time the whispering poles struck home. It was not long
before the whipping began to produce deep lacerations on my
back, arms, and legs. The pain became so extreme that I was
relieved to feel myself losing consciousness and hanging by the
ropes on the barbed wire.

19

After the flogging, I was carried into my cage and laid on the bed board. The soldiers had nailed a pair of crude wooden leg stocks onto the boards. I had regained consciousness by the time Old Dad entered the cage and chiseled two holes in the bed board on either side of my neck. Forming a piece of structural steel into a U, the guard fitted the hoop snugly around my neck. He then formed eyes at either end so that a pin could be slid through under the board. This secured the hoop to the bed board and kept me from lifting my head.

From now on I would sleep with my legs in the stocks and the iron hoop heavy against my neck. The two new devices made me dread the long nights. Before, I had become so good at untying myself at night that I sometimes would be able to enjoy a few hours with the ropes loosened, even when there was no chance of an escape attempt. Those nights were over now.

The stocks were badly installed, being placed too low. My thighs, legs, and buttocks were forced into a reverse bend, and my upper legs became numb only a few hours after I had been secured for the night.

By morning, when it was time for me to use the hole in the ground, I could barely walk. I had to shuffle along without picking up my feet. I guessed that the stocks were not deliberately installed to induce this agony, but they were certainly creating a physical problem that would hamper my efforts to escape.

The discomfort of the new confinement devices made me all the more determined to try another escape. Within twenty-four hours of my capture, I was already analyzing my five days at large in the jungle, rethinking my behavior, and using my newly-found knowledge about the area to plan better escape routes and travel-and-sleep schedules.

I was not kidding myself that my chances of making it were very good, but I was convinced now more than ever that if I

stopped resisting and accepted the conditions of my confinement, I would never survive.

I reminded myself repeatedly that someday I might be returning home to people who would want to know how the disgraced
Marine had handled himself in a POW camp. I wanted to be able
to tell them that I hadn't given up.

They kept me pinned down twenty-four hours a day for several
days. I was allowed to sit up and drink my soupy rice, but then
was put right back down after finishing. My legs became so
unusable that I had to lean against the barbed-wire-wrapped cage
to move to where I was allowed to urinate. On the third or fourth
day I was surprised when they didn't pin me down after the
morning rice was finished. Apparently I was only to be fully
secured at night.

Aware that my recent escape attempt had not been the first,
the soldiers meant my punishment to be severe enough to make
me never again consider escape. I received no medical attention,
even though the lacerations and bruises on my back caused me
considerable pain. They would not even allow me to wash off the
blood that had dried into a crust on my shirt and pants.

I noticed blood in my urine, probably owing to blows in the
area around my kidneys, and I also had become badly constipated.
The aftereffects of near starvation for several days, coupled with
the constipation and difficulty in urinating following the beating,
had caused my hands, feet, and ankles to swell. When a guard
offered me salt to alleviate my constipation, I turned it down,
fearing it would aggravate the toxemia.

During the first few weeks after my recapture, I was in such
poor physical condition that the neck hoop seemed the least of
my problems. As my back began to heal, my urine to clear, and
my bowel movements to become more regular, I recognized that
the hoop constituted my chief obstacle to escape. It was the most
difficult challenge I had faced as a prisoner. Rope, bamboo, and
wooden stocks were one thing, but steel was another. It wasn't
just an obstacle to escape; it was an instrument that pinned me
down so unalterably that it became a mental problem. More than
ever before, I felt at the mercy of the rats, leeches, snakes, and
other creatures that crawled into the cage at night.

I soon discovered that I had been sitting each day on the
solution to the neck-loop problem. The dirt floor of my cage
contained fine quartz crystals. I placed dampened nylon strands

from the remnants of my socks in the dirt. When the strands dried, they were crystal-coated and ready to be used as makeshift flexible saw blades. I took to loosening my hands again after the guards left the cage at night.

I devoted whatever time I could stay awake at night to running the improvised saw back and forth on the inside of the hoop. After a full week's work I noticed with satisfaction that a small groove had appeared in the metal. It would be a very long process, perhaps months. If I wasn't discovered in the meantime, eventually I would make it all the way through.

It was about the middle of May when I was taken from the cage and given a haircut. For the first time since I had become a prisoner, I was given a professional shave with lather and a straight razor. I was then carried down into the valley, where I was allowed to bathe in the stream and to wash my blood-encrusted clothing. The ill-fitting stocks had completely destroyed my ability to walk.

The guards were preparing me for the arrival the next day of a young NVA officer who inspected the cage. With a professional eye he sketched its construction, including the alterations since the last escape. Talking with camp officers and guards, he also sketched the cage as it had been before I had broken out. He showed me the pre-escape drawing and I indicated it was accurate. I guessed the young soldier was a staff officer assigned to investigate the escape and to make sure that something was done to prevent a recurrence.

When the officer left the camp and did not return, I assumed he had been satisfied with the alterations to the cage.

Three days after the officer's appearance, a truck pulled into camp after nightfall and its occupants came up the hill to my cage carrying flashlights. I was told to gather my personal items and to put on my tennis shoes, which were now modified so that they could not be tied and would fall off if I attempted to run. At this stage, such a precaution was unnecessary, because the numbness in my legs scarcely permitted me to walk. After stumbling, falling, and being carried down the hill in the darkness, I needed help from the soldiers to get into the uncovered back of an army truck.

Sergeant Harnavee was already in the truck. We hadn't seen each other in months, and I was genuinely glad to see the Thai soldier. His rangy frame was thinner now, but his square-jawed face still reflected serenity and forbearance. We exchanged smiles across the truck bed.

"You try to escape again?" the Thai asked.

"Yes," I answered.

The conversation was cut short as a twenty-soldier squad climbed into the back of the truck with us. They were a new bunch. I didn't recognize any of the faces. They stood along the staked sides, to which large tree limbs had been affixed for camouflage. There was no cover on the truck, and the guards didn't seem to care whether Harnavee and I could see where we were going. The truck rolled out of camp, down the road to the Dien Bien Phu valley, and turned onto the road. I could not suppress the hope that we were going to Hanoi to join other American prisoners. I had been a prisoner for just over a year now.

Sitting on my gear in the truck bed, I felt my neck hoop in the darkness beside me. The soldier who had packed up my belongings in my blanket had apparently shoved the neck hoop in, expecting me to carry it to the next camp. I knew I would never have a better opportunity to get rid of the detestable iron collar than now. With the soldiers standing over me, I picked up the loop and threw it as high and as far to the side as I could, into the darkness. I heard it strike the ground, but none of the soldiers made any sign of hearing it. I sat there in silent exultation, the adrenaline pumping as if I had just escaped. In a sense, I had. Reinforcing steel wasn't in great supply in the jungle, and the chances that I would see another such hoop were slim.

The truck lurched on, stopping at numerous military checkpoints in the Dien Bien Phu valley. We arrived at a new army camp, which I estimated could be no more than twenty miles from the old one. The new guards removed Harnavee and me from the truck. We were then blindfolded, but not before I saw that the camp was situated in another canyon that opened onto the main valley. From here on, the journey was to be on foot. My legs would not support me.

The soldiers rolled me into a blanket and tied it to a bamboo pole. Two men picked up the pole, and I was taken up the canyon on a trail that climbed into the mountains. Assuming we were not going far, I counted footsteps to give me an idea of how far we would be from the base camp. I gave up after reaching a thousand.

About ninety minutes after leaving the truck, the party reached my new place of confinement. My hopes of seeing other prisoners at this new site were dashed when the soldiers took off my blindfold. The moonlight illuminated a jungle slope much like the one I had just left, and before me was a recently constructed bamboo cage. Harnavee was taken a few hundred feet farther down the valley, where presumably a similar cage waited.

Doi Sai Two was better designed and constructed than Doi Sai One had been, and thus would be tougher to escape from. The long side of the structure was now open, facing the guard's lean-to, giving them a better view of me at night. The cage was larger than the last one, and was furnished with a bamboo-slat bed. Wooden leg stocks were installed, but I found immediately that they were better designed than the last ones and would cause me little discomfort. The new guards didn't seem to miss my neck hoop as they placed me in the stocks for the night.

One of the new guards, seeing my bare feet sticking out without benefit of mosquito net, gave me an old pair of trousers to stick my feet into. The next day I improved on the idea by tying knots in the trouser legs.

The absence of the neck hoop and the more comfortable stocks enhanced my chances of escaping. Not only had the chief obstacle to my freedom been removed, but my legs were losing the numbness induced by the previous stocks.

During the ensuing weeks, every task I undertook was somehow tailored to facilitate my escape. I borrowed needle and thread from the guards to repair holes in my mosquito net. I sewed on cloth patches that would be large enough to help shield my movements from the guards when I made my move at night.

I studied every pole and opening in the cage. Finally I decided that the weakest point was where the stocks, which could be locked from the outside, entered the cage in back. With some work on the bars, I guessed I could make a hole large enough to slip through.

I had become adept enough at untying my neck and wrist ropes that they presented little challenge, but the stocks were a real problem. They were secured outside the cage at their hinge point by a long bolt that would have to be unscrewed and removed before they could be opened. Luckily, the hinge point was on the back of the cage, away from the guards' lean-to. The locking point of the stocks was on the guards' side. It consisted of a large bamboo peg driven in place by a wooden mallet at night.

Although I could reach the head of the large bolt while sitting up at night, I couldn't reach the nut itself on the other side of the stocks. One night I was actually able to turn the bolt by hand, but felt the nut turning on the other side. Some kind of tool had to be devised. The barbed wire that covered only the cage door seemed suitable. Watching the guard carefully, I spent hours bending a section back and forth until it snapped off.

During the nights, when I had loosened my wrist ropes, I fashioned a small wire wrench that would allow me to turn the bolt. I first made a hexagon, estimating the one-inch sides of the large bolt head by the joint in my thumb. Then I put a bucket-like handle on it, through which I could put a bamboo pick for turning leverage. The problem remaining was to hold the nut so it wouldn't turn with the bolt.

I managed to get a two-foot length of bamboo into the cage after leaning it against the thatch in back one day on my return from the hole in the ground. I worked patiently to split the end, hoping the tension of the piece would hold the nut from turning. Finally, after weeks of work, I had a long-handled tool that could be inserted through the bars and extended to the bolt.

Every night that the opportunity presented itself, I practiced unscrewing the bolt. I was careful not to let it drop irretrievably to the ground, where the guards would find it the next day. About six weeks after I had been placed in the new cage, I was ready to make a move. I immediately put my twenty-point plan into operation.

Night after night passed, with never the right combination of conditions to allow an escape try. I became increasingly impatient. I would lie there at night, listening to the hum of a generator from the army camp down the canyon. I could hear that movies were being shown to the soldiers.

Though I was now being allowed to exercise for a few minutes each day by sweeping around my cage, the long nights in the stocks were becoming intolerable. Desperate to make a move, I decided to abandon the twenty-point system and to go as soon as any reasonable opportunity presented itself.

The opportunity came on the night of August 17, when a steady rain battered the foliage and crowded the two guards into the lean-to. These were not particularly inattentive soldiers, and I had not been able to save any food or water to take with me, but the noise of the rain and the darkness of the night offered a chance to slip away.

I untied my wrist and neck ropes. Removing my wrench from the thatch, I slipped it under the mosquito netting and out through the bars. Little by little I turned the bolt. The bamboo held the nut and soon I felt it fall off into the mud. I then pulled the bolt out and let it drop. There was no turning back now; I was on my way again.

With my pulse pounding and my own natural instincts telling me this was impossible, I was not going to allow myself to abort another escape attempt because I had lost my nerve.

Taking my blanket, my tennis shoes, and the rope I was tied with, I slipped out of the hole in the back of the cage and started up the hill behind it, on a trail made muddy and slippery by the rain. I had seen the soldiers take the trail during the day, sometimes not returning for hours. It was a struggle to make it to the top without being heard. I stopped for a moment to catch my breath.

There was a log embedded in the narrow path near the top of the ridgeline. I stepped out uncertainly and was almost across when the banks supporting it collapsed. I fell with a thud, then rolled down to the stream, crashing through the underbrush as I went.

It was enough of a commotion to alert the guards. Though I managed to stay hidden for a few minutes in the bushes, they soon found me with their flashlights and returned me roughly to the cage. When I had been retied tightly and returned to the stocks, the guards hung a lantern on the cage. I spent the night listening to the rain and staring at the illuminated interior of my cage.

I felt like crying. I had come so close to getting away. A few more steps and I would have been heading down some jungle trail while the guards were still huddled in their lean-to. Now I could expect more punishment. From experience I knew something would happen in the morning.

I was still lying there tied when several of the guards showed up at the lean-to carrying shovels. In just a matter of minutes they dug a foxhole of sorts. An officer I recognized as the camp commander came up to inspect the hole about midmorning. I was beginning to wonder if they were ever going to untie me.

The camp commander came over to my cage and peered at me through the bars. He then motioned for the guards to get me out. I was taken from the cage and stood up outside while the camp commander harangued me vehemently in Vietnamese. Behind the officer stood the guards, still holding shovels and glaring with undisguised hostility at me. My escape reflected on their performance as guards, and it was likely they had already been reprimanded.

When the officer had completed his lecture, he motioned me toward the hole and ordered me to get into it. I assumed the hole would be covered by bamboo poles and thatch to form a small dugout prison. I climbed in and sat down. At least it did not appear I was going to be beaten.

The officer motioned for me to stand up. As I did so, the first shovelful of earth plopped in around my feet. Then the next, and the next.

When the dirt had reached my knees, I tried leaning forward and back and moving my toes and feet to give my limbs some breathing room. When the officer discovered what I was doing, he struck me on the shoulder with a bamboo cane. It was a frightening experience, standing there watching my body disappear beneath the damp black dirt.

Soon the hole was filled to my waist, then my chest, then my shoulders. When I could feel the dirt clods touching my lower jaw, the soldiers stopped. The officer walked over, straddled my head, and tamped down the earth above my shoulders.

Because I had not been standing perfectly erect when the hole had been filled, I was now leaning forward down the hill at about a five-degree angle. It was just enough to increase the pressure on my chest and make my breathing more difficult. Even so, this seemed better than the beating I had taken before, and I doubted that they would keep me in such a position for more than twenty-four hours. I was mistaken.

20

As the first day passed, I realized I was to be given no food or water. The steadily falling rains, soaking my longhair and beard, provided enough moisture to keep my mouth from becoming parched. When I asked for something to eat or drink, the guard responded by tossing a dirt clod that hit me on the back of the head. I was facing away from him, toward the slope that led down to the soldiers' camp.

The ants and other insects that crawled over my head, exploring my nostrils and ears, would have driven me crazy at one time, but fifteen months tied down at night in the cages had taught me to ignore the itches and aggravations of crawling insects. The situation improved when the chickens from the nearby camp, losing their fear of the human head sticking out of the ground, reoccupied the area. Occasionally the chickens stopped to look me squarely in the face before continuing their search for bugs.

As the hours dragged by, I kept my mind occupied by reliving experiences from my childhood or my years in the Marines. I had always had an exceptional memory, but I surprised myself at how vividly I could summon the past.

The sun climbing through the trees marked the passing of the second morning in the hole. In my mind's eye, I watched the green haze fade into a black-and-white collage, the black became mountainous images in a field of snow...

Beyond the barren, snow-mottled North Korean mountains below me, I could see the jagged coastline and the cold gray expanse of Tongjoson Bay stretching eastward into the Sea of Japan. A few miles north of Koji Point I could make out the coastal indentation of the seaport of Wonsan.

It was November 16, 1952, and I had been orbiting now for more than two hours in an AD-3 Skyraider equipped with an extra fuel tank on its belly and a camera on its wing. As the morning sun climbed, flight after flight of Marine fighter-bombers attacked the power station of the Wonsan dam that towered above its reservoir.

Though I had turned twenty-one only a few months before, I was already a flight leader. With two escorts I had arrived at today's target early to make a photo pass. That first run had attracted a lot of ground fire, and I could see now that the ADs making their bombing and strafing runs were getting the same reception.

My job was to hang around until the strike was over, then run in over the target for some more pictures. When the last bombing run was completed, I headed inland, then came around to make a low pass from the west with my cameras clicking. They had done some damage, all right, lots of fire and smoke, enough so that I wasn't sure I had gotten it all on film.

Since I hadn't taken any antiaircraft fire, I decided to try another pass headed inland, this one lower. Again there was no gunfire. By this time I was fairly sure I had all the photos I needed, but I was feeling so exhilarated by the success of the strike that I couldn't resist yet another pass. Foolishly, I rolled up into a big, acrobatic wingover and wheeled the AD onto a final run that would take me over the powerhouse and out over the hills that sloped down toward the ocean about fifteen miles away.

Squeezing the camera trigger and strafing the target myself, I saw the dam flash by beneath me and then felt the aircraft shudder from antiaircraft fire. I had taken hits behind the cockpit, in my right wing, and in my engine, which was spewing smoke. By the time I called in my Mayday and reported my position, the prop had stopped turning. I horsed the crippled Skyraider over the last ridge and then saw the ocean in the distance and ships on the horizon, but I was still miles short of the beach.

Another AD pulled alongside me, its pilot radioing that my engine was on fire and advising me to jump immediately.

Like all Marine pilots, I was equipped for the eventuality that I would have to bail out over enemy territory. I packed a Smith & Wesson .38 revolver, a canteen, and a survival kit that included a cloth map of North Korea and a "blood chit" identifying me to North Koreans as an American pilot and promising a reward if I was returned to the South. But the power plant was hundreds of miles above the Thirty-eighth Parallel, where the front lines were then situated. Bailing out here meant that capture was a virtual certainty.

"I'm going to try to make it over the water," I told the pilot in the other AD.

I cleared the surf by only a few hundred feet, much too low to bail out. I would have to ditch. Having opened the bubble canopy to ensure a quick exit, I put the plane down about two hundred yards offshore in heavy swells that brought green water into the open cockpit before the Skyraider's forward motion was stopped.

I climbed out over the windshield and slid down the engine cowling into water so cold that my legs were numb almost immediately. I wasn't wearing a survival suit—just a leather flight jacket over a heavy woolen shirt, Marine Corps-issue, and a pair of woolen flight pants over flimsy dungaree trousers.

My Mae West and small life raft inflated without difficulty, but I had scarcely climbed into the rubber boat before I heard popping sounds coming from the beach, and then little blurps as rifle slugs struck the water nearby. Slipping into the sea again, I turned the raft over, blue bottom up, and stayed behind it, listening to the gunfire and watching several ADs from my air group circle overhead and make runs on the beach. Because of the swells, it was hard to see what kind of vessels were nearby, but I had seen both fishing boats and warships before the plane hit the water. Floating helplessly in the sea, I knew I would belong to whomever reached me first, and I hoped friendly ears had heard my Mayday.

Then I heard the guns of a warship open up from seaward. As the swells took me up, I caught a glimpse of an American destroyer shelling the beach. The potshots from the beach stopped, and in a few minutes I climbed back into the raft. I lay in the bottom of the bobbing raft, colder than I had ever been and vomiting from having swallowed too much salt water.

I was getting nowhere at ridding the raft of water when I heard the chugging of a small craft and was greeted with the welcome sight of a gray whaleboat manned by American sailors. Two of them were standing in the bow, holding Thompson submachine guns. Then the boat was alongside, and strong arms grabbed me and swung me over the gunwale. After the pair with the Thompsons shot up the raft and sank it, we headed back toward the destroyer.

Soon I was in the small dispensary of the USS *Kidd*, a destroyer. After I was dry and in some warm clothing, I asked to be taken to the bridge to thank the commanding officer. I noted with amusement that the stenciled letters on the back of the skipper's foul-weather jacket identified him, appropriately, as Captain Kidd.

Captain Kidd suddenly turned into the North Vietnamese officer standing there looking at me. Had my eyes been closed? I couldn't remember. He turned, said something to the guard, and went back down the hill.

As the hours went by, I decided to try imagining a bus trip to be taken from Los Angeles to Maui. A plane trip would have been too fast. I felt myself drift into fantasy until I could feel the bus vibrating beneath my feet, smell the exhaust fumes, and see Kingman, Flagstaff, Tucumcari, and Amarillo sliding past the green-tinted windows. Slow down, look around, don't go so fast down that road. Lots of time to be aware of what's around me. Into my mind rushed the perfumed scent of a girl sitting in the seat in front of me, the plastic decor of a bar visited when we stopped at Albuquerque, the kindly face of a middle-aged lady who chatted with me as we rolled across northern Texas.

By what I thought was the third day, I was having a hard time maintaining my concentration. My last recollection of the bus trip was being stranded on the wrong side of the Mississippi River with no money for the ferry. In my dreams I was back in uniform. I would die as a Marine.

I had not knowingly slept since being placed in the hole, and when I started to doze off during the day, dirt clods from the guards jarred me awake. I tried to move my arms, legs, and body to keep the circulation going. It seemed I could feel a little air suck down around my chest. But the rain compacted the earth so that movement was almost impossible. The buried part of my body became numb, and that condition, along with the lack of food and sleep, caused my mind to play tricks.

I had become nothing more than a detached head, which in one wild hallucination bounced and rolled downhill, knocking down NVA soldiers as ff they were bowling pins. One lurid fantasy followed the other, and by late afternoon on the third day, I seemed on the verge of losing control of my senses altogether.

My wits and strength started to come back when, before dark on what must have been the third day, a guard poured a bowl of warm rice soup in my mouth. When the bowl was empty, I tilted my head back with my mouth open, indicating that I wanted

I flew an AD-2 Skyraider in Korea in 1952. The Douglas Skyraider was still being used in Vietnam twenty years later. It had been given an ejection seat and redesignated the A-1. (USMC photo)

On my 77th mission over North Korea, November 1952, I was shot down, but managed to get out to the sea to be rescued. The mission was a success, however, and Maj. Gen. Vernon Megee, USMC, awarded me the Distinguished Flying Cross. (USMC photo)

I was the first Marine second lieutenant to fly one hundred combat missions in the Skyraider. Here I'm wished good luck by Lt. Col. R. Huizenger, USMC, Commanding Officer, Marine Attack Squadron 121, VMA 121, Korea 1952. On the cart is a 1,000-pound general purpose bomb. The Skyraider carried 6,000 pounds of ordnance on a typical mission. (USMC photo)

Lt. Col. R. Huizenger pins on my fifth Air Medal after my one hundredth mission over North Korea. (USMC photo)

My Pilatus Porter PC6A on the airstrip at Son Ton Du, Thailand, April 1965, one month before my capture. Gathering of natives was common in Laos as well as Thailand. Note the large wingspan. The Porter could land at forty-five m.p.h. on a strip the length of a football field. This field is actually a dry rice paddy with the dikes knocked down.

Of the Americans released from Hanoi, North Vietnam, only nine had been captured in Laos. On March 28, 1973, the last day of the formal POW exchanges, we left Gia Lam terminal in Hanoi. I had been a prisoner 7 years, 10 months, and 7 days. I am in a dark sweater to the right of Lt. Col. Robson USAF, the uniformed officer who signed for our release. (USAF photo)

Once I became an outpatient at Balboa Naval Hospital, Nancy Rusth, my "rehab" nurse, and I dated regularly. This was taken at Caesar's in Tijuana about three months after my return. We were married at the Naval Hospital Chapel on February 23, 1974. Jim Bedinger, my first cellmate, was my best man.

Thai prisoners, captured in Laos, were released from North Vietnam on September 29, 1974, over a year after the Americans had left. In a show of contempt for their captors, most of them threw away their release clothes prior to boarding the Air America C-123Ks that picked them up in North Vietnam. (Air America)

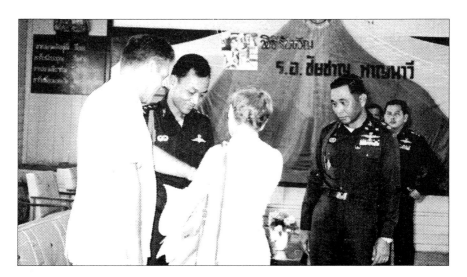

Chai Charn Harnavee, second from left facing camera, captured with me on May 21, 1965, as a sergeant in the Thailand Special Forces, was commissioned an officer on his release in September 1974. Former POW Lt. Col. Laird Gutterson, USAF, and his wife were present at the ceremony. (C. C. Harnavee)

Chai Charn Harnavee received several decorations from the U.S. Air Force for his aid to American prisoners in Vietnam. He is the only foreign national soldier to have his portrait on the wall of the U.S. Air Force Headquarters section of the Pentagon. This picture was taken when he was promoted to major. (Royal Thai Army photo)

After leaving the Marine Corps in 1961, I flew a variety of helicopter missions around California for three years. This Bell 47-J Ranger was chartered to NBC News Service in Los Angeles. (NBC News photo)

The Bell 47-G2 was the standard air transport for close-in offshore oil rigs for many years. I flew this one on a Global Marine/Shell Oil project off the coast of California, north of San Francisco, in early 1964.

When I made captain in 1954, I was only twenty-two years old. (USMC photo)

T/Sgt. Jim Alford, Capt. "Horse" Lowrey, Cpl. Rex LeFevre, myself, and Lt. Jim Miller (left to right) with the solid brass helms wheel and pedestal from an American tanker, the U.S.S. *Suloid,* sunk by a German submarine off North Carolina in 1942. Photo was taken at Marine Corps Air Facility, New River, North Carolina, November 1958. (USMC photo)

My first chance to see
Chai Charn Harnavee,
after last seeing him in
Hoa Lo Penitentiary,
Hanoi, March 1973, was
in Thailand, January 1983.
It was a very emotional
meeting for both of us.
(Bangkok Post)

Ernie C. Brace

more, and the guard brought me another helping from the camp below.

The relief was only temporary. The fourth day passed without food or water, and by the fifth day I had lost all feeling below my neck. I feared now I might be paralyzed.

The most intense concentration could not produce a twinge, tingle, or muscle contraction in any part of my body. I tried not to let the soldiers see how worried I was. The same guard who had fed me two days before brought me another bowl of soupy rice on the fifth day just before dark.

The sixth day passed, and then the seventh dawned. Though my mind was not entirely lucid, I had kept track of the days, and I believed it was now August 25. The sun had not been up for more than a few hours before I saw jungle boots and shovel blades around me. The guards were finally digging me out. I was relieved, but afraid of what had happened to my body.

When they had removed the dirt down to my waist, I flopped forward uncontrollably on my face, like a rag doll. What I feared had come true—I had lost my motor functions, including my ability to remain erect. With a guard holding me, the dirt was removed down to my knees, and the soldier in charge instructed me to climb out of the hole. It was an impossibility.

My brain was feverishly sending signals, but they weren't being received down below. When it was clear that I could not do it on my own, the NCO ordered two guards to pull me out of the dirt by my armpits. In the next moment I found that not all my senses had been numbed. When the joints in my arms and legs were extended, the pain was excruciating. I screamed loud enough that my voice echoed back across the valley.

When they laid me on the ground next to the hole, I examined my mud-encrusted body with horror and disgust. Where the mud had flaked away, the skin was wrinkled and gray. Small pus-filled sacs, the result of continuous contact with the damp soft, covered my body. With as much concentration as I could muster, I tried to move my hand, but it didn't stir, resting there in the dirt as if it belonged to someone else.

Before I realized what was happening, two guards pulled me to my feet, thrust my arms over their shoulders, and dragged me down the mountain toward the stream. The voice that was screaming was mine, I knew, yet the spasms of pain were so intense that I hadn't been aware I had opened my mouth. With my lifeless legs dragging through the rocks and brush, my toenails were tearing away from my shoeless feet.

When we reached the stream, I was told to remove the black pajamas I was wearing, but try as I might, my limbs wouldn't respond. Finally the guards removed my clothes and pushed me into the cold, shallow stream.

They poured pans of water over me to rinse off the encrusted mud. Little streams of blood flowed away from my feet where some toenails had been ripped off. I drank deeply from the stream, quenching my thirst for the first time since I had tried to escape a week before. I kept my bleeding toes in the cold water until the blood stopped flowing. When I had been dressed in my wet clothes, two more guards arrived, and the four soldiers carried me up the hill to my cage. I was now placed in the stocks twenty-four hours a day, with my neck rope tied, but there was no need for either. I was in no condition to sit up, let alone try an escape.

During the next few days, I ate and drank everything that was given me, hoping to regain my strength. The week in the hole had savaged my body more than even the soldiers had expected.

My skin color turned from gray to a swollen, unhealthy pink. I had neither urinated nor had a bowel movement for several days. My scrotum enlarged to the size of a softball. Toxemia was aggravating an already grave condition. Fever, headaches, and convulsions joined my partial paralysis and skin infections.

By the third day out of the hole, my physical problems had grown so acute they were affecting my mind. Organic psychosis, a doctor would call it. But there was no doctor. I withdrew from reality. I was no longer aware of those around me, of who or where I was, or of time passing. I just lay there, day after day, my eyes open, my body wasted, and my consciousness gone.

The next thing I can remember vividly is awakening to find a medic injecting medicine into my arms. Looking around the cage, I saw five or six empty vials lying where they had been tossed, indicating I had been under treatment for several days. The labels said the vials had contained vitamin B-1.Though I was still partly paralyzed, some of the feeling had begun to return to my hands and feet.

After I received another shot the following day, I felt the first urge to urinate since my attempted escape. Unable to control myself, I liberally wet my trousers. My nose was apparently functioning well; it was the worst smell I had ever experienced.

Instead of being upset, the guard treated the incident as if it were an occasion to celebrate. He called the senior NCO, who seemed pleased that I was responding to the medicine.

A few days later I was helped to the latrine, where I had my first bowel movement, another cause for celebration. On the way back to the cage, I asked the NCO the date. When the soldier finally understood what I meant, he took a stick and wrote "19-9" in the dirt. Three and a half weeks had passed since I was taken from the hole. I remembered little of those days.

During the next few weeks my bodily functions returned to normal and the toxemia began to disappear. The paralysis in my legs persisted, but I regained the use of my hands and arms. It was not long before I could sit up and feed myself.

Before my last escape attempt, I had tried to cultivate relationships with guards, even though none of them spoke English. My efforts had produced loans of needles and thread and other minor conveniences that made life in the cage a little more comfortable.

My prospects for escape were certainly increased by being friendly. I reasoned that an unfriendly guard was likely to be more alert than a friendly one. I also knew that the Vietnamese words I was picking up might help me someday as an escaped POW. Now that my legs were virtually useless, I decided that the best strategy would be to stop attempting to communicate with my captors altogether. It was not that I resented what the guards had done to me; their treatment of me had come from the punishment I knew would result from my attempts to escape. It was evident that since my removal from the hole, they had been trying hard to keep me alive. This was a time to lie low and regain my strength, and I guessed I would have the least difficulty if I began a period of complete silence.

As the weeks passed, my appetite increased. The food here was a little better than the fare of rice and bamboo shoots I had received in the other two cages. These soldiers embellished it with a better selection of local plant life, which included gourds.

Most of the food we ate was grown right around us. I couldn't help being impressed by the way the guards took full advantage of the resources available to them. They never wasted anything. They collected my urine, along with theirs, in bamboo tubes. It was used as an ammonia fertilizer for the camp garden. On occasion they also collected the contents of the hole in the ground, which they sprinkled with ash daily, and used it as manure. The ash treatment seemed to keep the large red ants away, which was a relief to me.

No longer preparing for an escape or communicating with the guards, I needed other ways of keeping my mind alert. I found myself engaged increasingly in mental exercises that could occupy me for hours and sometimes days at a time. I created, and then solved, complex mathematical problems in my head.

The calendar became an obsession. I figured the number of days I had spent as a prisoner and marked the passing of holidays ranging from Memorial Day to the Chinese New Year. I was now thirty-five years old. My birthday, August 15, had been just two days before my last escape attempt. It was the second I had observed in captivity. When the birthdays of Ernest, Patrick, Michael, and Cary arrived, I tried to picture myself at their parties, which now were in some imaginary Stateside home.

Sometimes I took myself on trips of pure fantasy. What would have happened, I speculated, had I left the Marines in the 1950s to fly for the airlines? A Korean War buddy, John Kaczynski, had done that, and I would put myself in his place. Recreating a scenario with meticulous detail, I would put myself in the cockpit of a TWA jet and fly it to Europe and back. I went through every detail of flight planning, preflight, takeoff, and landing. I talked to my copilot and flirted with the stewardesses. It was always sad when a journey ended and I came back to the reality of the cage.

Other times I reconstructed major portions of my life, bringing back important events and memorable moments so vividly that they almost seemed more real than the cage and the jungle surrounding me. Given my patience and a seemingly endless reservoir of memories, I found I could reconstruct movies and novels, sometimes summoning the dialogue line by line.

I relived every moment of the time in 1958 when my Marine scuba-diving pals and I recovered the solid brass helm wheel and pedestal from a sunken American freighter off the Carolina coast. It had been torpedoed by a German submarine during World War II. I felt the chill of the Atlantic Ocean in November through my wetsuit, and pictured Horace Lowrey descending alongside me through the shadowy green water. I re-experienced the discovery of the 1,900-foot vessel lying broken on the murky bottom in sixty-three feet of water off Bogue Inlet. I remembered the atmosphere of alarm and excitement when I and other members of the diving team, called the MerMasters, ran into several large sharks. We fired our spear guns, and I recalled the thud in my ears as the power head exploded. The spear hit the gray side of a shark no more than half a dozen feet away. The event was as real as if I were actually there again.

I recreated the challenge of detaching and raising the large, heavy, barnacle-covered wheel that had kept its watch from the ocean's floor for nearly two decades. Newspaper accounts had treated us like heroes. One article had concluded that the Marine divers would "relive the day of the raising a thousand times." Few members of the team would devote as much time and care to that as I now did.

In October of 1966, a visitor arrived unexpectedly in camp. I could tell that the soldiers wished they had had an opportunity to clean and shave their prisoner before bringing me down the hill for interrogation. By this time I had spoken to no one for months, and I decided on the way down the hill that I would maintain my silence.

I was delivered to a smartly uniformed middle-aged officer seated at a table under the trees. He was a high-ranking officer, I concluded. The soldiers treated him with unusual deference, and his shoulder boards were more elaborate than anyone else's in the camp.

"Sit down," the officer told me in English, gesturing toward a stool.

I did not react, behaving as if I hadn't heard. When the guards jerked at my arm and pointed at the stool, I sat down.

"Now, what is your name?"

I did not reply, but simply looked up into the trees.

"I said, what is your name?" The voice was louder.

When I failed to answer the second time, one of the guards struck me a blow that knocked me off the stool and onto the ground. Sitting up in the dirt, I watched as the guards talked to the officer. One of them tapped his head, indicating that I was crazy. The visitor ordered me returned to my cell. It was a small victory, but I went to sleep that night satisfied that I had completely fooled what must have been at least a full colonel as well as guards who had been watching me for months. For a professional pilot, I felt, I was not a bad actor.

With the passing of October, the monsoon rains ceased, and then November came and was gone. It was almost Christmas when the air attacks began. I heard what I guessed were American F-105s thundering overhead, then felt the shock of the bombs exploding. When some of them fell in the camp itself, I hoped that the bombing was in response to intelligence that I was being held there. Why else would they hit this remote encampment so heavily? When the guards came up after a bombardment, they gestured angrily at the sky and then at me, suggesting that I had once flown the airplanes that were attacking them. A few months before, I might have tried to explain that I had not flown bombing missions. But now I kept my silence.

On New Year's Day, 1967, only a few days after American planes had bombed the camp, a large two-engine cargo plane painted in jungle camouflage colors appeared over the main camp. It was so low I could see it through the bamboo bars below the thatch of my roof. It began "free-dropping" supplies at low altitude from a large open door. Five more times the plane appeared at about one-hour intervals. It was dropping supplies to the troops in this area. Though it had no military markings, I recognized it as a Russian IL-2, delivering supplies picked up near Hanoi.

That evening a couple of guards showed up and gave me a new red blanket whose manufacturer's tag read, in English, MADE IN CHINA, COTTON WASTE PRODUCTS. In the weeks to come, I noticed that all the guards had the new red blankets that had apparently been dropped by the IL-2.

For the first time since I had been taken from the hole, I felt well enough to do something again with my hands. Despite the tropical climate, there were many nights during the winter that I lay shivering in forty-degree temperatures. I had longed during those times for a coat or a sweater. Now that I would not need my old wool blanket to cover me at night, I decided I would make a coat out of it.

I used sharp rocks, smuggled into the cage, to fashion bamboo needles. Separated strands of fiber from the frayed edges of the old blanket provided thread. The fabric was so old that I was able to tear it along the lines of the pattern I had established. At first I was going to make a poncho-type wrap, but that was too fast. I needed projects that took time.

Practically the only sewing experience I had was gained in patching projects in earlier cages, but I learned quickly. Soon I was devoting large parts of my days to the task. Fascinated by my new-found inventiveness and industry, the guards followed my

progress each day. Some asked to see the needles and other implements I was using.

After more than a week, the sewing was completed. Now I
devoted myself to fashioning bamboo buttons. The completed
jacket might not win me any awards at the Michigan State Fair,
but it fit quite nicely and made me more comfortable on the cold
January nights.

Though the guards had seemed amused by my new coat, the
camp officer was not. Visiting the cage about a week after the
project was completed, the officer noticed the coat and immediately summoned more guards. When they arrived, I was taken
from the cage and steadied on my weak legs by soldiers on either
side of me.

Obviously convinced that I could not have completed the coat
without help, the camp commander angrily demanded an explanation from the guards. They all started talking at once. When I
saw they were trying to convince the commander that I had done
the job by myself, I tried to demonstrate how I had made the
coat, showing him remnants from the blanket and several of my
bamboo needles. I even stitched some torn cloth. The CO was not
impressed, and for a time I feared that the coat I had spent so
much time on was going to be confiscated. Yet the officer, angry
and disgusted with the guards, allowed me to keep the jacket
when I was returned to the cage.

21

The new year of 1967 went by rapidly. Before I knew it, the cold nights and chilly days of winter were replaced by the warm, humid days of spring. I had always thought there were no seasons in the jungle. Living in a bamboo cage was teaching me that there definitely was a delineation of the seasons. I was now using my blanket-jacket as a pillow.

On a warm, sunny April morning, I saw Harnavee being taken past my cage and down into the valley with all his possessions. It was the first time I had seen him since our move to these cages last May, almost a year. For a few minutes I feared that after nearly two years of imprisonment, the Thai and I were being totally separated. Shortly, additional guards showed up at my cage, and soon they were gathering my possessions and bundling them.

While one soldier removed the stocks from my cage, another cut a bamboo pole for me to use as a walking stick. Taking the stocks meant we were not on our way to Hanoi, I was sure. It took two men to carry each section of the stocks. Seeing that my tennis shoes were now nothing more than rubber soles with a toepiece, the guards provided me with several stringy pieces of bark, which I used to tie the shoes to my feet. When I had been tethered with an elbow-and-neck rope, the guards took me down the trail to the camp below. We took the path over which I had been carried, rolled in a blanket, about a year before.

Going down, I saw camouflaged huts stacked with boxes of ammunition on both sides of the jungle trail. The Marine in me stored the information in my head for retrieval later. I observed many thatch-roofed ammo sheds, open-sided, with bamboo floors set off the ground, spaced on either side of the valley about a hundred yards apart.

Stopping frequently to allow me to rest, the party made it to the main base camp about ninety minutes later. Seeing it for the first time in daylight, I estimated that the camp could accommodate as many as three hundred soldiers in the huts that bordered a drill field hidden from the air by the trees.

After a fifteen-minute rest at the base, we took a path up the side of a hill and climbed for several minutes before stopping for a rest on a knoll that commanded a view of the entire Dien Bien Phu valley. We rested on the edge of antiaircraft battery emplacements that had been abandoned for some time. Looking down at the pastoral scene of rice paddies and quiet villages, I found it hard to picture it as a battleground where thousands of men had died in just a few historic weeks in 1954.

Below us, its gravel surface overgrown with brush, stretched Hong Cum airfield, the 5,000-foot runway that had supposedly served as the last point from which battle-weary French Foreign Legionnaires managed to escape from the Viet Minh who encircled them. Beyond the airstrip, I saw Harnavee and his guards climbing into the mountains on the other side of the valley.

We walked down into the valley, crossing the old French runway, and then followed Harnavee's group up a trail leading into the hills. An hour and a half of climbing brought us to a new place of confinement, situated, as usual, on a slope above a small army camp. My guards installed my stocks in a well-built cage surrounded on three sides by a fence of crisscrossed bamboo poles. Even if its fourth side were completed, the fence was not sturdy enough to stop an escaping prisoner, I thought, but the loosely tied poles certainly would make a racket if someone disturbed them in the night.

Harnavee and I could not see each other's cages because of a curve around a small knoll, even though we were less than fifty yards apart, closer than we had ever been before. For the first time a single lean-to served as the sentry headquarters: from his halfway point, the guard could see both cages. However, he was far enough away now so that he could not monitor my every movement. If I could get my legs in better shape, I thought, I could get out of this place.

Since physical exercise at previous camps had been so limited as to be practically nonexistent, Harnavee and I were pleasantly surprised to find that we were required to sweep up around our cages and to police the paths leading to the guards' lean-to. Not only did this give me the chance to strengthen my legs, but it permitted me to communicate, if only by exchanging gestures, with the Thai.

No amount of survival training can help to cope with the lone-liness of solitary confinement. I longed for the company of other prisoners. A wave, a salute, or a smile from Harnavee, as we worked along the paths, lifted my spirits in a way I could never have imagined before I had been captured.

Spring and summer of 1967 passed uneventfully. With each passing month my physical condition improved. Though walking was still difficult, I was no longer exhausted after a few moments of work around the cage. I now looked for projects outside to permit me to extend the few minutes of exercise we were getting each day. When the sweeping of the path was completed, I kept the fenced area of the cage clear of new vegetation. I always left enough so that there would be something to do the next morning.

Though the guards visited the cage regularly, both day and night, the lean-to itself was far enough away to permit me to fashion bamboo picks to untie my hands at night. I had no intention of trying to escape at this point, but by loosening my neck and wrist ropes after I had been tied tightly for the night, I could sleep much more comfortably. It was risky, I knew, but the guards usually did no more than check a few times each night to see if I was in the cage, and never checked my ropes. Moreover, I had become so skillful at retying myself that I thought I could handle all but the most improbable situation.

The improbable happened on a quiet evening in September. Awakened by the arrival of a guard on his night rounds, I felt him tug on my neck rope before I could scoot down to take up the slack. He grunted at the discovery it was much too loose. Then the flash-light shone into the cage, and I frantically began retying my wrist ropes under the red blanket. It was too late.

The guard yelled down the hill for help, and soon I was yanked from my cage, stood up in the moonlight, and slapped around by angry guards who obviously thought I had been trying to escape. Even if they could have understood my frantic explanation, they were in no mood to listen. They put me back in the cage for the night, tied me securely, and hung a lantern on the door. Every few minutes a guard checked my ropes.

Untied as usual in the morning, I tried to dispose of the bamboo picks I had used to untie myself. I had not completed the job when the guards took me from the cage and inspected it. While his fellow soldiers watched, the guard who had been on duty the night before tied my hands exactly as he had when he prepared me for the night. Then, producing one of the picks he had found in the thatch, he motioned for me to try to untie myself.

Thinking that my punishment might be less severe if I cooperated, I untied myself with such ease that it startled the guard and sent the other soldiers into paroxysms of laughter. Seeing the anger and embarrassment in the guard's eyes, I realized that I had committed a bad mistake. I knew enough about face to recognize that this Asian had lost some of it the night before, and I, who was the source of his embarrassment, had just made things worse. The soldier's fist slammed into the side of my face, sending me stumbling.

They picked me up and stood me with my back to the bamboo fence. My neck rope was passed through the fence to a soldier on the other side. The soldier with the wounded ego delivered a beating with such ferocity that I feared I would be permanently injured. His fists slammed into my unprotected groin repeatedly. The neck rope kept me from doubling over.

When I thought I could not endure any more, I let myself hang by my neck rope in an attempt to convince the soldiers that I was badly injured. Feigning injury or unconsciousness had worked before, and it seemed to be working now. The soldier on the other side of the fence released the neck rope and let me drop.

Lying on the ground with my breath still coming in gasps, I thought the punishment was over. The blows to my chest and groin had hurt me, but I could tell he hadn't inflicted serious damage. I rose to my hands and knees. The guard's foot smashed into the side of my head. Something exploded inside like a phosphorus shell in the dead of night, and I lost consciousness.

I came to as the soldiers were dragging me back into the cage. Even though the sun was still climbing in the sky, I was tied up tightly on my bed board, as if it were already night. I spent the rest of the day and night in that position, without food or water.

The bruises from the guard's fists eventually healed, but his vicious kick to my head had devastating consequences. Within two weeks I began to lose motor skills in my right leg. Then the paralysis moved up the leg, through my groin, and down my left leg. A few days later I felt the numbness begin in my hands and then move up into my arms.

I had experienced some bad moments during my imprisonment, but never had I felt so helpless and afraid. I awoke each morning dreading the loss of the last few motor skills I possessed.

When you had a problem in the cockpit, there were procedures to follow, checklists to examine, buttons to push, but here the situation seemed out of my hands. The soldiers could see that I was ill, but they didn't know how to treat me, and there was no doctor in the camp.

By the middle of October I could no longer reach up to the ceiling of my cage to take down my mosquito net. By the first of November the only task I could perform was to push rice into my mouth, provided the bowl was placed close enough to my face. The guards quit taking me to the hole in the ground after I couldn't stand up, much less walk to get out of the cage.

Sometime in November I lost control of my bowels and kidneys, and the cage was soon a putrid mess. The guards wore handkerchiefs over their mouths and noses whenever they came near. None of them seemed to have the stomach to clean either me or the cage. I sat or lay in my own filth day after day.

I was unable to move without help, and oblivious of the flies and other insects attracted by the excrement, and now my sickness and degradation began affecting my mind. By December I was drifting in and out of lucidity as if it were a house I only visited. Incredibly, the guards continued to confine me in the stocks and tie my hands day and night. I no longer cared.

I felt like praying, but months before I had rationalized that God hadn't put me here and God wasn't going to get me out.

The long days and nights continued without change. The man who once thought there was no crisis he couldn't weather gave up hope and lost all feelings of self-worth. I remembered how my father had told me that none of the Braces had lived long enough to collect their Social Security, and now I seemed to be following in their footsteps. My condition was so wretched and my prospects for recovery so dismal that I wanted, and needed, to die.

On December 10, my son Cary's birthday, nearly three months after the beating at the fence, I tried to strangle myself on my neck rope. It had been stretched tight anyway, and all I had to do was pull a little harder with my neck.

I must have passed out. Sometime later I became conscious of a warm feeling. I awoke to find that I was once again urinating on myself. My debasement was complete. Perhaps I had needed to strike bottom, because the next day my head cleared and I began again to fight for my life. The only person in the world who could help me was the man who had stared back at me from the bathroom mirror in Chieng Mai on the morning before I was captured, two and a half years before.

"You're going to rehabilitate yourself," my mind told me. "You're going to walk again. You're going to get out of here." The words became a kind of litany, and in the next few days I incorporated their hopeful message into a poem I composed in my head. I recited my creation virtually every day, and drew strength from it:

> I'm just a prisoner in a cage
> I have no name, I have no age
> The guards, they don't know what I've done
> All they know is I'm a captured one

> They captured me in '65
> And I guess it's lucky I'm still alive
> For I've tried to escape three times in all
> And I'd go the forth. . . but I'd have to crawl

> They buried me once for seven days
> And that was supposed to mend my ways
> But I still have that urge to try, you see
> But now I don't have the legs to carry me

> My feet are in stocks, my neck's tied to a pole
> What food I get is shoved in through a hole
> At night I lie down and my hands are tied
> And the rope is stretched to a post outside

> Now I've been sick and almost died
> And I've had to crawl to get outside
> I wasn't helped in any way at all
> In fact I was beaten while held against a wall

> But I'll leave here alive, I know that now
> But I don't know when and I don't know how
> And I'll see my family once again
> But I don't know where and I don't know when. . . .

22

Buzzing loudly, the hornet flew into the cage and began frantically searching for food. I had watched these bright yellow-and-black hornets before. They were after the giant black spiders that lived in the thatch. When one of the spiders dropped from the roof thatch onto the dirt floor, the hornet was on him instantly, back arched and stinging viciously. The lean body moved in a frenzy over the dying spider, not giving up the attack until its prey lay motionless. Now the hornet could be more deliberate. It carefully removed each of the spider's eight legs, discarding them. Then, tucking the swollen body under its belly, reminding me of a lumber carrier, it began the journey to one of the vertical poles of the cage. Its grotesque cargo seemed much too large. I had seen hornets climb the poles before, to get enough altitude to fly away. I knew it would have to climb as high as possible to be able to fly with this load.

The hornet was on its way up the pole when I noticed a dark green lizard watching the ascent with emotionless, yellow-slit eyes. Its green back was curving around the pole and the front legs leaving the ground. The red tongue flicked out, and both the hornet and the spider were in the reptile's mouth. Banging its tail on the ground as if to help it close its jaws over this double lunch, the lizard moved off into the jungle, pieces of insect hanging out of both sides of its mouth.

Such brutal little scenarios repeatedly brought home to me the realities of my own struggle for survival in the jungle. The hours I spent studying insects and animals around the cage helped keep my mind alert during the end of 1967 and into 1968. Unable to move in a cage whose stench I had now grown accustomed to, I became an expert observer of the anatomy and behavior of the mosquito, the takeoff and landing characteristics of the common fly, and the eating habits of the ground beetles around the cage.

I learned not to be alarmed when the lizards and bright green bamboo snakes ventured near. And I looked forward to the daily visits of my only friends in the camp, the dogs who hung around, scavenging for food. They, too, lived a precarious existence. Occasionally the soldiers would butcher one of the dogs to eat. I felt a kinship with these homeless curs.

When I wasn't watching insects and animals around the cage, I occupied myself with my mathematical problems, making them progressively more complicated and complex. I drifted into the past, challenging my memory each day for more tidbits that lay hidden in the recesses of my mind, waiting for the right signal to bring them out.

Though my mental attitude had changed for the better since my suicide attempt in December of 1967, my physical condition had not improved with the arrival of the new year. In January 1968 a doctor unexpectedly arrived in the camp and gave me a cursory medical exam. I thought the disgusting, foul-smelling cage would be cleaned and that I would be allowed to bathe for the first time in several months. The only result of the doctor's visit was the application of some winter-green-smelling ointment on my paralyzed legs. Even so, I was not complaining. The strong-smelling stuff masked the odor of the cage.

I was convinced, now more than ever, that no one was going to extricate me from my misery but myself. I began my own conditioning program-very limited at first-in an effort to regain control of my limbs. Each day I devoted time to the challenge of moving a finger, a hand, or an arm. The progress wasn't apparent at first, but by February even the guards were impressed. Now, when I ate, I could hold on to and manipulate the chopsticks well enough to feed myself normally.

Determined to use the hole in the ground again, I crawled the thirty or forty feet every morning. I began pulling myself upright on the outside of the cage and making part of the journey by walking unsteadily on my spindly legs. By the end of February I had regained control of my bowels, an achievement that made me feel like celebrating. Soon I was walking unaided for very short distances.

My fortunes took another turn for the better in the first week in March. The guards who had beaten me and then watched me deteriorate without doing much were transferred. They were replaced by an NVA unit whose soldiers took much more interest in the condition of their two prisoners. The new guards were better disciplined, groomed, and uniformed than their predecessors. I could tell they were not satisfied with the way Harnavee and I had been treated.

On the day after their arrival, the new senior NCO came up to the cage from the camp below, wearing a uniform so impeccable that it looked out of place in the jungle. Shocked by the odor of the cage and my appearance, he immediately summoned a crew of guards from the camp below. I was taken from the cage and ordered to remove my clothes. A soldier picked them up with a stick and took them off-to be burned, I guessed. As I sat there naked, shivering in the cold March air, the guards cut my tangled, matted beard and hair with a pair of Chinese hand clippers, leaving me completely bald.

A few minutes later I was helped down the path to the stream, sat on a bamboo bathing platform, and given my first bath in nearly six months. As they poured bucket after bucket of cold water over me, the soldiers required that I scrub myself until the new bar of soap they had given me was half gone. Then they instructed me to rub myself vigorously with matted grass they provided. The grass removed the dead skin still left from the scrubbing. By the time the bath was completed, my skin was raw. I was as clean as I had ever been in my life.

I was given a pair of clean, well-patched, army-type trousers and a green shirt whose buttons, pockets, and undeteriorated fabric seemed too good to be true. An old pair of clean tennis shoes, their backs removed to prevent running, completed my outfitting.

The pleasant surprises were not over. Upon being returned to my cage, I found it had been cleaned. Six to eight inches of fresh dirt had been placed on the floor, and the cage itself was covered with a fine white ash, the residue of a caustic wash. My red blanket had been washed and placed to dry on the bamboo fence. As I stepped back into the cage, a guard pressed a small, heavy green blanket into my arms.

I went to sleep, still in the stocks, hoping that I would not wake the following morning to find that all this was a dream. I was so grateful that I had to thank my captors, and I broke my silence of more than twelve months. The misery of the last few months made a cold bath and a clean cage in the jungle seem more luxurious than a room at the Ritz. My morale soared.

You're going to make it, Brace, I told myself as I lay looking up at the thatch. You're going to make it.

My condition continued to improve in the next several weeks, and by the first week in April, Harnavee and I were allowed to work together, clearing brush between our cages and cutting down the banana trees nearby. This was the first time we had been allowed to work side by side, in a situation where we could actually exchange more than gestures.

I noticed a different, more relaxed atmosphere in the camp now, and began to harbor hopes that the end of the war might be near. Since the first of April I had heard neither the drone of jet bombers overhead nor the popping reports of the antiaircraft emplacements in the valley. From my working area I could see that the camp below was much less carefully camouflaged than it had been before. Even the camouflage foliage on my cage was being applied more casually. It would not be long now, I told myself. The war would soon be over, if it wasn't already. I had been a prisoner three years now, and no war involving the United States had lasted more than about four.

When the brush-clearing project was finished, I found that I had cleared off enough foliage to permit me to see a patch of blue sky through the bars from my cage. It was a small thing, but the window of blue was an added tonic to my spirits. I lay on my back by the hour, losing myself in the clouds and azure distances, dreaming of what it would be like to go home.

In the three years since I had been captured, my four boys would have grown so much I wondered whether I would recognize them. Cary would be in the first grade, Michael in the fifth, Patrick in the seventh, and Ernest would be entering high school. Remembering that I had four boys waiting for me was always a source of comfort, even though it pained me to think they were passing their formative years without me.

Would Patricia be waiting for me when I came home? I was enough of a realist to have my doubts. By now I had accommodated myself to the probability that the letter I had written her a few months after my capture had not been delivered. Patricia was young, beautiful, and not possessed of the temperament to wait out long years for a husband whom she probably thought was dead, anyway. Another woman might wait, but probably not Patricia. I did not condemn her. That was the way she was, and that was life.

The summer of 1968 passed without restoration of the air activity. My hopes for repatriation got another boost on September 2. Relatives of the soldiers visited the camp. To me it was a sure sign that the NVA didn't expect any hostile air activity. Civilians—men, women, and children—toured the area and were even allowed to visit the cages and look at the prisoners. As I stared back at the civilians, I realized these were the first women I had seen since arriving at my first cage some three years ago.

One little, large-eyed girl came to the cage and looked in at the pale, hollow-cheeked white man whose legs were in stocks and whose neck rope was tied to a horizontal bar. Timidly she handed me a piece of candy wrapped in a banana leaf.

I smiled, and thanked the little girl in Vietnamese. The escort, an elderly NVA officer, addressed me in that language. The only word I could make out was "Hanoi," but that was enough to send a surge of adrenaline through my veins. If I was going to Hanoi, repatriation couldn't be far behind.

"When?" I asked in Thai.

"Soon," the officer replied in the same language.

Before the civilians left that evening, there was a party in the main camp. As I lay listening to the laughter and singing, I told myself that I also would be celebrating before long. The civilians left, and the camp returned to normal. September passed without change.

On October 8, a new group of visitors arrived at the camp. I guessed they must be very important since the guards had taken me down to bathe the day before, and were preparing their own uniforms for an inspection. They lined up with their rifles on each side of the path leading up to the cage and saluted the entourage of high-ranking officers when they climbed the hill to inspect the cages.

The inspection was brief and cursory, and soon the delegation departed. They apparently ordered the two prisoners to be brought down the path for interrogation.

I watched Harnavee go first, and could see him seated unsteadily on a stool, answering questions. It sounded as if they were speaking English. Though I could hear only portions of the interrogation, I could tell that the officers were accusing the Thai of being a pilot.

After Harnavee had been returned to his cage, the guards came for me. One of them untied the door while the other knocked the pin from my stocks with the bamboo mallet. They took me down the hill with my hands tied behind my back. I made it only part of the way down the hill, and then the strength in my legs left me. I fell hard on the trail, unable to cushion my landing because my hands were tied.

Seated at a table next to the guard hut, the officers watched the guards help the rubber-legged prisoner down the rest of the hill and escort him across a small log bridge spanning a stream bordering the camp. It was obvious I was in no condition to escape. The senior officer, whom I guessed was at least a lieutenant colonel, ordered my hands untied.

Placed on a stool facing the officers, I was asked, in English, to identify myself and to state my age. When I told them I was thirty-seven, the interrogators looked startled.

"You look much older," said the officer who was translating.

"I wouldn't know," I replied. "I haven't seen a mirror for years."

The officer spoke to one of the guards, who produced a small mirror from his shirt pocket and handed it to me. I was shocked. Staring back at me was a face I didn't recognize. The eyes were sunken, the cheekbones were sticking out, and the six-week-old beard was flecked with gray. Shaken, I handed the mirror back to the guards.

Then came the annoyingly familiar questions. They were still trying to get me to admit that I was a "colonel in the CIA."

"The CIA story was made up by a Buddhist in Moung Sai," I said. "Each time you've brought it up, I've told you it wasn't true." I wasn't sure that the translating officer understood. The man's English was so shaky that when I told him I had worked for "a contract company of the USAID," the interpreter leaped to the conclusion that I had been attached to a U.S. military outfit.

"Yes, company! What is the number of your company?"

"Bird and Sons."

"No number?"

"No, no number, just name, Bird and Sons."

I made a motion of a bird flying in the sky, and pointed at the sun. He seemed to think that was a logical name for an aviation company, but still thought it was military.

Despite my efforts, I couldn't seem to get the notion across that I was a civilian. I wasn't sure at this point that it mattered to my interrogators. They seemed more concerned about my resistance as a prisoner.

"How many times you escape?"

I wasn't sure how I should answer the question. If I admitted the truth, and they weren't aware of it, the revelation would do me no good. On the other hand, if they caught me in a lie, I might be punished. I decided to interpret the question as applying only to the cage in which I was currently being held, and to the fact that I had never made it completely out.

"None," I said, as nonchalantly as I could.

I could see the interrogator bristle at the answer. The interpreter called me a "criminal," and then demonstrated that the officers had been briefed about my behavior in the cages.

"You have escaped many times, and you have therefore been punished by being placed in leg irons," the officer said sharply. But, he added, the Vietnamese government had decided to be lenient with me. I was now to be taken to a "new place" where other prisoners were held. I would receive "much medical attention," be allowed to get plenty of exercise, be given reading material "to improve your mind," and be permitted to attend "classes" with other POWs.

I could hardly believe my ears. Perhaps the war was over! Even if it wasn't, the prospect of joining other Americans after so long alone in the jungle made me giddy. I had to force myself to remember that I had felt the same way a month before, when the elderly officer had suggested I would be going to Hanoi "soon." I had been disappointed when nothing came of that, and I knew I must be careful not to put too much stock in the promises of my captors.

When, in the early evening, I heard the visiting officers leave the camp, I was crestfallen. I'd been deceived again. Other than a good evening meal, the routine of tying me in and knocking the pin in to lock the stocks was the same as always.

The next morning I found we were leaving, after all. Harnavee and I were awakened before daybreak, told to gather our few belongings, and fed a good breakfast. Before being helped down the path to the camp, I took a last look at the cage that had been my home as well as my place of torment for the last year and a half. I noted with relief that the leg stocks were being left behind.

We walked through the camp, which was being dismantled. The path led into a meadow. Two guards helped me along. They had removed my neck rope when I left the cage. It seemed strange not to be wearing a collar.

In the meadow a new Soviet-made command jeep was waiting. Wearing aluminum blindfolds tied in back with string, Harnavee and I were placed in the back and seated on the floor. I could see out on both sides of my nose; obviously the model for the aluminum blindfold had had a very small nose. Six guards sat on bench seats, three to a side. The two officers had crowded into the front beside the driver.

The jeep rolled down a sloping dirt road and out into the larger valley of Dien Bien Phu.

23

The blindfold constituted only a minor obstacle to my vision. By tilting my head back, I could see anything I wanted. If the soldiers noticed that I was peeking from behind my blindfold, they didn't do anything about it. Facing forward in the jeep, I read the odometer before the jeep left camp. I noted that we had gone thirty-eight kilometers before stopping in a town the signs identified as Moung Pon.

The soldiers bought a bag of oranges and gave each of us one. The jeep continued its journey down a road so bumpy and chuckholed that Harnavee immediately became carsick. This required frequent stops for the miserable prisoner to vomit beside the road.

I had hoped we were headed for the North Vietnamese capital, and when I saw the sign saying "Hanoi—540 km," I felt like cheering. Hanoi, I knew, was where most of the American POWs were being kept. There had been only a handful of American pilots in Hanoi prisons when I was captured in 1965, but I knew that the years of bombing must have produced some more. Once in a while, the guards had shown me copies of the People's Army newspaper whose front pages were adorned with pictures of downed American aviators and "box scores" purporting to tally the number of downed planes.

I remembered seeing, early in my imprisonment, that the figure of downed aircraft had reached 366; the next time I was shown a paper, the tally was more than 1,000. Even if the figures were exaggerated, it seemed likely that a sizable number of American POWs were being held in the capital city.

Though the signs of the war were everywhere, the jeep drove on in broad daylight, the soldiers seemingly unconcerned about the clouds of dust swirling up behind them. When they encountered bombed-out bridges, the driver wheeled the jeep along the stream bank until they reached the fording areas marked by upright poles in the water. Then the vehicle would cross the stream just down-stream from the poles, over an underwater roadbed of rocks built by the industrious North Vietnamese.

The roads were in dreadful condition, and more than once the soldiers had to get out and push the vehicle through the mud. Road crews were in the process of repairing the worst spots.

The NVA soldiers seemed as disciplined in their behavior toward civilians as they had been more than three years before, when I had traveled from Boum Lao through the jungles to my first cage. Once, when they got into a heated roadside argument with two boys over the price of their geese, the soldiers finally threw up their hands in exasperation and drove off without the geese. Guerrilla forces on both sides of this war would have taken the whole flock, I knew. That night, stopping at a village along the road, the soldiers negotiated with the female proprietor of an inn-like building for the evening meal and lodging. Eventually they came to a deal, but I had no doubts by then that the soldiers would have left the woman alone if she had refused them service. When kids who lived near the hostel began pegging dirt clods at Harnavee and me as we waited in the jeep, the soldiers stopped them immediately.

The Thai and I were placed in the same room for the night, giving us our first opportunity to converse in nearly three years. It was an experience to cherish, this simple act of talking with a friend in English after so many years. Harnavee wanted to hear every detail of my escape attempts. For the first time I had someone with whom I could share my adventures. When I had finished, my Thai friend told me that the escape attempts had resulted in harsher treatment for him also, including the introduction of legs stocks to his cage following my second and longest venture more than two years before. Yet he showed not a hint of resentment.

By this time, both of us assumed that we were on no prisoner-of-war lists that would advise our families that we were still alive. We guessed that our having been captured in Laos by the NVA was the reason. Harnavee feared that as a consequence we could be locked up forever, without anyone knowing of our existence.

"If you escape, will you return for me after the war?" he asked me.

I promised him that I would, but I also reminded the Thai that of the two of us, Harnavee was the better prepared for an escape, since he was younger, in better physical shape, and knew the language. Yet he had never tried. The Thai simply shook his head.

"I am not afraid of what will happen to me in prison," he said. "Buddha will provide."

As grim a turn as the conversation had taken, I did not feel that either of us would remain prisoners much longer. Everywhere were signs that I was sure meant the war was over: the relaxed attitudes of the soldiers, the fact that we were not tied in any way in the jeep, the driving in broad daylight, and our apparent transfer from the cages to Hanoi. It would not be long now, I thought, before we would be repatriated. Any escape plans would have to be weighed with that fact in mind.

We slept the night in loosely tied ropes that seemed more for show than for restraint. In the morning we were fed our first hot breakfast in years, a rice dish served in a sauce with pork and bean sprouts. On our way out to the jeep, we were pelted with more dirt clods by the same kids who had harassed us the night before. Though the soldiers ran them off again, the incident upset me enough to produce an angry flush in my cheeks. With the war over, or probably close to it, one didn't expect that kind of hostility, even from the kids. As the jeep drove away, I could still see in my mind the looks of hatred on the faces of the boys.

The guards obviously bore us no ill will. On this second day of traveling, we were allowed to sit with the soldiers on the bench seats in back, rather than on the floor of the jeep. Concerned about my complaints of constipation, they stopped at a bombed-out military outpost a few miles down the road. The officer left Harnavee and me behind with two guards, and drove off to get assistance at what I later learned was probably the POW prison at Son La. When they returned they were followed by another jeep whose passenger examined me. He told me to take some pills that he had wrapped in newspaper.

About midday we reached what I guessed must be the Noir River. The banks were scarred by large, recently made bomb craters. Because no bridge spanned this three-hundred-yard-wide water-way, vehicles had to be ferried across on a long barge powered by a tugboat. Though traffic was already waiting on both banks, the guards and their prisoners were given priority. As soon as a bulldozer nudged the ferry to the bank, the jeep drove aboard.

We had continued on the other side for only a few miles before we had to be ferried across another section of the twisting river.

The corrugated texture of the poor roads changed to smooth blacktop after the second river crossing. We soon rolled into a city. It was the largest town we had seen so far, and I thought it might be the outskirts of Hanoi. We drove for nearly ten kilometers through residential areas and shopping streets. Hidden under the trees on both sides of the road were thousands of fifty-five-gallon gasoline drums, painted blue with red tops, and stacked ten barrels deep. If a bomb struck this concentration of gasoline, I thought, thousands of civilian residents would die in the explosions and fire.

We went beyond the town, so it wasn't Hanoi, I concluded. The density of the population in the countryside increased dramatically. We were about an hour out of the city when the jeep left the main road, traveled about five miles, and pulled up under some trees. As Harnavee and I sat alone in the jeep with our blindfolds still in place, we looked out the sides to see the officer sign some papers for a guard we had known from the last cage. With a handshake from the officer, he went off across the rice paddies carrying his AK-47 and full combat pack. Harnavee thought he was going on leave.

The soldiers waited for dusk, chatting in the late-afternoon shadows and snacking on oranges that they shared with the POWs. When the sun was down, the jeep returned to the main road and traveled a short distance before pulling off into some tall grass that hid dozens of gasoline drums. As an attendant helped the soldiers fill the jeep's tanks, I looked beyond this fueling station to an adjacent field where several truck bodies had been set up on empty oil drums.

The fake trucks were obviously serving as bait for a flak trap. Antiaircraft installations undoubtedly were hidden in the trees along the edge of the field. I guessed American aviators must have taken the bait, because the field was pitted by large bomb craters. The hidden drums of this fueling station, only a few hundred yards away, had apparently escaped detection.

The jeep continued down the road through the growing darkness for only a short distance before the traffic began growing heavier and the highway merged into a very wide, tree-lined street. Then the lights of the city were flashing past. They were the bright lights of a metropolis whose inhabitants didn't fear the bombs of an enemy. Soon we found ourselves alongside an old

French-made electric streetcar. It had four units in all, and was clanking and grumbling toward the city center, its civilian passengers looking down curiously at the jeep and its blindfolded occupants.

From the cafes and other business establishments we could hear music. This was no city at war, I thought excitedly. Peering around the blindfold, I saw streets crowded with people busily going about their everyday tasks.

We threaded through the bicycles, pedicabs, and honking motor vehicles for nearly an hour before stopping to allow the officer to ask directions of a policeman. Soon we were at the stone gates of what appeared to be an old French prison. When the officer produced his papers to the sentry, the large, wooden, steel-braced doors were opened. The driver wheeled the jeep into a courtyard and parked, and the soldiers got out to find someone in authority.

They left their AK-47s behind them in the jeep, but the Thai and I were convinced by this time that the war was over, and made no move toward the weapons. When the guards returned, they were trusting enough to ask us to pass their weapons down to them from the jeep.

Still blindfolded, we were as yet too weak to walk well. We were half-carried and half-dragged by the soldiers across the courtyard, down a hallway, and into a room, where we were seated on the floor and warned not to speak. Our blindfolds were removed, and then our guard left the room. I saw we were in a room with a large hook hanging down from a high ceiling. The hook, I thought, had probably supported a chandelier.

We sat on a red tile floor in a dirty room with faded yellow walls. A door whose painted-over window contained a peep-hole was the only entrance. An eye was watching us through the peep-hole. A table and a stool were the only furniture in the room.

In a few minutes a short, dark, chubby NVA officer, with a wandering right eye that one noticed immediately, strode into the room with a book under his arm. Looking down at us with an expressionless face, he motioned for us to stand. When he saw we were unable to stand up by ourselves, he addressed me in English.

"Get on the stool."

I crawled across the floor and managed to stand, using the stool as a support. Then the officer addressed us both.

"You are not to be curious about anything you hear in this place," he said. "You are now prisoners and you have no rights."

After a few more words of introduction, he began questioning me, disputing as usual my contention that I was a civilian. "We have other information," he said. "Date of capture?"

"Twenty-one May 1965."

The answer brought the interrogator's eyes up from his notes.

"'Sixty-five? No, this is 1968."

"I was captured in 1965," I repeated.

"Where you been?"

"Somewhere in the jungle," I answered.

When the interrogator had finished with me, he left us alone in the room, and I looked at my Thai friend and smiled. Harnavee smiled back, but shook his head sadly. "No, the war is not over," he said.

He was right. It would not be long before I learned that the reduction in air activity I had noticed during the recent months was the result of a partial bombing halt ordered by President Johnson. The war was far from over.

We had been brought to Hoa Lo Prison, the large, high-walled penitentiary in the center of the city that the American POWs called the Hanoi Hilton.

The courtyard we had driven into was in the "Heartbreak Hotel" section, and we were now near "New Guy Village" in one of the two torture chambers of the prison. This was Room 18, the "Meathook Room." It was named for the hook in the ceiling from which trussed POWs were hung, sometimes upside down, for long periods. The man who had just interrogated us was one of the most sadistic officers in the prison system. The POWs called him "the Bug."

24

I was blindfolded again and carried out to the courtyard of the large prison. There I was put in the back of a waiting truck. Harnavee did not come with us, and I felt as if I were leaving an old friend behind. I hadn't really met him until the day of capture, we'd never been able to engage in long conversation, but there was a bond between us that would exist forever. Besides, I sometimes felt guilty about having placed him in this position.

While we waited for a driver, a soldier gave me a bread roll stuffed with cooked vegetables, pork, and lettuce. *My God*, I thought, *it's bread.* It was the first I had seen in three and a half years, but my enthusiasm dimmed when I tried to bite into it. My bridgework had been loosened as a result of the beating after my first escape attempt, and I could no longer bite down on anything substantial without considerable pain. I broke the hard bread into tiny pieces and was eating it a piece at a time when the truck engine started.

We drove out the gate into the night and maneuvered our way through the city traffic for about ten minutes before entering another gate and courtyard.

I was carried by some guards into a large building that looked like a house. I could still see out around the blindfold. When I had been brought inside and the blindfold had been removed, I found myself in a large and more ornate room than the one with the hook. The room looked as if it belonged in the residence of a wealthy family. A large fireplace on one wall had tall Oriental urns on each side that dominated the room. In the center was a large table with a white tablecloth. The two guards who stood at attention on either side of the table seemed to serve the same decorative function as the urns; they were frozen in position.

I was seated on a stool when two officers entered the room. One of them, whose features suggested he had French blood, clutched a sheaf of notes in his slender hands. When he was behind the table, he looked down at the notes, then up at me. His face was friendly, and his tone not at all intimidating.

"You are intelligence agent?" he asked in English.

Here it came again. "No," I said wearily, "I'm a civilian pilot."

"How much money you make?"

Instinct told me to give them a lower figure than was the case. "A thousand a month," I said.

"That is very much," came the response. Then a raised eyebrow. "You get paid as much as a colonel."

Though I didn't take the bait, I prepared myself to answer the accusation that I was a colonel in the CIA, but the interrogator changed his tack.

"You have been a prisoner a long time. I think you are one of the first men captured in this war."

The observation gave me a chance to interject a question of my own. "What is the situation? Is the war over?"

"We will explain the situation to you shortly," he said.

"Will I be allowed to write my wife?"

"We will discuss that later also." He seemed unperturbed by my questions.

"Have you received mail from my wife?"

The officer laughed. "Yes, she has probably written you many times, but whether it is here or not, I do not know. I will check and see."

Then, in a stem voice, he advised me of the prison regulations. I was to treat all camp officers and guards with courtesy, and was to bow from the hips when I met a North Vietnamese anywhere in the prison. I was to furnish full and clear answers to all questions asked by the camp authorities. And finally, I was not to attempt to communicate, either by talking, tapping on walls, or using other means, to the other "criminals" in the camp. If I did, I would be severely punished.

I nodded soberly, but inside I was rejoicing. For the first time I was being placed with other Americans. How many years had I longed for this moment?

After the officer had asked some questions about my health, he signaled the guards to get me to my feet.

"The men now prepare a room for you," he said. "I will talk to you yesterday." When the other officer corrected him, he smiled. "I should have said "tomorrow!"

Blindfolded again, I was helped out of the building and across a large open space. After we had turned a few corners, we stopped while a guard unlocked a padlock. I heard what sounded like a wooden bar scraping against metal, and then a door banged open. This blindfold was of black cloth. I couldn't see out around the edges.

I was lifted over some waist-high obstacle and dropped onto a concrete floor. Someone stepped in beside me and jerked the blindfold off.

The glare of a bare light bulb hanging from the ceiling temporarily blinded me, but in a moment I saw that I had been dropped through a window into a rubble-filled room whose only door had been bricked up. A wide board set on two sawhorses, my bed board, was in the corner of the room. The window I had been dropped through was set in a concrete wall whose cracks revealed crumbling brick. A mosquito net tied to nails in the concrete-covered brick wall was over the bed. A black bucket sat in a corner, the floor around it stained from years of use and bad aim.

The Vietnamese guard who had dropped me into the room glared down at me with such hatred that I felt a cold chill. A harsh kick propelled me on my hands and knees toward the bed board, which almost collapsed as I climbed up on it and sat down.

When I had complied with an order to remove my clothes, another guard came in with newer prison pajamas and a pair of sandals made from tires. He inspected my body for bugs and infections, then painted iodine between my toes and fingers. Taking a needle and syringe from his bag, he showed me a vial with a large B on it, broke the end off, filled the syringe, and administered the shot in my arm.

Before the guards left, they indicated how I was to use the refuse bucket and warned of the dire consequences of scratching or tapping on any of the walls. Then the guards stepped out through the window, over which they closed heavy louvered French shutters braced with a heavy wooden bar. Finally I heard the metallic click of a lock being snapped shut.

I spread the blanket out on my bed board, made a pillow from my extra clothes, and lay down in the darkness. It had been an exciting and exhausting day. I was not so sure, now, that my repatriation was near. This room didn't strike me as a temporary holding cell. And I was disappointed that I had not found a roommate with whom I could share this new place of confinement. But I was now in the same prison with other Americans, and that thought was immensely reassuring.

Though the bed board seemed harder than the bamboo slats I had slept on in the cages, there were no leg stocks, no ropes binding my wrists, and no neck loop. I was tired enough to fall asleep almost immediately.

At dawn the sound of a hammer striking steel broke the silence of the camp. The cadence of the gong started slowly, becoming more rapid as the noise level rose to a crescendo. The guard with the look of hatred, whom I dubbed "Nasty," unlocked the window and handed me my breakfast jug of hot water and a piece of hard bread.

The gong signal, Nasty indicated, meant that all prisoners were to get up, fold their blankets neatly, and do some exercises. Though I could not even stand up without using the wall for support, I welcomed the chance to try to strengthen myself.

Having been told to stay on my bed board, I had my breakfast on my knees, with my back against the wall. In the last few years my twenty-four-hour confinement in the leg stocks had not permitted me to sit with any back support, and now by comparison the concrete wall seemed as comfortable as an easy chair.

I heard a radio playing in the distance, perhaps over loudspeakers, and realized that I was listening to American popular music. Then I heard the voice of an Oriental woman reading the news in English. I could make out only a few of the words. I spent the rest of the morning listening to the loudspeaker and trying to walk around the room. When the music stopped, I could hear the sounds of people moving about the camp. I was able to peek out the louvered window to the left or right, but could see nothing more than the space between my building and what must have been the outer wall. The gong sounded again some hours later, more softly this time, and the guard rapped his knuckles on the louvered window. "Sleep, sleep," he said. It was time for a noontime nap.

25

No sooner had I lain down than I heard tapping on the wall. It was in the old "shave and a haircut" rhythm, but without the "two bits." If I had needed any more evidence that Americans were nearby, I had it now. I couldn't help smiling.

After a few moments of silence, the same signal was repeated. I realized the sender expected an answer. I eased my way off the bed and crawled along the wall to the spot where the tapping had come from. When the next "shave and a haircut" came, softly but distinctly through the wall, I came right back with a tapped "two bits." The answer brought a series of rapid tapping that I couldn't understand. I retreated to my bed board, thinking I might have been gulled by a guard into breaking the rules on my first full day in camp. I lay on my back, staring at the ceiling, my heart pounding.

The tapping had ceased and I feared the window would burst open at any moment and a guard would be coming in to punish me. There was only silence. Then the tapping started again.

"Shave and a haircut..."

Whoever he was, he was persistent. I remained on the bed board, unable to see where this was getting us.

Then came a long, slow series of taps, which seemed almost like a code. Confused, I started counting the number of taps in each unit, but that made no sense. Then I realized I should be saying the alphabet, one letter per tap, and that the last tap in a series was a letter in a word. I got the word "wall" on the last series, but that was obviously only part of the message. The strain of trying to understand the tapping and the worry of being discovered had left me bathed in sweat.

The tapping began again. This time I was ready at the beginning. "A, B, C, D..." The message was clear: "Put ear to the wall." I slipped off the bed board again and returned to the spot where the knocking was loudest. Pressing my ear to the wall, I heard a voice on the other side speak distinctly but quietly, in a tone that suggested he had been repeating his message in vain.

"If you hear me, buddy, knock two times."

I knocked twice, my heart in my throat. The slightly bored voice on the other side became so excited the words seemed to tumble out on top of one another.

"I've been trying to raise you all day! Are you a new prisoner? Do you know the tap code? I guess I'd better tell you how to answer."

My eyes were filling with tears, and I was smiling so hard my face hurt. This was the first American voice I had heard since the day I left Chieng Mai, three and a half years ago.

"Give me one tap for 'no,' two taps for 'yes,' and three taps if you don't know,' the voice told me. I gave him two taps.

"My name is John McCain. I've been a prisoner over a year. Have you been a prisoner long?"

Two taps.

"You a pilot?"

Two taps.

"Navy"

One tap.

"Air Force?"

It was like a game of twenty questions, and McCain was good at it. He soon established that I was a civilian pilot captured in Laos in 1965. He immediately thought I was CIA, but said he wouldn't ask.

"Now," he said, "I'm going to tell you how I'm talking to you. Take your tin cup and wrap your shirt around it. Leave plenty of cloth around the mouth and press firmly against the wall. Do you want to try it?"

One tap: "No."

"You do want to communicate, don't you?"

Two taps: "Yes."

"Do you have a cup?"

One tap: "No." Then he explained the tap code. "Shave and a haircut" was the signal to come to the wall, and "two bits" was the "go ahead" reply. McCain's voice came through the wall as if it belonged to an instructor in a classroom.

"Divide the alphabet into five groups of five letters each. Leave out the letter *K*. The five key letters are *A, F, L, Q,* and *V*. They are group headings. The letter *A*, the first letter in the first group, would be tapped 1-1. The letter *B*, first group and second letter, would be 1-2. The letter *R*, fourth group, second letter, would be 4-2.

" 'McCain' is tapped 3-2, 1-3, 1-3, 1-1, 2-4, 3-3. Are you getting it?"

I was getting it. The years of working mathematical problems in my head helped me to visualize the tap code in my mind. It looked like this:

	1	2	3	4	5
1	A	B	C	D	E
2	F	G	H	I	J
3	L	M	N	O	P
4	Q	R	S	T	U
5	V	W	X	Y	Z

I was able to tap out my name to John before the gong sounded, ending the nap period. I spent the rest of the day and much of the next working to become proficient in the tap code and listening intently by the wall as the voice from the next room told me about my new place of confinement.

The Americans called this prison camp the Plantation. Americans, being Americans, also named all the buildings. It was a walled, tree-covered estate whose large mansion was surrounded by warehouses, utility buildings, and workers' quarters. The square two-story "Big House" in which I had been interrogated had been the residence of the mayor of Hanoi during the days of French colonialism. The compound had since been converted to a military truck-repair facility and then, apparently only a few years before, into a POW prison. John McCain and I were confined in the south end of the "Warehouse," the largest of several confinement structures in the compound.

The Warehouse was a long, low building that looked from the outside like a barracks, but whose interior was divided into cells. McCain was in 13 West, whose door opened onto the main courtyard, and I was right behind him, in 13 East. Most of the cells were not divided. My window entrance opened onto a space between the Warehouse and the outer wall. To my right, through the louvers, I could see part of a wash area. It was an area where POWs were likely to visit, I thought. My room was in an out-of-the-way place, McCain informed me.

Most of the eighty or so American prisoners at the Plantation were housed in the Warehouse, but there were enough of them scattered around the rest of the complex that establishing communications among them had been difficult.

Small numbers of POWs were housed in buildings the POWs called the Corn Crib, the Gunshed, and the Movie House, McCain told me.

The senior officer among the prisoners was Colonel Ted Guy. Since McCain's communication bloc at the south end of the Warehouse was cut off by an empty room to the north of our two, he had been unable to get in touch with him. McCain assumed that Commander Dick Stratton was in charge.

Stratton had already issued directives to the Plantation inmates, but the communication system wasn't well enough developed to link up all the disparate parts.

The importance of establishing a communications system was critical if the chain of command was to work. The only resistance effective for most was to communicate. Contact with other prisoners was needed to reinforce the guidelines for POWs contained in the Uniform Code of Military Justice.

Tortured and beaten in isolation, some prisoners were not sure what was acceptable behavior. Those who did not have the guidance coming down through a chain of command often were the ones who wound up cooperating with the enemy.

Practically everyone, McCain said, had been forced into admissions that went beyond the name, rank, and serial number limitation set by the code.

A few POWs were voluntarily cooperating with the North Vietnamese, making anti-American broadcasts and accepting in return privileges not extended to the rest of the POWs. When peace delegations from the United States and elsewhere visited the Plantation, a few of those prisoners were routinely placed in a special building the POWs called the Showplace, a cleaner, well-ventilated, more attractive place of confinement that visitors were led to believe was permanent.

PLANTATION

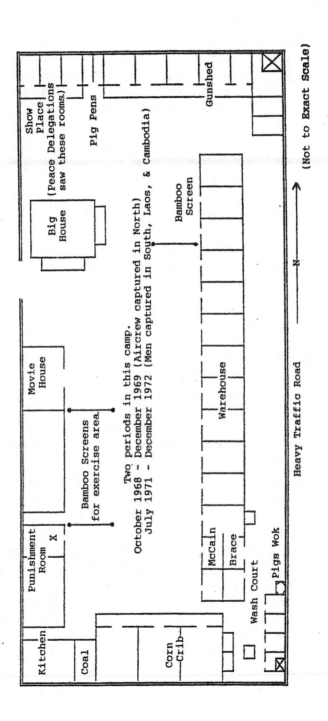

Show Place
(Peace Delegations
saw these rooms.)

Pig Pens

Gunshed

Big House

Bamboo Screen

Movie House

Bamboo Screens for exercise area.

Two periods in this camp.
October 1968 – December 1969 (Aircrew captured in North)
July 1971 – December 1972 (Men captured in South, Laos, & Cambodia)

Warehouse

Punishment Room   X

Kitchen

Coal

Corn Crib

McCain

Brace

Wash Court

Pigs Wok

N

Heavy Traffic Road

(Not to Exact Scale)

A few days after my arrival, I was issued the tin cup I needed to transmit my voice through the wall. Following the instructions given me by McCain on the first day, I immediately began communicating with the Navy pilot almost as easily as if we were speaking on the phone.

For me, who had lost touch with the world for more than three years, the long daily discussions were exhilarating. We had to be extremely careful, McCain warned. Prisoners in solitary were not supposed to speak, whistle, or make any other noises. We stood over our buckets on either side of the wall. If a guard opened a peephole to look in, we would appear to be using the bucket. I was astounded by how well I learned to interpret the shadows that came through the louvers. I could tell well before a guard got to the window.

Lieutenant Commander John McCain brought me back into the world of reality. The wall was like a confessional booth. Both of us found ourselves telling each other things we would never say to anyone else. When John started to tell me what a great hero I would be when we went home, I felt compelled to tell him about my court-martial. It was probably one of the few times I felt sorry for myself.

John briefed me on world events, including the war situation. Then he related what he knew about the other Hanoi POW prisons, their treatment of the prisoners, and the existing POW chain-of-command structure and communication system.

John chronicled the deepening involvement of the U.S. military forces in Southeast Asia since 1965, and advised me of the rise of Nguyen Cao Ky to prominence in Saigon and then the election of President Thieu in 1967.

Though he had been captured in October of 1967, McCain had been able to keep reasonably well informed of the conduct of the war through clandestine communication with more recent "shoot-downs," and by listening to the propaganda news broadcasts that were piped into his cell.

He knew, for example, that the Communists' Tet Offensive of the previous February and March had triggered a domestic outcry at home and that President Johnson had announced he would not run for a second term.

In July, General Westmoreland had been replaced by a tank man, General Abrams. An important election was shaping up for

November, when Vice-President Hubert Humphrey and Richard Nixon would vie for the presidency. John was interested in politics and explained the issues of the upcoming election to me.

He told me that hundreds of American POWs, most of them Navy and Air Force pilots, were being held in and around Hanoi. Many were at Hoa Lo, the huge French prison that seemed to be the first stop of many American shoot-downs. Smaller prisons the POWs called Alcatraz and the Zoo completed the prison system in Hanoi, according to McCain.

More Americans were held just outside the capital city, at places known as the Briar Patch, Faith, D-1, the Rockpile, and Sontay. POW intelligence had it that there was also a mountain prison many miles north of Hanoi, along the China border, called Dogpatch. McCain had never before heard of any prisoners captured in Laos or held in the Dien Bien Phu area.

Many of the prisoners in Hanoi were being held in solitary, McCain told me. Some POWs had roommates, or were housed in cellblocks where they could see each other. Though any communication between cells or compounds was strictly forbidden, a surreptitious communication system using the tap codes and other devices was helping to keep the POWs in touch with one another. The shuffling of prisoners between camps, usually when they got caught communicating, provided valuable information, not only on the camps, but also on who was a prisoner.

Solo treatment was given troublemakers, senior officers, or special cases. Certainly I qualified on all counts. I was a civilian captured in Laos by NVA troops who weren't supposed to be there under the Geneva Accords. I had repeatedly tried to escape from my cages. That I should be in solitary, hidden away in the far side of Warehouse 13 where no other prisoner could see me, did not surprise John McCain.

The Navy pilot also was a special case. He had been uncooperative with the prison authorities, and his prison experience had been especially difficult as a result.

John Sidney McCain III was the son of a four-star admiral who was, at the time of John's capture, the Commander-in-Chief of U.S. Naval Forces in Europe. His grandfather had also been an admiral.

John's carrier-based A-4 Skyhawk had been hit by a surface-to-air missile over Hanoi, and he had been upside down when he ejected. Pulled from Western Lake in the center of the city, he had suffered two broken arms and a broken left leg from flailing when he punched out at near sonic speed.

One of his angry captors had broken his left shoulder with a rifle butt and another had bayoneted him in the foot. Taken to Hoa Lo prison, he was subjected to days of intermittent interrogation and torture at the direction of the same interrogator with the wandering right eye whom I had met. The Bug had allowed McCain to lie for four days in his own body waste, his broken bones and wounded foot untreated.

When his captors learned he was the son of an admiral, they immediately took the "Crown Prince," as they called him, to the hospital. There he spent several agonizing weeks being treated by doctors who used no anesthetic to set his broken bones.

The young naval aviator had attracted enough attention to draw the presence of General Vo Nguyen Giap, North Vietnam's Minister of Defense, who stared wordlessly at the bedridden prisoner, then strode from the room. Even as John lay confined to his bed, the Bug visited him in an effort to persuade the flyer to make a tape recording that they could use for propaganda. When he refused, he was slapped and even punched as he lay in bed.

He finally had been placed into the prison system with another prisoner who was to bathe, feed, and generally nurse him until he was able to fend for himself. Once able to take care of himself he became an "uncooperative prisoner," and was "a bad influence on his cellmate." They sent him to the Plantation, where he was now in solitary confinement, like myself.

26

John had been placed in solitary at the Plantation because of his uncooperative attitude. He continued to get pressure to produce propaganda tapes or make appearances to peace delegations. Some days he would tell me, through the wall, not to worry if he wasn't in his room for a while. He was refusing, he said, to appear before another peace delegation, and he would probably be spending some time in the punishment room on the other side of the courtyard.

Now that I had someone to talk to, my spirits improved immeasurably. Since I had no radio speaker in my room, John would come up on the wall every morning after "Hanoi Hannah" had signed off. He would give me his "music, news, and lack of sports" reports. For hours every day we told each other jokes, or exchanged stories about ourselves. John told me about his grandfather, who may have been the model, John believed, for the character of Torrey Rockwell in the novel, *In Harm's Way*.

When we realized we were using up our stories too fast, we made a pact to try to tell a movie to each other on Sundays. Sunday was always a quiet day in the camp, and there were few guards on patrol. None of the prisoners got out for exercise on Sunday.

When you don't worry about where your next meal is coming from, or what clothes you're going to put on today, it's easy to concentrate on a movie you have seen in your past. Both of us were amazed at how much dialogue we could remember. We even used accents to enliven the telling. It was a feature to look forward to on

I soon learned that I had fewer privileges than any other prisoner in camp. I was not allowed to exercise outside in the courtyard, as were other prisoners. My food and water were brought to my window and left by some other prisoner or guard. Then the bar was dropped, the window opened, and I could pick it up. I set my bucket out in the morning when the guard brought my water, and picked it up after some other prisoner had dumped it and rinsed it out.

My only time outside the cell was to use a wash stall in the courtyard immediately outside my door. I was not allowed to attend the propaganda lectures and movies I occasionally heard in the larger courtyard on McCain's side of the Warehouse, and I was never given the reading material that the other POWs were permitted to see. Though some prisoners, including McCain, were allowed to send and receive mail on a limited basis, I was not. I was approaching my fourth year of captivity, and my family still had no idea whether I was alive or dead. Early on, I had decided not to worry about those things over which I had no control. There were enough immediate problems to concern a prisoner.

On Christmas Eve of 1968, the Vietnamese prepared a room where the prisoners were taken in small groups. Some prisoners had decorated a tree, and some were allowed to sing Christmas carols. A special meal that went beyond the usual soup with pork or vegetable bits was given to most. One of the few times I felt sorry for myself was when I learned from McCain that I was the only prisoner in the entire camp who was not allowed to visit the Christmas Room and didn't get the special meal. I was convinced that my captors were making every effort to conceal my presence from the other prisoners.

I knew that McCain and I would be punished, should our daily communications be discovered, but my lack of other contacts gave this one crucial importance for me.

The camp had learned via a propaganda broadcast that President Johnson had declared a complete bombing halt of North Vietnamese targets as of November 1, and the Plantation was awash with rumors that the POWs would all be going home soon. I was now worried that I might not be going with them. Why else would they be so intent on disguising my presence here?

My first opportunity to get my name to the outside world came on a chilly morning in February of 1969. I heard an American talking to a guard near my window, and went over to peer out through the louvers. I saw a tall, gangly, bespectacled prisoner helping a guard prepare a pot of pigs' food in the area by the wall outside my window. When the guard walked out of sight, I spoke softly, calling the young man over. McCain had told me about this young sailor.

"You're Hegdorn, aren't you?"

'Hegdahl-Doug Hegdahl. And you must be Brace, the civilian."

Though I could see Doug by peering sideways through the louvers, he could not see me. In true prisoner fashion, developed by the need to survive in this environment, Doug faced away from me and appeared to be busy with the pigs' food as we talked softly. He could watch to see if the guard returned through the wash court, while I could maintain a lookout the other direction along the wall. A cough was the danger signal recognized by all prisoners.

For me, there could not have been a luckier contact with an American prisoner. Douglas Hegdahl was a twenty-year-old from South Dakota, who, as a seaman apprentice aboard the cruiser Canberra; had fallen overboard on the night of April 6, 1966. He had been fished from the water by Vietnamese fishermen and taken to Hanoi, where he was to become an important figure in the story of American POWs in that war.

Because of his youth and the circumstances of his capture, the North Vietnamese had offered him an early release based on "humanitarian considerations." Hegdahl had turned them down in compliance with the instructions of the senior POW officer. But now, he told me, he had been given another opportunity to go home, this time in August, and Colonel Ted Guy, the senior officer at the Plantation, was urging him to take release so that he could bring out the list of prisoners being held. Hegdahl had been held in three different prisons and had memorized a list of some 150 American POWs, including all of the eighty or so inmates at the Plantation.

"I repeat the names every night before I go to sleep, to make sure I don't forget them," he told me.

We were interrupted by the return of the guard, but when he wandered off again, we resumed our conversation.

I explained that I had been held in the jungle for three years and had not been allowed to write to my family. Though I didn't need to, I asked that Hegdahl include my name on the POW list and get in touch with my family when he returned to the States. He had planned on doing that anyway, and this encounter simply gave him more material to relate.

I recounted, in as much detail as I had time for, what had happened to me since my capture. I gave him the name of my Thai friend, Harnavee, and told him about the Laotian POW who had been left in Moung Sai. The State Department could pass that information on to the appropriate governments. Hegdahl promised to memorize the names and make sure they got to the right people.

The young man also provided useful information for me and for the other members of John McCain's communications bloc. John had assumed that Dick Stratton was the de facto senior ranking officer in the camp, but Hegdahl's revelation that he was taking orders from Colonel Guy suggested that the colonel had been communicating all along, but hadn't been able to get in touch with the south end of the Warehouse. The guard returned, and Doug went with him somewhere.

As soon as Doug had left, John rapped me up on the wall, and wanted to know if I had a roommate now. I told him no, and explained about talking to Hegdahl. John was excited about the details I had learned about the camp.

As the months of 1969 dragged by and the peace talks in Paris seemed bogged down, I was becoming one of the most active communicators in the camp. McCain would report to me occasionally about the POWs in camp who were cooperating with their captors and getting special privileges. We were convinced that such behavior could be held to a minimum through better communication. Often it was the prisoners who were isolated who would start cooperating.

John and I devoted some of each day to communicating, in an effort to help extend Colonel Guy's chain of command to the various buildings in the prison complex.

Though some of the POWs considered it reckless to do so, I was known to speak from my cell window to passing prisoners in an attempt to exchange or pass on information. The dishwashers from the Gunshed, at the north end of camp, would walk by my window followed by a guard. Sometimes the lead man would stride right out, leaving the guard and one or two prisoners trailing by twenty to thirty yards. We could get a few snatches of conversation in that way.

Each of the prime communicators in the POW system had his own code name. McCain was "Crip," reflecting his still crippled condition, Hegdahl was "Mug," Dick Stratton was "Whiz," and I was "Stol," the acronym for the short-takeoff-and-landing aircraft I had piloted.

In August, a couple of American POWs in the Corn Crib were caught passing magazines through a hole leading from one cell to another, and the "communications bust" resulted in my being moved next door to room 14, a cell previously occupied by the guards as temporary sleeping quarters. Ironically, the move increased the possibilities for communicating in the south Warehouse "comm" bloc. By placing my tin cup in the corner that adjoined three other cells, I could talk to the prisoners in all of them simultaneously. McCain was catty-corner from me, in 13 East. Guy Greuter and Bob Craner, a couple of Air Force shootdowns, were on one side in 14 East. In my old room were Navy pilot Tom Hall and Air Force pilot Mel Pollock. John and I were still solo.

In the ensuing weeks, we six POWs not only exchanged information but played games from room to room. Chess and checkers took up hours of our time. Each room had its own playing board, and the players were proficient enough with the tap code that they could tap their moves to their opponents, rather than calling them through the cups. At one point the communicating became so furious that McCain, the senior officer in this comm bloc, warned everyone to ease up. He feared that too many games might result in a bust that would sever their links with each other and other parts of the camp.

Later in the month we got the word that Hegdahl had been given an early release, with the blessing of Colonel Guy. I knew that it would not be long before my family found out that I was alive.

The rumors of a negotiated peace had been rampant in the camp for the entire summer, and each morning McCain would relay the latest news dispatches that Radio Hanoi deigned to broadcast. By this time the Vietcong had joined the negotiations, and President Nixon had announced the first of several major U.S. troop withdrawals in the name of Vietnamization.

The mounting American combat casualties were broadcast frequently. By March of 1969, the radio said, the number of American combat dead exceeded those of the Korean War. On September 4, a camp officer came around and advised the other POWs that Ho Chi Minh had died. He didn't come to my cell. The next few days, he told them, would be days of national mourning, and he warned the POWs that they should do nothing to antagonize the guards, who were wearing black armbands and were visibly upset.

If my special status meant the Vietnamese were trying to keep me a secret, it also seemed to keep me from the beatings and torture that most prisoners experienced sometime soon after their introduction to Hanoi prison life. Perhaps it was because I was a civilian, but I sensed, too, that the allegations linking me to the CIA may have worked to my advantage in Hanoi, where my interrogators spoke of the agency with a mixture of awe, hatred, and fear. Whatever the reason, I was never tortured during my visits to the "Big House" for attitude checks or other business. During 1969 I was interrogated three times by the smooth-talking officer we knew as "Frenchy."

During a July visit to the mansion, I was required to fill out a mimeographed form with questions about my personal background. McCain, and the other prisoners I communicated with, had prepared me for the questions, and I told the truth except with respect to my combat duty in the Korean War. That didn't seem to be a prudent admission to make to Asian Communists.

I was able to use Hegdahl's knowledge of my existence to my own advantage during an interrogation session in November 1969. An older man I had not seen before was trying to get me to make a tape recording acknowledging the criminal nature of American participation in the war. I refused. The interrogator responded with a threat.

"We know you have not written home," he said. "We could shoot you and dump you in a hole. No one would know where you were."

"My family knows where I am," I replied.

"How do you know?"

"I spoke to Doug Hegdahl before he left."

The startled officer leaped to his feet and summoned Frenchy, who demanded to know the circumstances under which I had communicated with the released Navy man. When I explained about the conversation through my window the previous January, and that Hegdahl had memorized the names of other POWs who were not declared prisoners, the younger interrogator seemed to lose the composure for which he was well known.

"You are in serious trouble," he told me.

But the punishment never came. Returned to my cell for the night, I was taken back to the Big House the next day and treated better than I had ever been treated before. Now that my presence would be known in the States, my captors would have to take a different attitude. A new interrogator gave me a beer and some candy, and demanded an explanation of why I had disobeyed camp orders by communicating with another prisoner.

"I thought it was important to let my family know that I was still alive," I responded.

Then, to my astonishment, I found myself being offered an early release along the lines of that granted Hegdahl. Since I had been captured in Laos, I would be required first to compose an apology for my crimes to the Prince of Laos, the Communist brother of Souvanna Phouma. Since Hegdahl's release, Colonel Guy had issued instructions that no more early releases should be accepted; all POWs should go home together. Though I was not bound by such orders, I felt it would be wrong for me to leave before the others, and I turned down the offer.

"I'll wait to go home with the other prisoners," I said.

Would I be willing to write the Prince of Laos, telling him I would like to be reunited with my family? I could see no harm in that gesture, and, accepting a pencil and paper, I sat down at a table and wrote:

Dear Sir:

I have been a prisoner for four years and six months and I have never been allowed to correspond with my family since capture. I would like very much to return to my family.

E. C. Brace

It was clear the interrogator was not enthusiastic about the contents of the letter, but he took it and said he would "see what could be done."

Prison conditions, especially medical attention, improved as a result of the Hegdahl release. My revelation to the interrogators, that Hegdahl had left with lists of POWs and the intention of revealing prison life as it really was, was later con-firmed by news media accounts of how Hegdahl portrayed the realities of prison life. The young Navy man had duped his captors into believing he was an ineffective farm boy, but the information he brought out forced the Hanoi prison system to improve its conditions.

Daily medical checkups at the Plantation became standard procedure. Each day there was a "How are you?" spoken through the cell door. The prisoners called the medic "Dr. Spock" in recognition of that famous doctor's antiwar activities. Treatment often came in the form of some token medication, but the prisoners were being taken care of better than ever before.

As 1969 drew to a close, McCain and I were communicating prolifically with others in the camp. I was acting as a conduit for messages between the Gunshed and the Warehouse. I would take notes or oral messages from the Gunshed crew and relay them to McCain, who would pass them on to the communications block at the other end of the Warehouse, which was commanded by Collie Haynes. There had been signs that the guards were catching on to the communications activity, but I hadn't taken them too seriously.

On the night of December 9 my door was jerked open, and the guard told me to get ready to move. Frenchy, who was supervising the transfer, waited outside.

"You are in bad trouble for communicating," he told me. "You are being taken to a harsher place."

Blindfolded, I was placed in the back of a truck with some soldiers and other prisoners. The vehicle had rolled out of the prison grounds and was heading through the Hanoi streets when I felt someone tapping a message on my thigh.

"Hi," said the message. "I John McCain. Who U?"

With tears forming in my eyes behind the blindfold, I worked my hand around to grasp my neighbor's hand, and squeezed out an answer. "EB here."

27

From the back of the truck I heard the sound of the large iron-strapped door of Hoa Lo prison opening. The noise reverberating off the sides of the short stone tunnel entrance told me I was returning to the Hanoi Hilton. One at a time, the blindfolded POWs were taken from the truck, marched through Heartbreak Courtyard, and into another part of the prison. My hopes for a cellmate were dashed when I was locked alone in a room with two permanent bed boards installed.

Awakened at sunrise by the familiar gong, I found myself in a room similar to the one I had left at the Plantation: It had a concrete-and-brick wall, crumbling with age, and a concrete floor. Barred windows, the lower half covered with bamboo screens, were on each side of the door. The most significant difference was that I now had a speaker in my room.

After I finished my breakfast fare of water and bread chunks, I was treated to propagandized news broadcasts that sounded as if they were being read by Americans. I knew the "news" wasn't reliable, and took with a grain of salt the reports that antiwar sentiment in the United States was turning every city into a battleground. But I was happy to hear outside news from any-where, and enjoyed the music that was played afterward.

I found out almost immediately that I was being treated more like the other prisoners here than I had been at the Plantation. I soon made contact with other POWs as I performed routine courtyard tasks that previously had been denied me. I was allowed out for a few minutes each day to dump and clean my refuse bucket in the latrine area. At the Plantation, my bucket had always been dumped by a guard or another prisoner. At this new place of confinement, I also was allowed to use the wash stalls in the courtyard. Occasionally, if the guard outside was inattentive, I was able to speak or tap to the POW washing in the stall next to me.

I had not been there long before I knew the name of the camp, its general layout, and something about its population. I was in a compound the POWs called Little Vegas, situated in one corner of Hoa Lo. It was just beyond the prison's receiving area, which we knew as Heartbreak. From the Vegas courtyard I could see the eighteen-foot gray stone wall, its four-foot-thick concrete top embedded with broken glass and covered with barbed wire.

Opening onto the courtyard were the cellblocks, the largest of which were the Thunderbird, the Desert Inn, and the Stardust. It always amused me the way we Americans named things, but here, as in all the camps, it served the purpose of locating the prisoners for each other and for themselves. Smaller buildings housed the Mint, the Riviera, and the Golden Nugget. I had been assigned Golden Nugget number 3, and soon learned that John McCain and an Air Force pilot named John Finlay were two cells down, in Golden Nugget number 1.

I found, too, that the POWs in Vegas constituted a special group. The highest-ranking officers, some of whom were among the earliest shootdowns of the war, were confined here, as well as some of the junior officers who had proved to be hard-core resisters, men who hit guards or had tried to escape. Some had previously been confined in a smaller Hanoi prison called Alcatraz, where they had spent twenty-four hours a day in stocks. On being transferred to Vegas they had quickly developed a reputation for being the fastest and most proficient tap-code communicators in the camp.

Since President Johnson's bombing halt of targets above the Twentieth Parallel in March of 1968, the number of new POWs had been reduced to a trickle. There was scarcely a man in the camp who had not been a prisoner for less than two years. They knew how to communicate in an environment where speaking wasn't permitted between prisoners. Everyone knew the tap code, and there were others who were experts in hand-signaling as well as scratching and coughing codes. Most of the prisoners were kept two men to a room, in cellblocks patrolled by guards.

Tap-code communication was frequent between adjoining cells, and an effective note-exchange system had been established between the various units, using the wash stalls and the latrine area as drop sites. The surreptitious communication permitted a military command structure to operate. The senior ranking officer at the time was Lieutenant Colonel Robinson Risner, a Korean War jet ace whose exploits as an Air Force pilot in

Vietnam had made him the subject of a Time magazine cover story in 1965, only a few months before he had been shot down in August of that year.

I had heard from John McCain about the Christmas Rooms that POWs had been allowed to visit at the Plantation, but I had never been allowed to visit them. As Christmas of 1969 approached, I learned from the camp officer during one of my "attitude checks" that I would be allowed to visit the Christmas Room and that I would soon be getting a cellmate. I was excited by both prospects.

On Christmas Eve I was escorted from my cell to a large room in another part of the prison, where a tree had been set up and decorated. The other POWs had either already been there or were yet to come. There was only one other POW in the room. He was a tall, slender, bespectacled young man with red hair, wearing a pair of prison grays that looked as if they had just been issued.

Lieutenant Junior Grade Henry J. Bedinger looked at the prisoner who was to be his cellmate and gasped. My God, thought the twenty-three-year-old Navy officer, he looks like the Count of Monte Cristo. Though he later learned that I was only thirty-eight, Bedinger thought I was an old man. My gray-streaked hair and grizzled stubble beard, with a gaunt face whose eyes seemed lost in their deep black sockets, gave him this impression. My legs were so infirm that I virtually staggered into the room. When I smiled in greeting to the young aviator, Bedinger noticed several teeth missing in front.

"I'm Jim Bedinger."

"Hi, Jim. I'm Ernie Brace."

We were allowed to talk for a few moments, and then I was handed a package that bad been sent me from my mother. Obviously, Doug Hegdahl had gotten in touch with her upon his return to the United States. There was no letter, but perhaps that had been confiscated. The package, which had been opened, contained a pair of slipper socks and some candy. The Vietnamese had taken whatever else had been sent. The return address read simply Mrs. Ruth Brace, which indicated to me that my father had died.

For me, it was a Christmas Eve to remember. After four and a half years of solitary confinement, in which I was never allowed to communicate with my family, I had in the same evening gained a cellmate and a package from home.

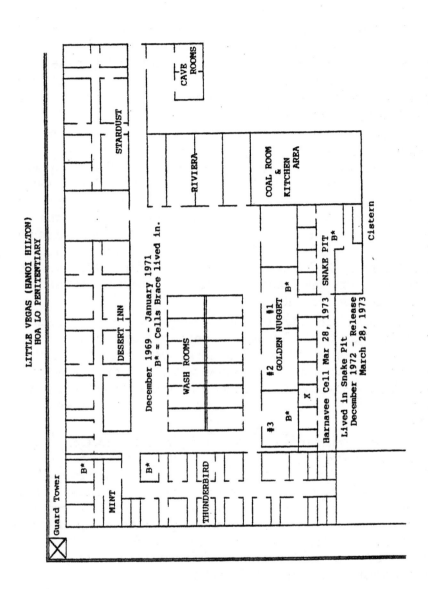

LITTLE VEGAS (HANOI HILTON)
HOA LO PENITENTIARY

December 1969 - January 1971
B* = Cells Brace lived in.

Lived in Snake Pit
December 1972 - Release
March 28, 1973

Harnavee Cell Mar 28, 1973

Jim joined me in Golden Nugget number 3. For the rest of 1969 we spent our days greedily exchanging information. Jim, a radar intercept officer in the back seat of a carrier-based F-4 Phantom, had gone down over Laos on November 22. He had up-to-date information about the war and the world that no one else in the camp possessed.

I spent hours briefing Jim on the situation in camp, the behavior expected of POWs, the military command setup, and the communications systems. Jim learned quickly that the appearance of his cellmate was deceiving. Even though I had always been in solitary, and had arrived in the Hilton only a few weeks before, I knew a great deal about the layout of the camp, its inmates, its routine, and how prisoners were expected to behave. Despite my civilian status, I still thought of myself as a Marine, and I already had become a part of the clandestine communication system that transmitted POW behavior policy from the SRO to the other inmates.

Communications in the camp were crucial, not only because they permitted the SRO to pass on policy, but because they helped bolster the morale and the will of the POWs to resist their captors' attempts to use them for purposes of propaganda. No two wars had the some type of POW conditions. For a variety of reasons, this war was very different from that of any previous American war.

I myself had not been mistreated physically since arriving in Hanoi, but I knew that virtually all of the prisoners captured in North or South Vietnam had been tortured or beaten during efforts by camp officers to get them to make propaganda tapes or statements to peace delegations. Prisoners had been tortured into making tapes in which they encouraged other Americans to refuse to fight. Some made "confessions" that they were war criminals, and repeated memorized answers before delegations of American war protesters visiting North Vietnam.

I outlined briefly for Jim the complicated questions facing POWs about the level and manner of their resistance. The Code of Conduct for Prisoners of War stated simply that POWs were to give only name, rank, and serial number. From the information available to the enemy through the press, and given their skill in the arts of torture and interrogation, few Americans were able to comply with the letter of the code.

Virtually every POW, sometimes after days of torture, had made some kind of statement. Most believed that the information they provided was nothing more than the enemy could have read in *Stars and Stripes*, the American servicemen's newspaper that was flown in daily to Hanoi from Vientiane and Hong Kong. They considered that the statements they made under duress would not be of much propaganda value to North Vietnam, because they would not be believed.

The tough question, I told Jim, was how much torture one should endure before admitting something, and what kinds of things it was permissible to admit. There were limits to what was considered acceptable behavior, and some of the prisoners had gone beyond those limits. Some, for example, were broadcasting propagandized news reports over the speakers, and others were voluntarily making propaganda tapes and visiting with peace delegations. In return, they were receiving privileges from their captors that the other prisoners were denied.

Jim was relieved to hear that the treatment of prisoners had seemed to improve since the death of Ho Chi Minh and the ascendancy of Premier Tram Pham Dong. Premier Dong had been to the Paris peace meetings and perhaps had been confronted with the revelations about prisoner abuse brought home by Hegdahl.

Having sketched for Jim the general situation in Hanoi POW camps, I explained that Robbie Risner's SRO policy for prisoner behavior at Little Vegas was to avoid aiding the North Vietnamese propaganda effort, but to protect yourself from serious injury.

"Say no, but with a smile," I advised Jim. "If you're forced to write or tape something, screw it up, get the names wrong, or louse up a detail, so that people hearing it will know it's not real." There already had been tapes read by prisoners who referred to "Senator Halfbright" and "Senator May Govern" that had gone out over the camp speakers.

Finally, I warned that some POWs had become convinced by their captors that the war was wrong. The advice of the SRO, I said, was simple: "If you believed in what you were doing when you were captured, don't allow your mind to be changed by what you might see or hear in prison. You won't get the whole story here."

I taught the young lieutenant the tap code, and soon Bedinger was proficient enough to tap out messages to John McCain and John Finlay in Golden Nugget number 1. I could see that my new cellmate was both bright and brash. Watching the bespectacled

red-head hammering away enthusiastically on the wall, I thought
to myself that this young man, who had been a college student
when I was captured four years before, was going to make an
excellent communicator.

As the only recent shootdown in the camp, Bedinger had
news about the outside world that the other prisoners would
welcome. I suggested we write a newspaper that could be covertly
circulated. Soon the *Vegas Gambler* was born. As Jim kept watch
for the guard, I penciled news onto large pieces of toilet paper,
using slang designed to mask the nature of the information to a
foreigner. Without the slang, I reasoned, a confiscated note could
be traced directly back to Bedinger, the only man in the camp
who could possibly have been its source. Thus the account of the
closing of the Suez Canal as a result of the Israeli-Egyptian Six
Day War began, "Big ditch closed, bears pissed 'cause they have
to paddle all the way around the horn." The stunning revelation
that astronauts had walked on the moon began, "U.S. made jump
like cow, July 69, two sat down." Passed from compound to
compound, through the common washroom facilities, the *Vegas
Gambler* constituted the only non-sanctioned news in the camp.
Often the paper was used to amplify or correct information
received by the POWs over the loudspeakers.

Little Vegas was filled with so many high-ranking officers
that I had dubbed it "the old folks' home" when I arrived in
December of 1969. My new cellmate was by far the youngest
prisoner in the camp. Jim soon learned that his tender age
worked to his advantage. Indiscretions and minor rule violations
that would mean punishment for the other POWs tended to be
overlooked if the perpetrator was "Bep," the guards' name for the
prisoner they thought was too new and too young to know any
better. Jim took full advantage of the situation, and soon he was
communicating so brashly that I wondered how long the guards
would tolerate it. At times he struck up conversations with other
prisoners within earshot of the guards, or yelled from his room at
POWs in the courtyard.

Jim's audacity and my experience made us into what an
intelligence document later would describe as "possibly the most
prolific communications duo to inhabit the Hanoi prison system."
When we weren't working on daily editions of the *Vegas Gambler*,
we spent our days tapping to other prisoners, flashing hand signals
from our cell windows, and writing notes with our aluminum

spoons on the bottoms of our plates. The plate notes were for the POWs across the courtyard, who were assigned to wash the dishes.

The position of the Golden Nugget, directly in front of the washing stalls, made our room the hub of a communications wheel, and we found ourselves relaying, as well as initiating, many messages from one unit to another.

Jim and I were relaying messages from the SRO, ordering that prisoners should no longer make recordings of "news" for broadcast over the prison radio. I had heard that my old friend Ed Miller, with whom I had gone through flight school, was in the Stardust, and that he had been making some of the broadcasts. Some characterized him as a turncoat.

One day when I was in the courtyard for a brief exercise period, I noticed that the guard had left the area, and struck up a conversation with someone I could hear exercising on the other side of a large bamboo screen used to separate the POWs from one another.

"Who you?" I asked, in the communications jargon.

It was Bob Schweitzer, one of Miller's roommates.

"Miller with you?" I asked, since I knew he was Miller's cellmate.

"Yes."

"Tell him Ernie Brace is here."

Schweitzer walked across the courtyard, talked to someone I couldn't see, then came back to the screen.

"Miller says he heard you were dead."

"Where did he hear that?"

"Marine Corps bar talk. He heard you were killed in Southeast Asia."

"Ask him if he's heard anything about my wife."

In a few moments, Schweitzer was back. "He's heard nothing."

"Tell Ed if he sees any more peace delegations to tell them that I'm not allowed to write or receive mail, and that I'm sure I'm not on any POW list."

Schweitzer agreed to pass on the request, but nothing came of it.

In the months to come, I gritted my teeth when I heard Miller's voice say over the prison radio that the prisoners were being treated well, and that they were allowed to send and receive mail at least once a month.

Like me, Bedinger was not allowed to receive or send mail. We both understood that our being captured in Laos was the reason. I had said as much during my "attitude checks" with the camp officers, the men the Americans called "Cat" and "Butch," and had requested repeatedly to be allowed to write home. The answer was always no.

It wasn't long before other POWs in the camp learned that Jim and I weren't allowed to send letters and that except for my lone package we had received nothing in the mail. Soon the other POWs were sharing their packages with us. A note in the drain of a washroom would advise us to check the spot "tomorrow." The next day there would be a new pair of sweat socks stuffed into the drain, gifts from prisoners who were receiving packages from home. I learned later that Colonel John Flynn was one of the sources of these gifts.

After Commander Mel Moore was moved into the cell adjoining ours, he sneaked various items to us, including a toothpaste tube full of vitamins that he had received in a package. Later, when Moore wanted to show his two neighbors the photos he had received of his two teenage daughters, the three of us came very close to being caught in the act of communicating. I had climbed on top of Jim's shoulders near the front of our cell, where I could reach over the concrete-and-brick wall through the thatch roof. Mel was to put the pictures in my hand, using a long stick. In the middle of the transfer, Jim saw a guard coming across the courtyard. Hanging by one arm, with Jim staggering around beneath me, I watched the pith helmet pass by the window and move out of sight. "He's gone," Jim said, and the transfer of the photos was completed.

Jim and I had learned through our communicating that we were not the only two POWs in the camp who were unfortunate enough to have been captured in Laos. A pair of Air Force pilots, Major Walt Stischer and Captain Steve Long, were being held in the Thunderbird, in one of the two-man rooms there. I had actually seen Long from my window as the blond-haired pilot used the wash stalls one morning.

A few weeks later, Jim and I were transferred from the Golden Nugget to another small cellblock, the Mint, situated next to the latrines in the far corner of the compound. We were there a short time, then they moved us again. This time we went into the Thunderbird, one of the major cellblocks that stretched along the base of the wall. There seemed to be no reason for these moves, but we were happy because it gave us new men to commu-nicate with. When we couldn't tap or flash signals, we watched the small, suction-footed lizards called "chinchucks" stalk flies on the ceiling of our tiny cell.

We had been in the Thunderbird only a few weeks before we were in trouble. Trying to communicate with another prisoner in an adjoining bath stall by talking through the floor drain, I was caught on the floor by a guard who opened the stall door unex-pectedly. Jim had been keeping watch, and was supposed to cough a warning should the guard appear, but something had gone wrong, and we were roughly returned to our rooms. The next day we were interrogated by the camp officer, who accused us of communi-cating and of failing to cooperate. Then we were taken to the punishment room called the Cave, so named because of its window-less, unlighted interior and its rough concrete walls. We spent several days there and then were taken back to our original building and put into Golden Nugget number 1, which in every respect was better than the cells we had occupied in the Mint and the Thunderbird.

The location of the Golden Nugget put two prolific communi-cators in the camp right back into a room where they could be most effective. We were soon communicating as avidly as before, and there were now even more ways to send messages.

In the summer of 1970, POWs were occasionally allowed to use a Ping-Pong table in a room between the Stardust and the Thunderbird, and a Vietnamese billiard table in the east end of the Riviera. Both spots became popular places for note drops. Even more important, the increasing concern of the camp officers about communications between wash stalls prompted the guards to cut the stall doors in half, leaving the tops open. This drastic action actually facilitated communication. The guard on duty could not see all the openings at once, and the open stalls permitted Jim and me, and anyone else in the Golden Nugget, to flash hand code to prisoners who trooped in each day from other parts of the camp to use the facilities.

The summer sun turned the cellblocks into ovens, and most of the prisoners were suffering from heat rash. The light-skinned Bedinger seemed particularly bothered, and soon developed a severe case. His skin became a bright pink that would blanch where one pressed on it. I kept my long pants and long-sleeved shirt on, despite the heat, and repeatedly advised my younger cellmate to do the same, rather than stripping down to his under-shorts.

"Look at the Arabs and the Foreign Legion in the deserts," I said. "You don't see them stripping down, no matter how hot it gets." I knew the long sleeves and trousers worked for me, but they may not have worked for everyone.

Soon the painful rash covered Jim's body. In some places the red pinpricks had turned into large running sores. He spent the days in agony, and the nights sleeping fitfully. One night I awoke to hear my cellmate leap screaming from his bed board. Before I could reach him, Jim began hitting his head against the concrete wall. By the time the guard rushed to the door, I was restraining my young friend.

"He's trying to kill himself," I yelled. "It's the heat rash!" The guard brought in a bucket of water, which we used to sponge Jim off and dab the blood from his forehead. Soon he had calmed down. Jim told me he had had a nightmare about ants crawling all over his body and biting him. He had leaped out of bed to try and knock them off. For the rest of the summer, the guards allowed Jim to have a bucket of water in the room at night. The sponge baths made the nights tolerable until the fall.

Later we found out the guys in the Desert Inn had been given an armpit thermometer to check a fever, and had found that the temperature in the cells stayed at almost 120 degrees during the day, dropping only to 110 at night, that summer of 1970. Most of the windows were partially covered with bamboo screens.

Though I had never seen the high-ranking officers who were housed in the Stardust and Desert Inn, I had heard much about them by the summer of 1970. Virtually all of them had come over from Alcatraz. They were able and prolific communicators and had survived the days when the torture and beatings were at their worst. Robbie Risner and Jeremiah Denton were there, as was Commander James Stockdale. Shot down on September 12, 1965, only four months after I had been captured, Stockdale had been a prize catch for the North Vietnamese. One of the highest-ranking officers to be captured, he was, at the time of his capture, the commander of Carrier Air Group 16, off the carrier Oriskany. He had survived years of torture and abuse.

As recently as the previous September, on the day Ho Chi Minh died, Stockdale had been caught communicating. He was tortured to near death in an effort to get him to admit his "guilt." Now, in

Little Vegas, he was one of the officers with whom Jim and I had been communicating, and occasionally had been the senior ranking officer.

One fall morning when Jim and I were using a wash stall, I heard noises in the one next door. Noticing that the guard was not in the area, I stood in the tub and caught a quick glimpse of an old man with gray hair and a face both haggard and strong. It was Stockdale.

I told Stockdale who I was and that my cellmate was Lieutenant Junior Grade Jim Bedinger. He said that he heard I was a Marine, but that I was captured as a civilian. I confirmed this and Stockdale said, "Consider yourself on active duty."

I replied, "Aye, aye sir."

Bedinger passed on some news about San Diego, and the current aircraft carriers in the Tonkin Gulf. Someone coughed loudly as a warning signal and we broke off communications.

It was about this time, too, that I ran into another "prize" prisoner. I saw John McCain face-to-face for a brief moment outside the interrogation room where I had been taken for my periodic attitude check.

I recognized the white hair and the slender, limping form that I had glimpsed once at the Plantation, and greeted my friend as we passed.

The camp officer was angry. "Do you know that man?" he demanded.

"Sure. That's John McCain. I knew him at the other camp."

"Do not speak to him," he said. "He is very important prisoner."

"I know. His father is an admiral." As one of the Laos prisoners, I felt I had to emphasize to my captors that there were POWs here who knew me, and would report my presence when they returned.

By the end of the summer, Jim and I were transferred again to the Thunderbird, and were advised of a "new lenient policy" that would allow the prisoners in that cellblock to visit each other during the day. Soon we were visiting daily with Steve Long and Walt Stischer, the other two "Laotians" in the camp, and found that they, too, were not allowed to send or receive mail.

The next few weeks provided the first group social activity I had enjoyed in five years. The four of us exchanged life stories and discussed for hours our special situation as POWs captured in

Laos. Our common concern that our families would think us dead and that we might not be released at the end of the war bound us together into a close-knit group. I gave the quartet the code name "LuLu" for communications purposes. It was an acronym for Legendary Union of Laotian Unfortunates. The LuLus used every chance we got to advise other POWs of our situation and get their assurance that the group wouldn't be forgotten if it should suddenly disappear before repatriation.

Jim's and my communicating had been curtailed dramatically when we were removed from the Golden Nugget. The location in front of the wash stalls brought its occupants into contact with prisoners from throughout the compound. The Mint and Thunderbird were not centrally located, however, and Jim and I found ourselves much less involved in the daily transmission and reception of messages than we had been previously. We continued to keep in practice by communicating in the courtyard, from one wash stall to another, or by conversing surreptitiously with other POWs separated from us by screens. Fall came, and the days passed quickly in the Thunderbird, where the LuLus played gin, bridge, and invented games with cards provided them by the guards. By this time I had tucked securely away in my memory the names of all the POWs in Little Vegas, knowing that the information would be useful after repatriation, should some prisoners not be returned. Though I did not have a complete list, I guessed there were some eighty Americans in Little Vegas, which seemed to be the only camp for Americans in Hoa Lo prison besides the receiving cells in Heartbreak.

That situation changed about Thanksgiving 1970, when the occupants of Little Vegas were startled and thrilled to hear a large group of Americans singing "God Bless America" in another part of the prison. Vegas was alive with excitement, but all anyone could do was to speculate about the identities of our new fellow inmates. One thing was for sure, there were a lot of them.

A few days later, when I was exercising in the courtyard, I saw a couple of new POWs being put into the Riviera. When the guards left the area for a few moments, I slipped over to make contact by standing in front of their door and pretending to speak to Jim.

"Brace here. Who you?"

"Bud Day here."

George "Bud" Day and his cellmate, Ben Pollard, were Air Force shootdowns who had just arrived from the large group we had heard singing in another part of the prison.

"Where are we?" Day asked.

"This is Vegas," I replied. "Robbie Risner is the SRO. John Flynn is senior to Robbie, but he's out of comm. Do you know about the other men who just came into this prison?"

Day did. He and Pollard had been housed with them until they got in trouble and were sent to Vegas. There were at least three hundred men in the new camp, which the Americans had dubbed Camp Unity. They had come from several prisons outside Hanoi, and were being held thirty or forty to a room in a large horseshoe-shaped compound in another corner of the prison. It was they who had sung "God Bless America" a few days before.

I slipped back to my own area of the courtyard, convinced that something important was happening in the war. The arrival of so many new POWs; their being housed together in large numbers rather than in individual cells; the newly relaxed Vegas policy permitting POWs to visit between cells during the day: all seemed signs that the peace talks were making progress.

A few days later Jim Bedinger tested the limits of the camp's newly established "lenient policy," and the LuLus found themselves in trouble. Jim and I were carrying bamboo poles on a work assignment in the courtyard when the young officer, as if by accident, knocked down a bamboo screen separating us from some prisoners we didn't know. When the screen crashed down, there was a moment of stunned silence as the two groups of prisoners stared at each other across the open space. Then Jim stepped over with an outstretched hand.

"Hi," He said. "I'm Jim Bedinger."

The guard exploded in anger. Screaming in a high-pitched voice, he demanded that the screen be replaced immediately. When Bedinger stood it up, he was on the wrong side, with the POWs that he wasn't supposed to see. That enraged the guard further. He returned the redheaded prisoner roughly to his cell. To make matters worse for the LuLus, Steve Long was caught communicating on the other side of the courtyard about the same time, and was also returned to his cell. When I was able to join Jim in the Thunderbird, he had already been interrogated. The young officer told me he had been told to prepare himself for transfer to "a dark place" where he would be kept alone, "away from other

Americans." Jim had never been in solitary before, except for a few days after his capture. As I picked out the best clothes for him from our common supply, I counseled my friend about what to expect.

"Don't take anything from them, don't write anything," I advised. "And if they force you to do something, screw it up." But I knew Jim well enough by this time to know that such advice wasn't really necessary.

The guards never came that day to pick up Jim, nor did they come the next day. Apparently the young man's behavior had strained, but not destroyed, the camp officers' new "lenient policy." I knew that other officers, especially the higher-ranking ones, had been subjected to the "straps and bars" treatment for similar behavior.

Though Jim had been spared solitary, the LuLus were punished as a group. For the next three weeks the four prisoners were not allowed out of their cells, except to dump their refuse bucket and visit the wash stalls.

Then, on Christmas Eve, the day Jim and I observed our first anniversary as cellmates, the LuLus were taken from their cells and allowed to visit the Christmas Room after the other POWs had come and gone. It was the first time we had been allowed out of our cells since December 3. We enjoyed the decorated tree and the cookies and candy. I had hoped for a package from Patricia or from my mother, but, like the rest of the LuLus, I was disappointed. I wondered how the one lone package from my mother had managed to slip through the year before.

When we were returned to our cells in the Thunderbird, we found that the rest of the POWs were being moved. Soon we were the only prisoners left in the cellblock. In the morning we were taken into the courtyard to find that we were the only prisoners left in the camp. The doors to the Desert Inn, the Stardust, the Golden Nugget, and the Riviera were open, their cells deserted.

We spent Christmas morning sweeping out the cells in the Thunderbird, and then we were moved into the Mint next door. We watched from the open door of the cellblock as a large group of Vietnamese prisoners, scraggly, barefoot, and filthy, were brought into the courtyard.

During the next few days the LuLus remained in the Mint, trying to figure out what had happened and why we had been left bhind. Bedinger spoke French, and ever the communicator, unsuccessfully to establish communication with the Vietnamese after he heard them singing French songs one evening. When a guard came into the cellblock and told us to prepare to move, we feared the worst. The other POWs had been taken somewhere for release, but, perhaps because the peace treaty did not cover Laos, we were being returned to that country to prison. We discussed the possibility of jumping out of the back of the truck we expected would be taking us back toward the border.

With our small bundles of belongings, the LuLus were taken blindfolded into the courtyard, arranged in single file, with a hand on the shoulder of the man in front of us, and told to move. We had spent our last day in Little Vegas.

28

Led by guards, the LuLus moved blindly through the courtyard, into passage-ways, then back into open air again. I could hear doors and gates opening for us, then closing behind. Soon we were in a large courtyard, then what seemed to be a smaller one, and finally we were walking down a long hallway. When the blind-folds were removed, we found ourselves in a small cellblock. I was placed in a room with Steve Long, and Jim Bedinger was paired next door with Walt Stischer. We put our buckets down in cells about ten feet by seven, with the only furniture being the concrete slabs that served as beds. The cement walls were scrawled with prisoners' names dating to 1928. Though we weren't sure where we were, we were relieved that we hadn't left the prison. Wherever this place was, it was better than Laos.

When the guard had gone, Steve stood on his bed and called out the vent into the darkened hallway, "Hey, any Americans in here?"

"Yeah."

"Who you!"

"John Flynn and Dave Winn."

Colonel John Flynn was the highest-ranking POW held by the North Vietnamese. He and three other colonels had been brought over with the others from Vegas on Christmas Eve and isolated in this small cellblock, presumably because they were the four highest-ranking POWs. By rank, Flynn clearly had been the SRO at Vegas, but since he had been out of communications, Stockdale, Risner, and Denton had assumed those duties.

Across from the colonels, we learned, were a Vietnamese pilot and two Thais, one of whom was my old friend Harnavee. The familiar voice greeted me from the darkness, and assured me he was doing okay.

None of the colonels knew where we were yet, but I assumed we must be in a cellblock in the horseshoe-shaped complex called Camp Unity that Bud Day and Mel Pollard had told us about in the Vegas courtyard. That would mean most of the men were being held together in large squad bays.

During the next few days we learned that our daily routine permitted us to leave our cells for a few hours each day for the purpose of dumping our buckets, using the wash stalls, and exercising together in the small walled courtyard outside our cellblock. Beyond the courtyard gate we could see a larger courtyard and what appeared to be the U-shaped complex that Day and Pollard had told us about. Rising behind our cellblock were the walls of the prison and the guard towers from which soldiers with AK-47s looked down.

The LuLus were responsible for washing the dishes for the entire cellblock. The job gave us the opportunity to see if anyone was on the other side of the wall in the washroom. Washing the dishes in the small wash area near the door leading to the courtyard, we waited until the guard had stepped out, and then I banged a "shave and a haircut" with my fist on the wall. We had guessed this wall might be the back of one of the squad bays. When I got nothing back, I tried it again. This time the "two bits" came banging back. I tapped out a "Who U?" and the reply was "Rm 1, who U?"

"I Brace. What camp this?"

"Unity."

"Put ear to wall," I tapped, and then began talking through the concrete wall with my tin cup, the way John and I had done at the Plantation. It worked, and our isolated cellblock was now "in comm" with most of the some three hundred men in the camp. Room 1 told me that it was the first of seven squad bays, each of which formed a section of the curving eastern wing of the horseshoe complex in the northwest corner of Hoa Lo prison. The large rooms were well organized and had excellent communications. Lieutenant Commander Leo Proffilet was the senior officer in room 1. They could send and receive messages through the wall to room 2, which in turn was in touch with room 3, and so forth.

Unaware of Colonel Flynn's presence in the small cellblock behind them, Proffilet and the other room commanders were reporting to the senior officers who had come over from Vegas a few days before. Those senior officers were now in the last bay, room 7.

They included Stockdale, Risner, Denton, and Vem Ligon. My friend John McCain was also in room 7.

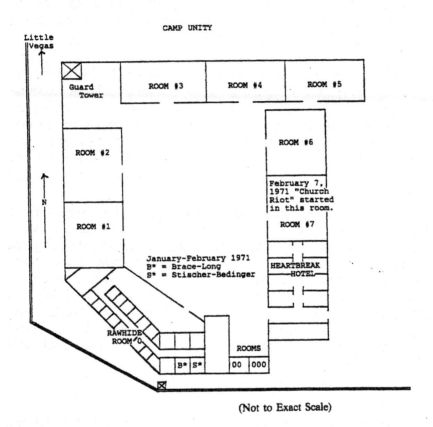

(Not to Exact Scale)

We set up regular communication procedures with room 1 through the washroom wall. Each day for a few minutes after the two meals, a LuLu member communicated with the squad bay while two washed the dishes and one maintained lookout. Our small cellblock took the code name Rawhide, and the numerical designation O.

A short time later, Steve Long discovered a peephole, concealed by a piece of wood shaped like a breadboard whose handle was nailed into the wall we shared with room 1. The first time Steve pushed the board aside and peered in, he found himself staring into an Oriental face and immediately covered the hole.

"Guard!" he told me in alarm, but it turned out he had been looking into the face of Terry Uyeyama, an Air Force pilot of

Japanese-American background. Soon we were using the peephole to talk and pass notes.

Meanwhile, the LuLus had also established comm with two rooms on the other side of them, bays that were beyond the medical room directly adjacent to Rawhide. By yelling through their windows when the guards weren't near, Bedinger and Stischer were able to get in touch with the nineteen occupants of a room that would be assigned the designation 00, and with the six or seven residents of 000, the last room on the western wing of the horseshoe.

Now that communications had been established with the rest of the camp, Colonel Flynn assumed command. Soon the LuLus were the conduit for a flood of communication coming in and out of Rawhide.

Though I was the only civilian in camp, I was assuming an enormous amount of responsibility as the SRO's chief communicator. Each day, when the guard left the small courtyard where the LuLus exercised, I sneaked back into the cellblock, lay down on the floor, and conversed under the door with Flynn and the other colonels. Outside, Bedinger would be stationed at the gate of the courtyard, ready to engage the guard in conversation if he should return unexpectedly. Stischer or Long would be stationed near the cellblock door to relay any warnings. Occasionally we switched roles.

I also conversed in this manner with Harnavee and his Thai cellmate. A South Vietnamese pilot, Lieutenant Dat, whose code name was Max, lived on our block in another cell. Max passed on the intelligence that the arrival of more than three hundred American POWs at Camp Unity from outlying prisons was probably in response to a U.S. commando raid on the prison at Son Tay earlier in November. The commandos found the prison empty, Max said, but the raid had probably prompted the North Vietnamese to centralize their prisoners in Hanoi. Sometimes Max could hear the radio being played in the guards' quarters.

Though communications between the SRO in his isolated cellblock and the rest of the camp were now excellent, we knew that a single communication bust could cut Colonel Flynn off. We were also aware that the senior officers in room 7, Ligon, Stockdale, Risner, and the others, had valuable leadership ability that shouldn't be wasted. We recommended to Flynn that a deputy camp commander be named from room 7, so that the command structure could continue if communications from Rawhide should stop. Such a move would also allow the experienced leaders in room 7 to continue to play a role in setting policy for the camp. It still left the last word to Colonel Flynn as to whether it should be put into effect. Flynn accepted the suggestion, and named Lieutenant Colonel Vernon Ligon as his deputy. Ligon's staff included Stockdale, Risner, and Denton.

Virtually all of the message traffic that Colonel Flynn received involved questions about POW behavior. The occupants of room 00, for example, wanted an SRO ruling on whether Lieutenant Alvarez, who had been a prisoner for seven years, should be allowed to accept an opportunity for early release. Except in situations like Doug Hegdahl's, the policy was that special favors or parole were prohibited by the Code of Conduct. Colonel Flynn reiterated that policy in response to the 00 inquiry.

The LuLus also passed on messages to Flynn asking guidance about the proper resistance behavior. Some messages from the squad bays suggested that the resistance be hard-core, that guards be harassed and massive escape plans devised. Others argued that the war's end was probably very near, and that the best policy was to keep a low profile in the hope of surviving our prison ordeal and making it home again. Such prisoners did not condone making propaganda for the enemy, but reasoned that POW admissions of war crimes were of little practical use to the enemy, and that the price of refusal-beatings with rubber hoses, strap-and-bar torture, or isolation in leg irons-was too high. Such issues were so complex that Flynn and the three other colonels had a difficult time formulating policy that could easily be transmitted through short notes or passed in brief conversations. They did pass on some general guidelines, but gave each cellblock commander the authority to handle any contingencies not covered by their policy. Often the Ligon-Stockdale group in room 7 found Flynn's policy on resistance less strict than that which they had been promulgating, and toughened the resistance policy about making propaganda tapes or broadcasts.

The six or seven POWs housed in room 000, the last room on the western wing, did not involve themselves in the controversy over prisoner behavior. Considered turncoats by the rest of the camp, they had supposedly made propaganda broadcasts of their own free will, and visited with peace delegations. Among them were my old Marine buddy, Ed Miller, along with Bob Schweitzer and Gene Wilbur. The LuLus got in touch with Miller's room by yelling from our cells. We tried to relay warnings to some of the newer men in the room that their cellmates were not following the guidance of the SRO, and would someday have to answer for their actions.

"Colonel Flynn says you are to quit cooperating," I had called out the window. "You shouldn't see any more peace delegations. Get yourselves squared away." At first the residents of 000 yelled back, but after a while, obviously annoyed by the persistent badgering of the LuLus, they stopped communicating.

In January 1971, a few weeks after Colonel Flynn had resumed command, I began a survey for him to determine the name of every prisoner in Camp Unity and those prisoners who had been elsewhere. The various units transmitted their rosters and other information by voice through the wall hole or by notes passed in the false bottoms of waste buckets, thrown over courtyard walls, or hidden in washroom drains. After three days I had a complete roster of the Camp Unity inmates, which included 339 American airmen shot down in North Vietnam, the four LuLus from Laos, one South Vietnamese airman, and the two Thais. The only Americans seen in the prison system who could not be accounted for were George Atterbury, Homer Smith, and Ted Guy, who had been SRO at the Plantation when I was there.

In the process of the survey, I collected a great deal of information about other prison camps in the area, and in addition to providing Colonel Flynn with the POW roster, I wrote daily full-page memos to the SRO, telling what I knew about such prisons as the Briar Patch, the Zoo, the Dirty Bird, and Alcatraz.

By this time, practically everyone in the camp knew of the LuLus, and of the efforts of the North Vietnamese to keep their existence a secret. Though the LuLus still were not allowed to send or receive mail, other POWs in Camp Unity shared the contents of the Christmas packages they had received a few weeks before. When the LuLus came into the small courtyard for our exercise periods, we found small gifts waiting for us on the clothesline: handkerchiefs, T-shirts, or a pair of socks with candy inside. One of the sources of the gifts was Colonel Flynn himself, who also exercised in that courtyard.

I had long since removed the dental bridge that the guards had knocked loose five and a half years ago, during the beating that followed my first escape. I now had only one of my front teeth left, and that one had developed a cavity. By the time we were transferred to Camp Unity, the tooth was painfully abscessed, and my mouth was swollen so badly that the guards took me to the medical shack that adjoined Rawhide. The POWs had dubbed the physician in charge "Dr. Spock" (the same name we had given the medic at the Plantation).

The doctor had reduced the swelling in my mouth by administering penicillin. After several days he decided the tooth had to be pulled. Though the physician meant well, he obviously knew very little about dentistry. The next few hours would seem like torture. Despite my efforts to tell him otherwise, the doctor insisted on inserting the novocaine needle directly into the gum area alongside my tooth, rather than in the fleshy area above. The shots were not only painful but useless. I scarcely felt any numbness in my jaw at all. Most of the novocaine simply ran down my throat, and in a few minutes I was having to vomit in a pail.

When the doctor began wrenching the tooth back and forth with his pliers, the pain was blinding. Yet the stubborn tooth would not yield. By the time the doctor was finally able to yank it free I was screaming, and was being held in the straight-backed chair by two guards. I was returned to my cell exhausted and ill, but I was relieved that the tooth was out. Over the years I had found I could think away any pain except for a toothache. I was now completely toothless in front.

By the end of January the guards had caught on to the communications activity in the camp, and the resulting crackdown cut our cellblock off from the squad bays. As a result, we were not aware that room 7 had organized a Sunday-morning religious service for February 7. We plainly heard the prisoners' reaction when the guards interrupted the services and took the senior officers out into the courtyard.

Hundreds of voices began singing *The Star-Spangled Banner*, then such songs as the Marine Corps Hymn, "Anchors Aweigh," the Air Force song, and "God Bless America." Still not knowing what had happened, the LuLus joined in.

When the men in the squad bays ran out of patriotic songs, roundrobin chanting began, starting with room 7.

"This is seven, this is seven, where the hell is number six?"

The chant grew louder as it was picked up by the younger, more energetic officers in 2, 3, and 4, and each successive squad bay tried to outdo the one preceding it. With only eight Americans in Rawhide, the volume dropped, but the colonels and the LuLus joined in as loudly and enthusiastically as we could.

"This is zero, this is zero, where the hell is double zero?"

The Zoo people in oo continued the chant, but it ended there. There was silence for a few moments while the rest of the camp waited for ooo to respond, then a loud cheer went up. Room ooo, which contained most of the prisoners who were making propaganda tapes, was silent.

As the round-robin progressed, the large courtyard filled with police wearing riot helmets and gas masks. Some were carrying tear-gas guns and others had rifles with bayonets fixed. Then the prison loudspeakers blared Vietnamese music that drowned out everything else, and the incident known as the Church Riot was over. For the rest of the day the prisoners were kept in their rooms, the music blaring relentlessly from the speakers.

It was after midnight when we heard the trucks in the prison, and then the guards were unlocking our doors and ordering us to "prepare to leave." Blind-folded and tied with our hands behind us, the four LuLus were marched through the darkness across the large courtyard and pushed into a waiting truck. Peeking from beneath my blindfold, I saw that about a dozen soldiers, commanded by a guard the POWs called Pepe, were crowded in with us. That seemed too large a contingent for a simple cross-town transfer, and I noticed also that the truck was loaded with cases of canned meat, both Bulgarian and Vietnamese. Moreover, the four refuse buckets stacked in the corner suggested that the LuLus were going to be put in solo at their new place of confinement.

Oh boy, I thought to myself, we've had it now. If we weren't on our way back to Laos, we certainly were headed someplace where we would need rations. Visions of the prison called Dogpatch, in the mountains along the Chinese border, came to mind.

29

Soon the sounds of the city were behind us, and the paved road turned to dirt. The truck bumped along for several hours before it pulled off into a field and stopped. We got out and were guided across some rough ground until a squeaking gate signaled our entrance to a new compound.

When my blindfold was removed, I found myself in a small concrete-walled room with an arched ceiling. The guard lit a kerosene lamp so I could see to stow my gear and rig my mosquito net over my bed board. There was no electricity in the room, no lights, no radio speaker.

I noticed that dozens of names had been scrawled on the bed board, but later inspection revealed there were no American names. The walls were covered with lumpy concrete bumps. It would be hard to tap, impossible to write on them. The guard didn't notice that I threw the rope I had been bound with under the bed after he untied me.

In the morning the get-up gong sounded in the distance. We wakened to find sunlight spilling into our rooms through tall barred windows that reached from our knees to the ceiling. Each of us was in one of four cells in a small square building in the center of a courtyard not more than fifty feet square. An eight-foot-high wall topped with barbed wire surrounded the area. No guards patrolled the courtyard itself, but armed soldiers watched from a guard tower that rose from behind the walls.

The prisoners' doors all opened to the outside, with no door opening on the same side of the building. Baffle walls prevented us from seeing each other out of our windows. The absence of a guard in the compound permitted us to converse freely, and we spent a lot of time during the first few days speculating on where we might be. Having done the POW camp survey for Colonel Flynn, I knew there were several camps around Hanoi. Briar Patch, Son Tay, Faith, Skid row, and Rockpile were all within a fifty-mile range. Since there were no other prisoners nearby who could tell us where we were, we began calling our new home "LuLu's Hideaway." It was not an altogether lighthearted designation. The name reflected the group's concern that we had been hidden in the countryside by a government that still didn't want to admit its troops were in Laos.

LULUS HIDEAWAY

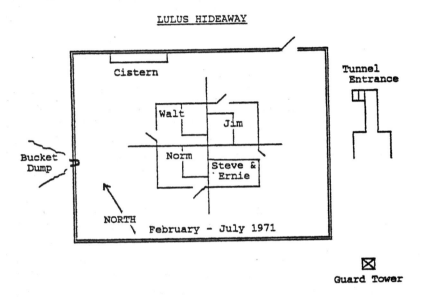

One of the first things I noticed about our new cells was that I could see the sky. Except for a few brief weeks when my cage in the jungle had offered an exhilarating patch of blue, my places of confinement had not afforded me the luxury of losing myself in the heavens. Now the tall windows offered me that delight, and the nights were even better than the days. Looking through the bars, I could see the Big Dipper for the first time since I was captured. Each night I followed the blinking white light of a satellite painting a trail across the sky.

There were other things to be said for this camp. One of them was that its discipline was more lax than that at Vegas or Camp Unity. Pepe, the even-tempered guard who had come with us from Hoa Lo, was in charge of the compound, and we found we could bend some of the camp rules without risking punishment. Told that we were to stay away from each other during exercise periods in the courtyard, the LuLus openly violated the policy by walking about the compound together, in full view of the guards in the tower outside. No punishment followed.

Soon the routine developed that we were all let out of our cells to wash at the open cistern at the same time. On the second or third day at the cistern I found an old piss pot of porcelainized metal—Walt called it a "thundermug"—in a pile of debris. It was caked with yellowish calcium deposits on the inside, but hadn't been used in such a long time that the calcium was rock-hard. We had all been using our small drinking cups to dip wash water, and I reasoned that something larger, with a handle, might be better.

The guard wrinkled his nose and tried to get me to put it down when he saw what I intended to do with the pot. I ignored him and banged the pot on the ground a few times, until the calcium broke up and flaked off the sides. Taking a small cup, I put some water in the pot and scrubbed it well, using handfuls of gravel. After rinsing it out, I started using it to souse myself down from the cistern. The rest of the LuLus didn't use it at first, but I noticed about a week later that they were all using the pot to wash with.

The food at the Hideaway was the best prepared and most plentiful that I had received at any time during my captivity. The hard bread of the Hanoi prisons was replaced with rice, well-cooked vegetables, canned meat, fish, and even an occasional egg. In the mornings the guards brought us a jug of water and a kind of pancake that was eaten with sugar. I found I was actually starting to gain weight.

The lax discipline in the camp and my improved physical condition prompted me seriously to consider escape again for the first time since I had left the jungle cages. Though I knew by the propaganda broadcasts in Unity that the peace talks were continuing in Paris, there was no assurance the war would end soon, or even that the LuLus would be freed with the rest when the treaty was signed. When I revealed my intentions to the others, Long and Bedinger indicated they would go with me. Stischer, the SRO of our small contingent, had a heart problem that he feared would not allow him to stand the days and perhaps weeks of exertion necessary for such an escape, but he gave the plan his blessing.

I immediately began to keep track of the guards' duty schedules and routines. I kept a record of the moon's phases so that we could scale the wall in the blackness before moonrise, and then use the moonlight to see by after we were free in the countryside. For food during the escape, we saved sugar that I hid in my room in the small plastic bags we had acquired from other POWs at Unity and Vegas.

We had been in camp less than a month before I noticed that a piece of structural iron reinforcing rod was hanging in the barbed wire atop a portion of the wall that was hidden from the view of the guard tower. If I could get to that piece of rebar, I could fashion it into a tool that would get me out of my wooden cell door, which was locked with a padlock. During an exercise period, while two LuLus were keeping a lookout, a third boosted me up far enough to permit me to grab the short piece of rod and hide it in my shirt.

That night, and in the nights following for three weeks, I lay in my room bending the steel rod back and forth until metal fatigue caused it to break. By grinding the ends on the concrete floor to sharpen them, I produced two crude wood drills that would permit me to bore holes in the door. I planned to drill a circle of holes around the piece of wood holding the hasp to which the padlock was secured. Once the hasp's wooden base was weakened enough, I would simply push the door open. Bedinger's and Long's rooms would have to be opened also. I thought I could easily pry the hasps off their doors from the outside.

Though most of the floor was concrete, there was a small patch of dirt in front of my door, and I dug a hole there to give me a hiding place for the tools. Along with the two drills, I buried the bags of sugar and the length of quarter-inch hemp rope that I had been tied with on the truck trip from Hanoi.

Knowing we would face many miles of walking after we had escaped the compound, I began removing my Ho Chi Minh rubber-tire sandals before going out for exercise periods, and I told Jim and Steve they would have to do the same. Despite Bedinger's protests that his mother had always warned him not to walk barefoot for fear of hookworm, we were soon circling the graveled compound daily, toughening our feet for the escape ahead.

Jim and Steve began having second thoughts about an escape try, and in early March, after a long discussion with me, they decided they were not going. The war was too close to being over, they felt, to justify the effort and risk involved in escaping into hostile territory from a prison whose location was not known. If I was going, I would have to go it alone.

That night I lay on my bed board and thought about what to do. I could understand why the others didn't want to go, yet I would probably never get a better opportunity to make a break than I had here at LuLu's Hideaway. I knew I was my own judge, and I didn't want to go home knowing I had passed up a chance to get away if it came. Even if I had been bound by the Code of Conduct, it was arguable whether I had a duty to go in this situation. Yet I still thought of myself as a Marine, disgraced or not. The Code clearly said prisoners should make "every effort to escape." I still had the tools buried in my room.

Goddammit, I'm going, I told myself suddenly. I'm going over the wall I may not make it, but at least I'll have tried.

Based on the moon's phase, June 1 was the ideal time to go. I would shove clothes under my blanket and pull down my mosquito net, hoping the guards would not notice that I was gone when they made their regular midnight flashlight check through the bars. I would bore through the cell door at about ten o'clock, after the first bed check. While it was still very dark, I would climb over a section of the wall that couldn't be seen from the guard tower, and set out across the countryside.

About an hour after going over the wall, I could be using the light from the newly risen moon to light my way. Heading in the direction of the tugboat or barge horns I had heard in the distance, I would try to find the river that had to be nearby. Knowing that all rivers in the Hanoi area led to the sea, I would swim and drift at night, and hide out in the day until I could get to the coast and signal a friendly ship.

In the next few days I spent my exercise periods going over and over the plan, making sure that I had selected the right place to go over the wall, and even jumping up once to grab the steel bar that I would use for a handhold. I dug up my tools and sharpened them some more, to make sure they would bore through the door in a short time, then reburied them.

On the night of March 8, my cell door suddenly opened and Pepe strode in. "Prepare to move," he said. "Quickly, quickly." I was taken around the comer of the building and pushed into the cell already occupied by Steve Long. The single large bed board in the small room hardly left any room to stand. After the guards made clear that Steve and I were now roommates, the door slammed shut.

"What's going on?" Steve asked.

"I don't know, but my escape tools are still in there."

Then Bedinger's alarmed voice called from around the comer.

"What has happened to Ernie? Where is Ernie?"

"I'm in with Steve. I'm okay."

We heard the guards return and put someone in my cell. When the soldiers shut the courtyard gate behind them, we tried tapping to the newcomer. We got no response. Then Steve called out, "New prisoner, say your name." The response was mumbled, unintelligible. Obviously the new guy was afraid the guards would hear, or that he was being tricked.

"It's okay. Don't worry if you're brand-new. The guards in the tower can't hear us. We'll talk to you tomorrow."

In the morning we called to the new prisoner again, and this time he identified himself as Major Norm Gotner, a navigator from an Air Force F-4 shot down over Laos during the invasion of that country the month before. We asked about his pilot.

"They killed my pilot," he said.

Gotner was not allowed out for exercise periods for the next few days, but the LuLus walked by to greet the new prisoner when we were let out to wash. We could see the major was upset and apprehensive; it was not the time to tell him that escape tools were hidden in the floor of his cell, much less ask him to dig them up. When Gotner passed on the news that President Nixon intended to withdraw all American troops from Southeast Asia within six months, I decided to scotch my escape plan.

The story Norm told us about the invasion of Laos was another reason not to go. Nixon seemed to be playing hardball, and we were convinced this would mean an early end to the war. The loss of my tools, and the news of what appeared to be a timetable for ending the war, made escape both impracticable and unnecessary.

The newest LuLu was an inveterate worrier who wasn't reluctant to communicate his concerns to the others during our conversations through the windows. Alarmed that he might have heart problems, because he could hear his heart pounding in his ears at night, we assured him he had nothing to worry about. The wooden bed board acted as a conductor of body noises and movements. It was one of our sources of entertainment to lie there and try to figure out what all the gurgles and plop-plop noises meant. Norm had a hard time adjusting to the grim jokes that helped sustain the rest of us.

He found no humor in Long's suggestion that the arched ceilings in the cells were like coffin lids, nor did he appreciate it when veteran prisoners described a trench being dug outside our cellblock as "our common grave."

But the LuLus enjoyed listening to Gotner's detailed accounts of the current war situation and his recollections of news events that had occurred since Bedinger had been captured almost a year and a half before. An Air Force missile man before he had come to Southeast Asia as a navigator, the Kansas City, Missouri, native knew a lot about the U.S. space program. He gave us a fascinating description of the Apollo flight during which an explosion in the capsule forced the astronauts to jury-rig some equipment in order to continue the flight.

When the new LuLu offered to draw some detailed sketches of the Apollo capsule, we warned him to find a secure hiding place. A few days later he was caught with the drawings, and the guards took them for "analysis." They were hardly blueprints, and contained little more than what might be picked up from a magazine like Popular Mechanics, but it was not the kind of information an American POW should be giving to his captors.

Of all the minor irritations of life at LuLu's Hideaway, the bedbugs were the worst. Watching Steve do sit-ups on our bed board one morning, I noticed dozens of bite marks on his back. An examination of my own body revealed the same marks. Checking the room for the source of the bites, we found hundreds of tiny bloodsucking red bugs trapped in the mosquito net and hiding in the cement walls. The tick-like creatures were so small that Steve and I hadn't noticed them at first. They were everywhere, and they seemed impossible to kill.

Steve and I began devoting time every day to the task of collecting the bugs, counting them, and dropping them into the kerosene in the small lamp we used for light at night. Even though we were on one large bed board, each of us had his own mosquito net to search through. Smashing some of the bigger ones would result in a drop of blood—our blood, we figured. We were depositing as many as two hundred bugs a day in the kerosene, and soon the lamp oil had to be replaced. After repeated complaints to the guards, the walls of the room and our rice-straw mats were splashed with DDT and the situation improved.

One night during the first week of May, all five of us were taken from our cells without warning and were blindfolded and wrist-chained. Then we were hurried roughly out the courtyard door to an excavation outside the compound. When the blindfolds were removed, we were told to climb down a ladder into a hole, then down another until we were about fifteen feet beneath the surface. A waiting guard at the bottom of the second ladder told us to crawl down a tunnel no more than three feet wide and four feet high, unsupported by shoring.

Bedinger, the first man into the tunnel, called back directions to the others as he followed the twisting passageway in the darkness. Once we had emerged into a subterranean room, some guards followed with a lantern and we heard the trap-door above us drop shut.

I was relieved to see the guards alongside us. At least they're not going to bury us, I thought. We tried to reassure Gotner, who was very upset and appeared to be praying.

We remained in the hole for nearly an hour before we were told to crawl back up to the surface. When we had been returned to our cells, we talked through our windows, trying to understand what the purpose of the drill had been. At first we assumed the tunnel was an air-raid shelter, but the bombing in the north had halted completely in 1968. Walt Stischer concluded that the tunnel was a hiding place for the LuLus in case of a commando raid designed to rescue us, similar to the one a few months before at Son Tay.

To counteract the scheme, Walt drew a map on toilet paper of the compound and the tunnel outside, using "ink" squeezed from the cotton balls soaked in purple merthiolate that he had been issued for treatment of athlete's foot. He placed a large X over the hiding place, with the notation "We are here!" He would leave the note on his bunk if we were ever taken unexpectedly from our cells again.

It was only a few days after the visit to the tunnel that a trio of English-speaking NVA soldiers arrived and began spending time in the courtyard each day trying to engage the LuLus in conversation. The three enlisted men, whom the LuLus named Mole, Smiley, and Buckles, the Three Stooges, perplexed us, because it was not clear whether they were an inspection team, interrogators, or simply observers. Whatever they were, Major Stischer didn't like them, and when they approached him for autobiographical information, he rebuffed them by saying that "all that information is available in Hanoi."

A few days later, when the three showed up in the courtyard to give Steve and me the weed-cutting tools we had been asking for, Walt apparently misunderstood what was happening and yelled from his cell to Steve and me to stop cutting the weeds around our cell.

"Don't do the bastards' work for them," Walt yelled. When I rushed over to the SRO's window and explained that we had asked for tools so we could get rid of the bug-infested weeds near our cell, Walt allowed us to continue. But the Mole had heard the exchange, entered Stischer's cell, and lectured him angrily. The major's contemptuous response was to turn his back and fart loudly.

The Mole had had enough. He called Buckles, who chained the major's arms behind him and stuffed a towel in his mouth. Then the pair began to beat him. We could hear the punches landing, the involuntary grunts from Walt that followed, and the crashes when the major's body slammed into the walls.

Immediately we began raising a commotion, yelling at the top of our voices at Buckles and the Mole, but also hoping our shouts would be heard by Pepe, the camp commander.

"Stop!" we cried. "What are you doing to that man? Get the officer. Get the officer. We protest! We protest!"

We tried alerting the guards outside the wall by yelling in Vietnamese, "*Bao Cao, Bao Cao!*" which meant, "Get the officer."

The fuss raised by us seemed to unnerve the two soldiers, who perhaps were not authorized to administer beatings. In any event, they left Stischer's cell and, after returning Steve and me to our cell, left the compound. The LuLus were particularly worried about Walt because we knew his heart was bothering him, but the major told the others through the window that he was all right.

The Mole and his companions were not through with the LuLus yet. About a week later the three soldiers came into the courtyard, and I heard them open a cell door around the corner. We heard Bedinger cough the letter I for "inspection." They were shaking down the rooms. Steve immediately hid the needle and thread and other items he had stolen from the guards in recent months. The door was pulled open and Steve and I were taken out and stood up against the wall with the other LuLus, while all the rooms were searched.

Though they searched Norm Gotner's room, the soldiers never found my escape tools buried in the floor. They did find and confiscate Steve's items and, worse, fished Walt Stischer's map of the compound and tunnel from his bucket, where he had hurriedly tried to disguise it as used toilet paper.

Walt was in trouble again, and after his behavior of the previous week it seemed likely that his next punishment would be worse than the last. Worried that Stischer's heart might be permanently damaged by another beating, I tried to take responsibility for drawing the map.

"Did you find the map I drew?" I asked the Mole, who looked up from the crumpled paper and raised an eyebrow.

"You didn't draw this map," he said.

When I insisted I did, the soldier gave me a pencil and paper and told me to duplicate the map. After I had finished, Mole took a look.

"Your map is not the same," he said. But he was not entirely sure, and after a long discussion among themselves, the three soldiers ordered everyone back into his cell. No one was punished.

On May 21 I observed the sixth anniversary of my capture. In the months we had roomed together, I had described Patricia and the boys to Steve Long in such detail that my cellmate must have had a clear picture of every one of them. But it was a picture now six years old, and I was having a difficult time converting three-year-old Cary into the nine-year-old he really was. And was it possible that eleven-year-old Ernest was now seventeen? I still had clear images of Patricia and my parents and sisters in my mind, but I wondered how they were dealing with my disappearance, how they were coping, how life had treated them in the intervening years. From the return address on the one package I got in 1969, I was sure my father had died. Had he died before he knew I was alive?

May passed, and the monsoon came on schedule. The rain hammered the cellblock roof and formed large puddles in the courtyard.

June went by uneventfully. Without warning, on the night of July 7, the guards opened our cell doors and told us to prepare to leave. In a few minutes the LuLus were aboard a truck, headed down the road. I had seen a camp commander I knew from Hoa Lo talking to Pepe just before we were put on the truck. He got into the cab, so I assumed we were headed back to Hanoi. Besides, we weren't taking any food with us, so we weren't going far.

We tried to assure an apprehensive Gotner that we probably were being moved back with other Americans, a good sign. If

Nixon's prediction had come true, the Americans should have been withdrawn from Southeast Asia by now, and we all would be going home soon.

Though I was looking forward to seeing other Americans again, I was sorry in a sense to be leaving LuLu's Hideaway. I had experienced more personal freedom at this camp than at any other. The food had been good, the discipline more lax than I was used to, and the camp commandant, Pepe, as lenient as we had any reason to expect.

We would never know for certain where we had spent these past six months, but from aerial photos shown us after release we would guess that we had been in an isolated portion of a country-side compound at Xiam Ap Lo, thirty miles northwest of Hanoi. Other POWs had called it the Briar Patch.

30

After a while the clanking streetcars and honking horns told us we were back in the city. The truck finally turned into a gate and the prisoners climbed out into a courtyard that only I recognized.

"This is the Plantation," I whispered to them. It had been a year and a half since I was here, but there was no mistaking the Big House looming in the darkness, or the long white warehouse in whose southern end I had spent more than a year in solitary, communicating with John McCain.

"This is an easy camp," I assured Gotner, not feeling as confident as I sounded. "Don't worry."

We were placed in a concrete-walled flat-topped building on the northern periphery of the compound. It was the Gunshed, I knew, and its cells opened onto a large courtyard bordered on the left by the Warehouse—the largest of the cellblocks—and on the right by the Big House, which served as the prison's head-quarters and inter-rogation center.

Straight across the courtyard, behind a seven-foot tarpaper screen that divided the expanse, was the third cellblock, which I remembered was known as the Corn Crib. The Movie House was on the right side of the courtyard, but there were no prisoners in there now.

The LuLus were placed in three adjacent cells of a four-cell block. Jim and I were in the easternmost room, with Norm by himself next door. Steve and Walt were beyond Norm in a room next to the fourth cell. They immediately struck up a tap-code conversation with their new neighbor.

In a few minutes Norm was relaying information to Jim and me.

"Walt says Ted Guy next door," Norm tapped. "Who he?"

I responded that Guy was an Air Force colonel who had been among those POWs unaccounted for when I had compiled the list of prisoners for Colonel Flynn in Camp Unity. He had disappeared from the normal prison system about the middle of 1970.

In the next few days the LuLus learned that the colonel had been taken south, where he had been kept for a time in bamboo cages similar to those in which I had been held. Apparently he had been captured in South Vietnam or Laos. Even the NVA wasn't sure, according to Guy. After the Son Tay raid, he was returned to the Plantation rather than to Unity, where he was now SRO of a POW population consisting primarily of Army and Marine enlisted men captured during the Tet Offensive of 1968.

He told the LuLus that he and his cellmate, an Army major named Art Elliott, had been kept in the Gunshed, isolated from the rest of the camp, and that the military organization was poor because the enlisted men wouldn't communicate. That, I thought, was a problem the LuLus could work on.

The most precious item among my personal belongings was the coat I had painstakingly created out of a blanket when I had been alone in the cage. It was the only thing I had left now from my years at the Doi Sai camps; a guard at the Golden Nugget in Little Vegas had confiscated my last sandstone carving, a clown, because Bedinger and I had been using it to write with. Not only was the coat the warmest piece of clothing I had, but it had become over the years a kind of symbol to me of my determination to survive.

On the morning following our arrival at the Plantation, the LuLus were taken out on the Gunshed porch while the guards inspected our personal belongings. I gasped in disbelief when I saw one of the soldiers start to leave with my blanket-coat. For the first time since 1965, when I hit the guard who had thrown my bamboo wedding ring into the dirt, I lost my temper. I grabbed the coat and tried to yank it away from the soldier, but the guard held on tight. A tug-of-war began.

"You son of a bitch," I blurted out. "Give me back my jacket!" I argued that the camp commander had seen the coat repeatedly during my first stay in the Plantation, and had never objected. "I've worn this jacket up to the Big House for interrogation!" I exclaimed. The guard insisted it was "not regulation," and finally jerked the coat away with a look that told me I would be in trouble if I pursued the matter much further.

Watching the scene from only a few feet away had been Ed "J.R." Leonard, an Air Force captain who was being held in a small punishment cell we called the Closet, in the eastern end of the Gunshed. Leonard called out a compliment to me, since I had just risked punishment by standing up to the guard.

"Balls, balls, balls," he said admiringly.

Then I heard the voice of Colonel Guy, whose cell door was only a few feet away.

"Remember," he said with an amused tone, "discretion is the better part of valor!"

The comments helped cool my temper, but I remained upset for days over the loss of my coat. It was almost as if I had lost a friend.

The LuLus learned that Leonard was also a Laos shootdown who had been denied the opportunity to write letters or receive mad. Colonel Guy feared that the North Vietnamese had no intention of releasing those POWs captured in Laos when the other prisoners were repatriated at the end of the war. To release the "Laotians" would be to admit that NVA troops had been in Laos for years. Therefore he always said he was captured in South Vietnam when asked in an interrogation.

Leonard brought the number of LuLus to six, and number seven was added a short time later when Jack Butcher, an Air Force pilot shot down in March, became Gotner's roommate.

Using our experience from Camp Unity and Little Vegas, the LuLus lost little time in establishing communications between Guy and the rest of the camp. Jim and I made the first contact with the other POWs when we visited the large washroom on the side of the Corn Crib at the other end of the camp. While Jim maintained a lookout, I climbed into a cistern and banged a "shave and a haircut" on the wall. There was no response the first time, but when I tried it again, two raps came back. I then put my tin drinking cup to the wall.

"If you hear me, buddy," I called, "knock twice."

Two knocks rang through the wall.

"This is Ernie Brace. If you are American, knock twice." Two knocks.

I told the prisoners on the other side how to use their cups, and soon I was talking through the wall to a couple of Army warrant officers in the Corn Crib. Having been brought into the camp when it was empty, the prisoners did not know the name of the prison or the building in which they were held.

"You're at a prison in Hanoi called the Plantation," I told them. "This building is called the Corn Crib, you're in Corn Crib number one. The long cellblock is the Warehouse. We're in the Gunshed, behind the screen, other end of camp. We're known by group as LuLu, since we were all captured in Laos."

"Is Captain Leonard with you?" they asked. When I told them he was in the Closet, the warrant officers explained that the captain had been housed with them, but was being punished for communicating. He was, they said, a pretty tough character.

Contrary to Colonel Guy's understanding, the prisoners in the south end of the camp had established a good communications system, but they had been unable to get in touch with the northern end of the Warehouse or with the senior ranking officer. Part of the problem, the warrant officers said, was that a group of turn-coats in the north end of the Warehouse had, in the past, reported any prisoner communication they saw to the guards. Some prisoners had been punished severely by the North Vietnamese, apparently as a result of information provided by the eight-member antiwar group.

I told the warrant officers, Frank Anton, Joe Rose, and Mike O'Conner, that Colonel Guy, the SRO, was with the LuLus in the Gunshed, and that his code name was "Hawk." I proposed that we set up a communication system, making sure that the antiwar group was not made aware.

It was not long before the note drops had been established in the washroom near the Corn Crib on the south end and in the latrine dumping area at the north end of the courtyard, near the Gunshed.

Except for the antiwar group in room 1 of the Warehouse, the camp was now unified under Colonel Guy's command. He immediately began issuing policy guidelines about POW behavior and answering questions from his men about what form their resistance should take. With Guy's blessing, I passed to each group the four-point policy developed by the senior officers at Camp Unity:

- Communicate at all costs.
- Do not deny or condemn your country or its leaders.
- Resist to the best of your ability, short of having bones broken.

- Do not make tapes or see delegations unless forced to do so.

The enlisted men that were suddenly brought under Colonel Guy's authority reacted enthusiastically. Morale improved and resistance stiffened. Some of the young men began surreptitiously saluting "Hawk" as they moved past the Gunshed during exercise periods. We heard stories of privates, corporals, and sergeants being punished for failing to bow to guards as prison regulations required, refusing to make tapes, or acting sullen during inter-rogations.

When Captain Leonard was taken from the Closet and placed with the other LuLus, the cell he vacated was used as a temporary holding room for new prisoners. The LuLus took full advantage of any opportunity to communicate with the new arrivals. I wrote notes to them on behalf of the SRO, rolling them up tightly and slipping them into the new prisoners' food. The food was always waiting on a plate when the LuLus were allowed out to pick up their dishes. Since the guards were nearby, the other LuLus had to engage them in conversation or otherwise divert their attention while I was inserting the note.

A typical first note to a new prisoner would tell him where he was and then say:

Have faith. We are organized. Expect many threats, but little physical punishment at this time. Expect stay in Closet for two weeks. Stick to Code of Conduct. Do nothing to further North Vietnamese propaganda. If you didn't think the war was wrong when you came, don't change your mind by what you hear here. Very easy to live by Code at this time. Stay away from group in first room, next building to your left. They are turncoats. Expect another note with further instructions by same method. Drop spoon when you set plate out if you receive this.

DESTROY IMMEDIATELY!

To the LuLus, the most disturbing aspect of Plantation life was the reward the antiwar group was getting for its cooperation. On weekdays, the group was allowed out into the courtyard from the get-up gong to the sleep gong. They had the run of the camp, with the exception of the officers' area in the Gunshed.

They could talk to any of the enlisted prisoners they wanted, and often tried to persuade others to join them in their activities. They were given powdered milk and beer once a week, items not given to the other prisoners. The LuLus could hear them singing "La Phong Vietnam," an NVA fight song, for visiting delegations in the Big House, and chanting, "Hey, hey, LBJ, how many kids did you kill today?"

The other prisoners had seen them in civilian clothes, presumably on their way to visits to downtown Hanoi. At Christmastime they decorated the trees in the Christmas Room and formed a choir whose carols were piped over the speaker system to the various cellblocks. They called themselves the Peace Committee, but the rest of the camp called them the "Peace Clowns."

They had a right to their beliefs. What I and the other POWs did object to were the special privileges the group enjoyed, and their apparent willingness to turn in their countrymen.

There were other prisoners who had concluded that America's participation in this war was a mistake, but had accepted no favors, nor did they constitute a danger to their fellow prisoners. Captain Floyd Kushner of the Army Medical Corps was one such prisoner. He was deeply opposed to the war, but decided against making any tapes. He advised the Warehouse 1 group that even though he agreed with their view of the war, they should not forget they were Americans.

Some of the messages that I relayed to Colonel Guy contained questions about whether other POWs should accept privileges similar to those given the antiwar group. Guy's response, sent out through me, was that no special favors were to be accepted unless they were given to all, and he informed the camp that he intended to bring charges against the antiwar group after repatriation.

By October of 1971 the guards had become aware of the prolific communication that was taking place in the washrooms in the south end of the camp, and began building another washing area on the north end, near the POWs in the Gunshed. Though the POWs were able to pass notes in the false bottoms of buckets that were exchanged at the latrine sites, the washrooms were the primary means of communication, and I could see that the new structure at the north end would seriously impair communications if an alternative system wasn't set up.

I advised Colonel Guy of the problem, and immediately went to work on a new communications system that would allow transmission of messages from the Gunshed to the Warehouse POWs, who also used the new washhouse. They, in turn, could pass on the messages to the south end of the camp. All this would have to be done without the knowledge of the peace group in Warehouse 1, who would also be using the northern washhouse.

It was mid-October when the Gunshed personnel began using the new facility. Jim and I found a loose brick in the floor of the structure, and drew the ancient Christian sign of the fish on it with a piece of limestone. The next day a smiling face had been added to the fish, indication that someone was ready to communicate. I wrote an anonymous note that instructed the recipient to wrap his messages in plastic and bury them in the mud beneath the brick. The next day the note was gone. Two days later, Jim found a detailed note wrapped in plastic and buried in the mud. We had made contact with a Marine sergeant, Jose Jesus Anzaldua, Jr., who was housed near the middle of the Warehouse cellbock and had communications with the northern end as well as the Corn Crib. Through Sergeant Anzaldua, whose code name was "Lobo," communications were established quickly enough so that the washroom change constituted no more than a slight interruption.

By this time I had become Colonel Guy's chief communicator, and had taken the code name "Moses," which was suggestive of my role as the man who passed on the Commandments from the mountaintop.

Christmas 1971 passed, and the LuLus again were among the few prisoners in the camp not to receive packages. We were accustomed to our situation by now, and had learned to live with it. I spent my seventh Christmas in captivity listening to the peace group singing carols over the speaker in my cell. The LuLus did get to visit the Christmas Room in the Big House.

It was during the holiday season that I passed on a message to Colonel Guy from an Army sergeant named Nathan Henry. Henry badly needed medical attention, and sought guidance as to whether he should agree to write statements for the North Vietnamese if that was the only way he could get it. Guy told me to respond that the sergeant had his permission to "do what is necessary" to get medical assistance.

The next day, when I was out in the courtyard during an exercise period, I noticed one of the peace group on the other side of a tarpaper screen. Knowing that the group had access to everyone in the camp, I spoke to the young enlisted man through the screen and asked him to relay the message that "Sergeant

Henry should do whatever is necessary to get the medical treatment he needs."

"Who says?" asked the young man.

"Moses," I replied.

I sensed by the tone of the young soldier's responses that it might have been a mistake to talk to him. Even though our conversation had been brief, and related to a humanitarian gesture, I had indicated there was a command structure operating in the camp. If this young private decided to pass on the information to the guards, Colonel Guy would surely be in trouble as the senior officer in the camp.

The next day my fears were realized. Colonel Guy was taken to the Big House. There he was tortured almost continuously for the next ten days and nights. He was locked in leg irons, flogged with a rubber hose, beaten with fists, and kept kneeling during one period for nearly eighteen hours. Finally he agreed to write the "confessions" and apology that were demanded of him. Sergeant Nat Henry, in the meantime, was placed in solitary in the Closet. The Peace Clown I had passed the humanitarian message to had turned both men in to the camp commander.

Having been returned to his cell, Colonel Guy was in bad physical and mental shape. Some teeth had been broken and he could barely walk. He passed the word to me that communication between cellblocks was to stop. It was too dangerous now, he said.

I could imagine how badly Guy had been treated, and was aware that continuing to communicate would be more dangerous than ever now. However, we still had an excellent note-drop system in the washroom that had never been detected. Keeping contact with the rest of the camp seemed more important than ever since the guards had put up a tarpaper screen cutting off the Gunshed from the rest of the camp. With the screen up, the LuLus could not even flash hand signals to POWs as they walked by.

To stop communications went against my interpretation of the Code of Conduct and the regulations promulgated by the senior officers in Vegas and Unity. I told Walt Stischer that I was going to continue to communicate despite Colonel Guy's order.

"I can't tell you to stop, Ernie," Walt told me. "You're a civilian. What you do is entirely your own responsibility."

During the next several weeks I kept the communication lines open, passing on information that I knew to be Colonel

Guy's policy before the communication bust. When, several weeks later, the colonel passed the word down to me that he was ready to begin limited communications again with the other cellblock, I told him the system was ready. I did not let on that it had never stopped functioning.

Spring 1972 came, and I observed the seventh anniversary of my capture. The North Vietnamese government put forth their ten-point peace plan at Paris, which it called "just and reasonable." According to Hanoi Hannah, it was just a matter of months before the world would welcome this initiative on the part of North Vietnam.

The LuLus were now being allowed to play Ping-Pong on the Gunshed porch occasionally after the morning meal. We had also been assigned jobs to do in the courtyard. Jim and I took care of the pigs that were kept in pens next to the cellblock and slaughtered occasionally to provide food for the guards and prisoners.

The radio speakers in the cells continued to be full of hopeful predictions about the end of the war, but soon summer arrived, and then fall, and the dramatic news of a signed peace treaty never came. Jane Fonda and Ramsey Clark visited the Hanoi prisons on peace missions independent of the U.S. government, and tapes of their remarks condemning the war were played to the POWs.

Critical articles about the American role in the war were pasted up on card-board and circulated to the cellblocks. I read pieces from such diverse American periodicals as *Time* magazine, *Life*, the underground newspaper *Speckled Bird*, the *Communist Daily Worker, and Stars and Stripes.*

Movies were now shown regularly in the courtyard. Some of them were American polemics such as Dalton Trumbo's *Johnny Got His Gun* or Vietnamese-made films depicting "the people's struggle" against the United States.

I didn't resent seeing the propaganda, I was delighted after so many years to have something, anything, to read, and to be attending movies and listening to tape-recorded voices from the outside world. With the propaganda came non-political treats from a camp management who now thought peace was on the horizon. The albums of popular American singers like Nancy Sinatra and Johnny Cash, as well as the works of Beethoven, Bach, and Brahms, were piped into our cells. The movies included Russian and Vietnamese science and educational films well as excellent Soviet-made film productions of Shakespeare's Othello and A Comedy of Errors.

The LuLus were allowed to attend the films with the rest of the POWs, though we were always seated by ourselves in the back after everyone else had arrived.

By October the atmosphere was still hopeful, and the LuLus noticed that the food and medical care were improving. Then, on October 17, came an event that seemed the best evidence so far that we would be going home soon. The POWs were each given a set of civilian clothes, loaded in public buses, and given a tour of downtown Hanoi. The atmosphere was cheerful and friendly. A tongue-in-cheek destination sign over the windshield of the LuLus' bus said, optimistically, HANOI, HUE, SAIGON.

Having been given a good briefing about what we were to see, we enjoyed the trip, though some of the routes seemed designed to show the destruction American aircraft had inflicted on the city. We were shown the French embassy, which was in shambles from a bomb hit, and an apartment complex that had been damaged by a string of bombs. We passed an old steam shovel that had been hit from the air, apparently having been mistaken for the surface-to-air missile site that was only a few hundred feet away. Along the sidewalks I could see the rows of cistern-like bomb shelters built into the cement in the downtown area.

The prison guards, also wearing civilian clothes and carrying pistols in small black bags, tried to point out landmarks in halting English. They took away the civilian clothes on our return to the Plantation.

As November neared, the prisoners were discussing the presidential race in the United States. Most of them seemed to back Richard Nixon, whose stated "peace with honor" policy seemed preferable to George McGovern's more dovish stance. McGovern, the POWs felt, sounded as if he would be willing to come to Hanoi on his knees to free them, and we didn't find that an appetizing way to end years of imprisonment. In the Gunshed, "SWD," meaning "Stick with Dick," was being tapped back and forth on the walls.

Even the guards were following the election, and they laughed uproariously when they learned that I had named a sow in the pigpen Agnes. They thought I meant Agnew.

About a month after Nixon's reelection, the peace talks broke off in Paris. Almost immediately, the Ping-Pong table disappeared and the attitude of the guards grew as chilly as the weather.

On the night of December 19, bombs began falling in the city, and I felt the ground shuddering beneath my feet. Norm Gotner was my roommate now, having been allowed to switch rooms with Bedinger several weeks earlier. The Air Force officer had served a tour as a B-52 navigator. He recognized the pattern of the falling bombs.

"Those are B-52s!" he shouted at me.

For the next half hour we listened to an almost constant roar of explosions, some of them not very distant from the Plantation itself. Chips of concrete began falling from the cellblock roof. I looked out through a crack in the door and saw a sheet of fire on the horizon.

The B-52s returned night after night, with smaller tactical aircraft sneaking in over the city on single bomb sorties during the day. The prison's air-raid gong always seemed to sound too late. It would scarcely be rung before a fighter-bomber would scream overhead at low altitude and we would be shaken by the concussions of bombs.

Sometimes the bomb strikes were so close that the POWs bounced on their bed boards from the concussions. Soon the guards were ordering us to crawl under our bed boards during the raids.

The LuLus stayed in their cells most of the day after the raids started, but we saw in the courtyard that the guards, now wearing steel helmets and carrying rifles, were digging foxholes in the courtyard with the assistance of the Peace Clowns. Then the Gunshed occupants heard a disturbance on their roof, and soon learned that an antiaircraft weapon, perhaps a 37mm gun, had been installed there. I could see its black snout sticking out over the roof. When it fired, the Gunshed reverberated.

A few days before Christmas, the guards opened our doors, gave us shovels and picks, and told us to dig bomb shelters in the concrete of our cell floors because of the "indiscriminate bombing" of the U.S. planes.

Norm and I found there were two layers of concrete below our floor. We dug through Christmas Eve, and on Christmas Day we finally completed a two-man foxhole about six feet deep. We were still nursing the blisters on our hands when, on the night of

December 27, a guard threw open the door and told us, "Prepare to leave."

Leave? We had just spent several days of backbreaking work on the hole. Concerned we were being taken somewhere to be hidden again, Norm and I used limestone to write the names of all the LuLus on the walls of our cells before we abandoned them. Then we stepped out into the courtyard, carrying our buckets and personal belongings. We were ushered into a waiting truck. The move, we learned later, was to make room at the Plantation for the B-52 crews who had been captured in recent weeks.

31

Neither blindfolded nor tied, the LuLus climbed into the back of a truck in which several of the Peace Clowns were already waiting. Putting these two units together even for a short ride was a mistake, I thought. Leonard was glaring at them, barely able to contain himself.

Almost a year before, Captain Leonard had spoken to several members of the Peace Clowns in the courtyard and ordered them to stop all forms of cooperation and collaboration with the enemy. On of them had responded with an obscenity. Within an hour, the Air Force captain had been jerked from his two-man cell and placed in leg stocks in solitary confinement. He had stayed there for eight months.

Some hostile words were exchanged as the truck rolled through the Hanoi streets, but the guards prevented anything else from happening. In a few minutes the truck turned through the massive gate of the Hoa Lo prison, and the prisoners got out into what I recognized as the Heartbreak courtyard.

We were marched into Little Vegas. The wash stalls had been removed from the courtyard and replaced by large water tanks at the end of each cellblock.

The LuLus filed through a new door in the rear of one of the Golden Nugget cells and into another small compound. We were placed in a four-unit cellblock whose door opened out into a small courtyard. We were soon calling our new home the Snake Pit.

Though we had expected very strict confinement now that the bombing had been resumed, the LuLus found they were allowed out in the courtyard together for several hours each day, and were permitted to talk with one another. We quickly established communications by tapping to other prisoners in adjoining cellblocks, and set up a note system for the exchange of information between the Snake Pit and Little Vegas courtyards.

The note-exchange procedure was simple but effective. The trees in the courtyard dropped large green nuts about the size of walnuts. We always collected a few to use in our comm system. We would toss a green nut, scored with an X, over the Golden Nugget into the Vegas Courtyard, where other prisoners from the Plantation were located. If it was tossed right back, it meant no guards were around. We then tossed a note inserted in an empty toothpaste tube over the building. The LuLus had used a similar system for communicating over the courtyard wall when they were handling comm for Colonel Flynn in Camp Unity two years before.

New Year's Day 1973 came and went, and the B-52 raids seemed to intensify during the first week of the new year. Practically every night the POWs could hear the bombs pounding the city.

In the first week of January the LuLus listened to an American POW read propaganda-type news over the speaker system. We had learned to be skeptical of what we heard, but when the voice announced on January 8 that a truce had been agreed upon for the withdrawal of American troops and the exchange of prisoners, we knew it was true. The LuLus joined in the whoops, yelps, cheering, and hollering that came from the cellblocks around them. Confirming the announcement was the fact that the bombing had halted completely on the seventh.

In accordance with the regulations of the truce, the text of the agreement was read word for word over the speakers. The LuLus listened carefully during the portions about prisoner releases for references to POWs captured in Laos. There were none, but we were cheered by the fact that the agreement specified that all prisoners were to be returned.

To clarify the situation, I asked the guard for permission to see the camp commander. When that officer met with us in our little courtyard, he dampened the enthusiasm of the LuLus considerably. "The truce," he said, "does not apply to your group." He told us the LuLus would not be released until there was peace in Laos.

As spokesman for the group, I argued that though we had been captured in Laos, we had always been held in Vietnam. The officer simply shrugged and left the courtyard.

I communicated this disturbing news to Colonel Guy, whom the North Vietnamese had now decided had been captured in South Vietnam rather than Laos. Now being held with the other former Plantation prisoners in Little Vegas, Guy responded that as soon as he was released he would get word to President Nixon about the LuLus.

If that didn't work, he would take the story to the world press. That assurance made the LuLus feel considerably better.

We had reason to be concerned. On the day we had heard the announcement of the truce agreement, my mother received a grim telegram from the State Department: "This confirms," it began, "that Ernest Cary Brace is not on the list of U.S. prisoners in Vietnam provided in Paris January 27, 1973." The families of other LuLus received similar news.

The LuLus got another member, our eighth, on January 17, when an Air Force pilot named Chuck Riess was placed in the cellblock. Captain Riess had punched out of his A-7 after a midair collision over the Plain of Jars in Laos on Christmas Eve.

On February 6 the LuLus got their last two members, two young missionaries captured in Laos a few months before and marched out of the jungles. Lloyd Oppel, a Canadian from Courtney, Vancouver Island, and Sam Mattix, an American from Centralia, Washington, had been captured after an NVA attack on the small village in which they were living. Two of their coworkers, both young women, had been killed.

The pair were never certain what they had done to merit such treatment. They arrived in Hanoi in debilitated condition, Lloyd suffering from malaria, Sam from typhus.

Welcomed into the small cellblock by the LuLus, the pair soon began conducting informal religious services for the LuLus.

There were now ten in the group, and two of the members, Ed Leonard and I, were sleeping on bed boards in the hallway outside the cells, but still locked into the Snake Pit.

On March 1, guards came into the cellblock and abruptly told the LuLus to take all their gear, including their buckets, and prepare to move. There were some tense moments among the LuLus—we feared we were finally being taken to Laos—but we soon found we were being transferred to another section of the prison named, by other prisoners, New Guy Village.

Situated in the northeastern extremity of the prison on the other side of the Heartbreak courtyard area, New Guy had been used as a holding area for many new POWs. Now its buildings were empty, and the LuLus were put into a large barrackslike room containing many bed boards and told to find a place. We later learned we were being taken out of the Vegas area while a group of the ex-Plantation prisoners was being released.

The guards were seldom around now, except to lock us up at night. The LuLus spent long days sitting at a table made of bed boards in the courtyard, talking and playing cards. Not long after the transfer to New Guy, Chuck Riess found that by laying a bed board on its end against a wall in our cellblock, he could climb up the slats and reach the ceiling. Pushing away the ceiling tile, he was able to climb up into the attic area beneath the roof.

He removed a loose piece of tile from the roof, producing a hole through which he could stick his head. From that vantage point he found himself looking down on the Hanoi street that ran along the prison's front wall.

Feeling he had pressed his luck enough for one day, Chuck withdrew his head and replaced the roof tile. His rooftop antics won him the LuLu "Brass Balls" award, bestowed on the member who demonstrated the most audacious behavior daily as the prison discipline relaxed.

When we heard some noises out on the street that sounded like Americans one day, several of us got up into the attic to take a look. In front of the main door, several buses were parked. Some American prisoners wearing civilian clothes filed out of the entrance and began climbing into the buses. One of them paused to look up at the gray walls of the prison he was leaving, and gasped in astonishment at the men in the roof, waving goodbye. He smiled, waved back, then climbed aboard. We ducked before the guards could see us.

After several days in New Guy Village, we were returned to the Snake Pit and found that our treatment seemed to improve with each passing day. Doctors visited us and prescribed medicine for some. The food got better and more plentiful, and the guards gave us free run of the courtyard, appearing only to lock the doors at night.

We were given our first Red Cross packages, which contained novels like *The Godfather* and *Love Story*, as well as combs, razors, shaving cream, vitamin pills, candy, toothpaste, cigars, cigarettes, bouillon cubes. Lipton noodle soup, and instant coffee. With the cigarettes there were matches. Using scrap wood from broken bed boards, we lit a fire almost daily in the courtyard to cook soup in our tin cups. The guards didn't seem to care.

By the middle of March we were back in New Guy Village, where we stayed for about five days and received the most encouraging sign so far that we would be released after all. We were fitted with "going home" clothes: Chinese-made khaki slacks, sport shirts and sweaters, and cheap, Russian-made shoes.

When we returned this time to the Snake Pit, we found that no Americans were left in Vegas. The place was tomblike. The LuLus were put to work cleaning up the Desert Inn, the Stardust, and the Thunderbird. When Jim, Walt, Steve, and I had lived in the Thunderbird back in 1969 and 1970, it had been all two-man cells. Now we saw that those brick-and-mortar walls had been knocked down to make large containment cells. We folded prison clothes that had been left behind and swept out the cellblocks.

In our ramblings around the prison we came across some more cells back near the Snake Pit. Chai Charn Harnavee was in one of them, along with a Thai tank man captured in 1972. The camp commander told me that the Vietnamese were negotiating with Thailand separately, and those men would soon be released also.

We were discouraged that we were the last Americans left in the prison. However, we continued to be treated as if we were soon to be released. Over a seven-day period we were given doses of vitamins C and B.

Finally, in the latter part of March, the camp commander called the ten of us to his office in the Heartbreak area. He announced without ceremony that "due to the lenient policy of the North Vietnamese government, you will not be taken back to Laos to be released, but will be released here."

The group would learn later that President Nixon had stopped the prisoner exchanges and the troop withdrawals because the LuLus were not among the prisoners listed to be released. When North Vietnam reluctantly agreed to release everyone, the exchanges and withdrawals continued.

Our last week at Hoa Lo was the tensest ever. All the LuLus were very nervous, and something had to be done to relieve the tension.

With the prison all to ourselves, we explored other court-yards and spent many hours playing games that were part of the "LuLus' Grand Master Tournament." We played the games to take up the time and to relieve the tension. The LuLu who compiled the most points gained in several types of competition would be the winner.

We played traditional games like chess and checkers, wild card games like "spoons" and "shit on your neighbor," and had stone-pitching contests. Lloyd Oppel was the overall champion and was crowned with a tinfoil coronet.

The LuLus were told on March 27 that they would be leaving the following day. I made my way through a courtyard gate to the cellblock where my Thai friend, Chai Cham Harnavee, was being held. Because the truce protocols did not include repatriation of Thai nationals, Harnavee and his Thai cellmate were not to be released at this time.

I assured my friend that I would do all I could to get him and his cellmate out. I would contact the Thai government as well as go to the U.S. State Department.

Characteristically, Harnavee seemed resigned to his unfortunate circumstances, but not depressed about them. Before we left, Jim and I pushed candy, shaving material, toothpaste, cards, and other items through the peephole to him.

We went back to our own courtyard to find that a sumptuous dinner was to be served the LuLus on our last evening in camp. Seated on tables in the Vegas courtyard where Bedinger and I had communicated so often, the LuLus were served turkey legs, vegetables, fish, and peach wine. A couple of guards ate at the table and refilled the LuLus' tin cups with wine when they were empty.

It seemed a strange and inappropriate way to end nearly eight years of captivity. We slept our last night in the Snake Pit with the cells and even the cellblock doors unlocked.

The next morning, as I hid my prison stripes in a cheap bag they had given us and put on my civilian clothes, one of the guards asked me if we were going to leave the books we received in the Red Cross packages. I said we would. One of the books was *Three Who Made a Revolution*, the story of Lenin, Trotsky, and Stalin. I hoped that one in particular would end up in the guards' hands.

After nearly eight years of captivity, there was no bitterness in me against my captors. They had punished me severely when I had tried to escape in the jungle, but it was punishment I had expected. For every guard who had abused me, there were several who had loaned me needles, taught me Vietnamese words, and given me extra helpings of food. I had felt after leaving Korea that I wouldn't mind living in the Orient someday, and though this had not been what I had in mind, I hadn't changed my views about the Orient.

When it was almost time to leave, Jim and I ran into the next courtyard and said goodbye to Harnavee, shaking the Thai's fingers through the small peephole. It was a very emotional moment, and my eyes welled up with tears.

The LuLus were led through the Golden Nugget, past my old cell, out into the courtyard, and past the Cave, where Jim and I had been placed after being caught communicating almost three years prior.

Then we filed into a receiving room in Heartbreak Courtyard. The camp commander met us with a smile and offered us beer. He chatted with each of the prisoners, asking me, "How long you been prisoner?"

"Seven years, ten months, and seven days."

He scarcely raised an eyebrow. "Oh," he said politely, "that is a very long time."

After the LuLus scowled into Vietnamese press photographers' cameras to deny our captors this one last piece of propaganda, we were taken out a small door in the large iron-strapped door of the Hoa Lo prison and placed on a bus. A crowd of Vietnamese watched from across the street.

The bus took us through the downtown area, then across a steel girder bridge so badly bombed that there was only one lane of traffic. On the other side of the river, we passed through a heavy-industry area that had been practically obliterated by the B-52s. I saw railroad cars on their sides, twisted track, and flattened warehouses. I thought, if only some President had had the courage to do this type of bombing back when it all began, how many lives on both sides would have been saved in the long run.

As we moved through bumper-to-bumper traffic to the airport, people on the street recognized us as POWs and yelled insults. I looked back without expression.

At Gia Lom Airport, we saw the tall tail of a U.S. Air Force C-141 jet transport rising behind the control tower. It was the most beautiful sight I had seen in years.

Television newsmen, who appeared to be French, clamored to get near us as we got off the bus, and the cameras were whirring when a soldier came running out of the terminal and

signaled the guards that the POWs were not to get off. The few
LuLus on the ground were pushed back up the steps, and the bus
drove off without explanation. It turned onto a side road and parked.

Most of us weren't alarmed, but the atmosphere was tense.
Then a motorcycle arrived, and the rider motioned the bus back
to the airport. This time we were ushered into the airport terminal,
which was jammed with spectators, and seated in a row of folding
chairs. In full view was the silver-and-white C-141. Nearby, an
American Air Force lieutenant colonel turned to us prisoners, nodded
and smiled, and turned back to the papers he was signing.

Colonel Robson had questioned Vietnam's original release
document presented to him for signing; it stated that all POWs in
Laos were now being released. The word all was unacceptable. So
while the LuLus waited in the bus, Colonel Robson negotiated the
release based only on the nine Americans and one Canadian included
in the present release.

After signing the release papers, Lieutenant Colonel Robson
walked over and asked the men to rise and follow him. When we
had left our captors behind and were with our U.S. Air Force escorts
together on the flight ramp, he turned to us and said, "Gentle-
men, you are now free men."

32

A flight-suited Air Force crewman with a southern accent met me a few steps out of the terminal and took my elbow and escorted me toward the plane. The C-141 was enormous. I had never seen such a large aircraft. Later I was given a photo of the LuLus leaving the terminal at Gia Lom Airport. It had been taken with a concealed automatic camera aboard the C-141. The pilot had lined the camera up with the terminal entrance by sighting past a spot on his side window before shutdown. The same camera proved invaluable in identifying various guards and camp officials.

As we went aboard, we were greeted by Lloyd Oppel and a representative of the Canadian government, who would be riding to Clark Air Force Base with us. "What took you guys so long?" Lloyd asked with a smile.

Flight nurses met us at the door, placed us in the airliner-type seats of the aircraft, and helped us buckle our seatbelts. Soon the big jet rolled out onto the runway, gained speed, and climbed into the air. We pressed our faces to the windows to try to get a look at the Hoa Lo prison and the Plantation, but there was too much cloud cover and haze. In a few minutes the pilots sent back word through the nurses that we had passed Haiphong and were now over the South China Sea.

Shortly after we passed Haiphong, the aircraft's radio operator brought back a message from an American aircraft carrier below us.

"Welcome back, Lieutenant Bedinger!" it said. Jim was the only Navy man aboard this flight.

We landed at Clark Field near Manila three hours later, and taxied up to a terminal area crowded with cheering people and festooned with signs saying "Welcome Home." As I left the plane, a pretty flight nurse named Sandy pressed her Air Force wings into my hand.

I followed Walt Stischer out the door and down the steps, where a line of senior ranking officers from every military branch waited to greet us. As a civilian, I wasn't required to salute as Stischer had, but I snapped a salute anyway, and the surprised colonel at the head of the line returned it. We were driven by bus, along roads lined with cheering people, to the base hospital.

On arrival at the hospital, the ever-efficient Air Force tried to place me in a ward away from the military. Only after Walt Stischer and Jim Bedinger protested vigorously did they agree to put me in a four-man room with them and Steve Long. I had lived with these men for almost four years, and now the military was trying to separate us. Reality that I was a civilian struck hard. Always a Marine?

It was at the hospital that I was greeted by Bill Mashburn, a representative of the Agency for International Development, who was to be my escort to the United States. During our first moment of privacy, Mashburn told me that he would have the overseas operator set up a call to someone in my family, but he said, "I think you should know that your wife remarried."

As much as I had tried to prepare myself mentally for that blow, it still hurt. That night I spoke to my son Ernest, now eighteen, who confirmed the news and added the information that his mother's new husband had been killed in an accident a few years after the marriage. A real surprise was that the boys now had a half-sister, born of Patricia's marriage while I was in the prison camps. He also let me know that Patricia was now living with a screenwriter in New York.

I wasn't the only LuLu to get this kind of news. Steve Long's wife let him know right away that they wouldn't be getting back together, either. The day was too important to us to let anything mar it, but this was hard to take.

After the call, I went up to the solarium, where I thought I would be alone. Steve was there, and he told me about what his wife had said to him. Through all the years of harassment, the leg irons, the beatings with bamboo rods, the rope burns, and the efforts they had made to demoralize us, neither of us could remember crying. Steve and I cried in front of each other in that quiet room.

Later that evening we helped Jim Bedinger celebrate his birthday in the cafeteria. The most popular meal for the returned prisoners was steak and eggs with lots of home-fried potatoes. I had a lot of thinking to do about my future, but I didn't feel like doing it quite so soon. Jim's birthday couldn't have come at a better time. I welcomed the chance to take my mind off my problems.

During the next three days in the Clark Air Force Base hospital, I was given a full medical examination. Of most importance, overnight they made a temporary bridge to fill in my missing teeth in front. A haircut and new clothing, which was now size medium rather than the large I had worn when I was captured, completed my transition back to civilian. I had weighed almost two hundred pounds when captured. I was now 145 pounds.

The military men all got new uniforms. I was fitted with a polyester civilian suit. I didn't even know what polyester was.

We all went as a group to the post exchange to purchase replacements of items we lost when captured. I found that the Rolex GMT watch the Pathet Lao had taken at Moung Sai in 1965 now cost three hundred dollars, triple the price I had paid for it. Mashburn, my escort, was apologetic, but said the U.S. government would reimburse me for no more than the original price. I bought a one-hundred-dollar watch.

The next day, after well-wishers in the crowd had placed leis around our necks, the LuLus got aboard another C-141 and began the last two legs of the journey home. A six-hour flight to Hawaii got us to Hickam Air Force Base in the middle of the night. I was surprised that the senior officers on the island were there to greet us. They visited with the group in a reception room, where hostesses offered soft drinks and hors d'oeuvres.

In the morning, when we arrived at Travis Air Force Base, near San Francisco, the news media were waiting. Having learned that I was the longest-serving civilian prisoner and that I had been buried in a hole after an escape attempt, television reporters asked me if it was true that I had been tortured.

"No," I replied. "A lot of the military were, but I was punished."

At Travis the LuLus were to head their separate ways, and soon I was saying goodbye to the closest friends I had in the world. I would probably never again know anyone better than I had gotten to know the other LuLus. I was glad that the closest friend of them all, Jim Bedinger, would be flying with me to San Diego, where we were to meet our families.

When I got off the Navy DC-9 at the Miramar Naval Air Station, I was greeted by a crisp salute and then a hug from a six-foot-four, two-hundred-pound Marine private who I could scarcely believe was my son, Ernest. He had been eleven when I had left

Chieng Mai so many years before. My mother and my sisters, Rose and Betty, were also in San Diego to meet me.

Patricia and the other three boys were waiting in the entrance of Balboa Naval Hospital. Tanned and trim, she looked as lovely as ever, and the boys were hardly boys anymore, but young men. Even little Cary, who had been three when I was captured, was now an eleven-year-old sixth-grader.

Because of the check-in activities at the Naval Hospital, Patricia and the boys only stayed a few minutes. It would have been hard to talk in front of the children, anyway.

The next day Patricia confirmed what I already knew, that she wasn't coming back. She was willing to let me have the boys if they would prefer to be with their father, but she hoped I would understand that she had raised them while I was gone, and that the ties were strong.

She told me little about her and our sons' lives while I was a prisoner, about the man she had married, the daughter that had been born, or the man with whom she now lived. I knew her too well to press for answers.

When she had greeted me at the hospital door, Patricia had told me, "I'm glad you're alive," and I didn't doubt it. There was no bitterness in me over her failure to wait for me; it had occurred to me even in the cages that it was expecting too much of her, given our relationship and her temperament. I was disappointed that she had nothing left of the $1,300 monthly payments she had received year after year from the U.S. Government under the War Hazards Act.

But what I could not understand was Patricia's apparent failure to make it clear to the boys that their father was alive, after she had been so advised. In 1967 she had received State Department notification that I had been identified by the Pathet Lao as one of the "bandit-rangers" being held by "Lao patriotic forces."

In late 1969, Douglas Hegdahl's information that I was alive and well in Hanoi had been relayed to her. None of this information had been passed on to the boys, according to them. My mother and sisters seemed to think she had encouraged the boys to believe me dead. These were not the kind of questions I wanted to pursue immediately.

My doctor, Navy Captain George V. Frankhouser, conducted an extensive diagnostic evaluation and concluded that my survival, from a medical perspective, was "an absolute astonishment." In his single-spaced, four-page official medical report, the doctor ticked off the ailments that I had survived during my POW tenure: insect, rat, and leech bites, chronic boils, malaria, acute diarrhea, ringworm, cervical strain from the neck rope, prolonged thigh and buttock strains, chronic weight loss, loss of bowel control, hairline facial fracture, severe swelling of feet, ankles, and hands. And, after the period in the hole, total body edema, blood in the urine, fat globules in the urine, loss of toenails, recurring nausea, skin pustules, hallucination, and prolonged disorientation.

Though I was allowed to move out of the hospital after three months, I remained an outpatient for the next nine months, bringing my total hospitalization time to a year. Besides the diagnostic evaluations, I underwent months of extensive oral surgery to correct dental problems stemming from my captivity, major anal surgery, a long and unpleasant treatment for intestinal disease, surgery for a bone spur in my nose, operations to remove large cysts from my hips, stomach, and back, and treatment for malaria.

There were other problems that the doctors could not do much about. Nerve-conduction studies of the lower part of my body confirmed what I already knew, I had permanently lost some of the feeling in my legs and feet. The doctor's whack on my knees produced no reflexive reaction. The scars from the insect and animal bites, and from the ropes, would, of course, be with me forever.

The scars inside, especially those from the revelation that my wife had remarried, were permanent too, but I was living with them. According to Frankhouser's report, "Psychiatric evaluation revealed the patient to be upset over his demolished family situation, but with psychiatric assistance he adjusted to this disappointment quite rapidly and became psychologically normal."

A pert, blue-eyed, beautiful young woman with short hair and a fresh Scandinavian look about her had much to do with my psychological recovery. A few days after Patricia Brace walked out of my life, Nancy Rusth walked in.

A consulting nurse for an industrial insurance company, she visited me in my hospital room to discuss my eligibility for receiving workmen's compensation payments. When she gave me her office phone number, I grabbed the opportunity to get her home phone also. A few weeks later I called to ask her if she would be willing to drive me around San Diego. She was, and soon we were dating regularly. I discovered she was a native of Klamath Falls, Oregon. She had moved from Portland to California after a divorce. She was eleven years younger than I, but the chemistry was right.

In May of the year of our return, I joined the other former POWs at a reception in our honor at the White House. Whatever President Nixon's involvement in the Watergate scandal may have been, I would be forever in the President's debt for having stopped the prisoner exchange at some political risk in an effort to assure the LuLus' release. When I met the President, I told him so, and he responded warmly.

The most exciting part of the occasion was seeing and speaking for the first time with dozens of POWs with whom I had only communicated by tapping or notes hidden in waste buckets or wash drains. There, in newly tailored uniforms, were Jim Stockdale, now an admiral, Colonel Ted Guy, and Colonel John Flynn. There, too, was Marine Sergeant Anzaldua, whom I had known only as Lobo at the Plantation.

Across the room I saw a slender, white-haired Navy commander whom I had seen just enough to recognize over the years at Hanoi. I made my way over to greet John McCain, the man with whom I had communicated through a wall for more than a year without seeing his face. As I shook John's hand, the memories came rushing back, and tears with them.

Strange that I wouldn't cry in front of the enemy, but now I couldn't contain my tears in front of friends.

I had not been back in Balboa Naval Hospital long before I got a letter from Terry Burke, the American adviser at Boum Lao whom I had assumed was dead. Terry was now an agent for the Drug Enforcement Agency and was stationed in Kabul, Afghanistan. He explained how he had escaped from the airstrip following the early-morning attack on the day of my capture, and how he had participated in the air searches for me and Harnavee. Remembering the beer I had promised to bring that day, Terry vowed that the two of us would "kill that case yet."

"I hope you're recovering fast and I'm sure you will," Terry wrote. "I always thought that you were a tough old bastard and I'm really glad you got a chance to prove it to everybody."

The rest of 1973 was a year of rest and recuperation, of medical treatment, intelligence debriefings, and adjustment to a 1970s lifestyle considerably different from the one I had left behind.

Though still an outpatient, I moved into a house on the beach with my three boys, and started to get to know them again. My relationship with Nancy grew and deepened.

In prison one does not worry about what clothes to put on, what to have for dinner, or any of the other day-to-day concerns of the average person. Now I was out, and each day contained a new series of decisions to be made.

One of my first concerns was to get a divorce from Patricia so I could marry Nancy—Patricia had remarried without divorcing me. Regardless of the newly accepted practice of unmarried people living together, I couldn't bring myself, or expect Nancy, to live in that fashion.

While in Arizona visiting my mother, I met a state senator who was also an attorney. During a discussion, when I mentioned my problem in getting a divorce, he asked where my residence of record was. I hadn't established California residence on my return, and my permanent forwarding address had always been my mother's home in Arizona. After a meeting with a county judge, it was decided I could get a divorce in Arizona with no problems. So I did.

By early 1974 the period of greatest adjustment was over. This would be a year of new beginnings.

With Jim Bedinger as my best man, and Admiral Jim Stockdale in attendance, Nancy and I were married on February 23 in the chapel of the hospital where we met.

Not long before, I had accepted a position as an executive with Evergreen Helicopters, an international air carrier operation based in McMinnville, Oregon. I would be taking Nancy back to her home state.

When I was discharged from Balboa Naval Hospital on February 28, 1974, I had a new wife, custody of my boys, and a new job.

Later in the year came the official removal of the stigma that had followed me from Quantico to Hanoi and back. Ironically, it seemed, the stigma had encouraged me to endure the worst my captors could deliver and come home with honor.

Citing my behavior in the prison camps, President Gerald Ford granted me full and unconditional pardon for my Marine court-martial conviction, and I received an honorable discharge. It was quietly done, unlike my ouster from the Marines, which had led to trumpeting headlines about the war hero tossed out of the Corps. But for me, the return of my self-respect was a triumph.

33

Seated on a platform facing the administration building of the Naval War College in Newport, Rhode Island, I looked out over the rows of senior naval and Marine officers who constituted the June 1978 graduating class. Had I remained in the Marines, I might be out there with them. I would be wearing a set of colonel's eagles on my collar and waiting to hear the remarks of the Secretary of the Navy and the congressmen who were among the official party. Then again, I might have died in Vietnam, as many of my peers had. The wind was sweeping away clouds that had earlier threatened rain. The day would be beautiful.

It was hard to believe that more than five years had passed since my return, yet Nancy and I had celebrated our fourth wedding anniversary only a few months before. It was reassuring to see her seated in the audience. In the special section for guests, Navy Captain George Frankhouser, my doctor from Balboa Naval Hospital, along with his wife, Judy, sat next to Nancy. The Frankhousers had become close special friends.

Much had happened in the intervening years. Sergeant Harnavee had finally been released in September 1974, more than a year after the last American POW. I learned after my own release that the Thai had made many American friends in the Hanoi prison system, where he delivered messages at extreme risk to himself. Like me, those former POWs had done what they could to get Harnavee released. When he was finally freed after more than nine years of captivity, he was commissioned as a major in the Thailand Special Forces.

Colonel Ted Guy had preferred charges against the eight members of the Peace Clowns from the Plantation, alleging that they had aided the enemy, had been disrespectful and disobedient to superior officers, and had conspired against their fellow prisoners. After one of the defendants died, the charges against the remaining seven were dropped by the Secretary of the Army.

"J.R.," Ed Leonard, a member of the LuLus, claimed an improper investigation had been conducted. He filed mutiny charges against the group. Those charges were dropped also. The members of the Peace Clowns were honorably discharged.

Jim Stockdale, as senior Navy returnee, filed charges against my old Marine friend, Ed Miller, and Navy Captain Gene Wilbur, claiming mutiny, aiding the enemy, conspiracy, soliciting other prisoners to violate the Code of Conduct, and attempting to cause insubordination and disloyalty. Though the Secretary of the Navy found merit in Stockdale's charges, he dismissed them because he thought a court-martial would disrupt the lives of the recently returned POWs and their families. The two men received letters of censure and were honorably retired from the service.

My old communications partner and first cellmate, Jim Bedinger, was now a lieutenant commander stationed in the Pentagon. He had been awarded the Bronze Star for his conduct in prison. Jim Stockdale, a commander at the time he was captured, was now a vice-admiral, and had been awarded the Congressional Medal of Honor for his performance as a POW.

While all this was happening, I had been quietly going about my work as an executive for Evergreen Helicopters. After a few years in the marketing division at McMinnville, Oregon, I was made president of a subsidiary company involving helicopter and fixed-wing operations, with headquarters in Missoula, Montana.

In that unlikely place, I visited with Vang Pao, the leader of the Hmong who had escaped Laos when it fell to the Pathet Lao in late 1975. He had resettled in the mountains of western Montana. The last time we had seen each other was on the airstrip in Long Tieng, when the guerrilla general had come out to inspect a broken tail wheel on my aircraft. Now the leader of the Secret Army of Laos was a farmer in the Bitterroot Valley. He told me the mountains reminded him of his home, where he and I had met more than a decade before.

I had returned to McMinnville to become vice-president for operations when I received the news that had brought Nancy and me to Newport.

I was to receive the Department of Defense's highest civilian award, the Medal for Distinguished Service, for my performance as a prisoner of war. Vice-Admiral Stockdale, now president of the Naval War College, had initiated the award, but the documentation had come from every part of the American military establishment. "In a society of heroes that survived the imprisonment in Southeast Asia," one letter said, "Mr. Brace was a legend."

My fellow prisoners wrote about my communication ability, my leadership, my example, and my guts; about how I had followed the Code of Conduct "to the letter" even though I was a civilian; and about how I had been "functionally a U.S. military officer of the highest caliber."

Stockdale, perhaps the most revered American POW of the war, said, "Ernie Brace is one of my own heroes."

The award ceremony was brief. Admiral Stockdale read the citation from the Secretary of Defense, Harold Brown, and pinned the medal on the lapel of my civilian suit. My thoughts went back to the grim day in 1961 when I had told myself to stand tall as I was dismissed from the Marines. I had been steadier on my feet then than my nerve-damaged legs permitted me to be now. And there was, of course, another major difference. Today, the officers looking up at me were on their feet, cheering in a standing ovation.

To

Ernest C. Brace

for distinguished public service while a Prisoner of War during nearly an eight-year period from 21 May 1965 to 28 March 1973. Employed as a civilian contract pilot in support of our Government's objectives in Southeast Asia, Mr. Brace escaped from his communist captors a total of three times prior to September 1966. After each escape, the rigors of his confinement were increased. In October 1968 he was taken to the citadel prison in Hanoi in such poor physical condition that he was unable to walk. There he lived in isolation as a high risk prisoner, eventually establishing clandestine communication with the American leadership in that prison. Although a civilian and not technically bound by the Military Code of Conduct, by his own aggressive example he was a continual force for the strengthening of the Americans' adherence to that Code. Despite the atmosphere of enemy harassment and brutal treatment, he continued to establish and maintain communications through many unusual and ingenious methods, which resulted in American and Allied prisoners presenting a posture of increased resistance to the enemy's wishes and at the same time improving prisoner morale. His ceaseless efforts in the extremely adverse conditions of the communist prisons of Southeast Asia demonstrated his professional competence, unwaivering devotion and loyalty to his country. Despite the harsh treatment throughout his long years of incarceration Mr. Brace's patriotism, determination and faith in his country are a tribute to the principles that made our Nation great and are worthy of the highest praise and recognition. I take great pleasure in awarding Mr. Ernest C. Brace the Department of Defense Medal for Distinguished Public Service.

Harold Brown
Secretary of Defense

February 15, 1978

Afterword

More than twenty years have passed since I started this book. Without the help of Charlie Hood, at that time Professor of Journalism at the University of Montana (and later the dean of the department), I might never have written more than a few short pieces based on my experiences. I met Charlie after seeing an article he had done in the local paper on General Vang Pao's new life in the Missoula, Montana, area.

People's lives seem to me to be predestined to travel certain paths. My life hasn't deviated all that much from what it might have been had I remained in the Marine Corps.

With Evergreen International, as Vice-President of Operations, I became involved in setting up an offshore oil operation for the Shell Company in 1974. The operation was based in Saigon and required my making multiple trips back to Vietnam that year.

While in Saigon I was also buying surplus Air America aircraft from their operations out of Tan San Nhut Airport and arranging for them to be ferried to Africa. Evergreen had acquired a contract for a United Nations World Health Organization insect-control operation in Upper Volta.

In 1976, I negotiated a contract for Evergreen to provide helicopter spray systems, pilots, and maintenance personnel to support the U.S. State Department's International Narcotics Control Program in Mexico. Many of the people I had worked with in Asia in the early sixties were now involved in narcotics control.

In 1978, the National Organization to Repeal Marijuana Laws, NORML, shut down our Mexican operation by getting an injunction against the State Department for endangering the lives of Americans. We were putting an herbicide, Paraquat 2-4-5T, on marijuana that was making its way into the States.

I left Evergreen in 1978 to take a better offer from Sikorsky Aircraft. In a marketing role for Sikorsky I found myself visiting the same old haunts throughout Southeast Asia. It was while doing a demonstration of the new Sikorsky H-76 gunship at Lopburi, Thailand, in 1983 that I once again met with Chai Cham Harnavee.

I had last seen him in the cellblock next to the Snake Pit in Hoa Lo prison on March 28, 1973, the day of the LuLus' release. It was a very emotional encounter.

In 1983 I visited the People's Republic of China for the first time. The U.S. Government had agreed that Sikorsky could sell to the Chinese a civilian version of the new UH60 Black Hawk U.S. Army utility helicopter, the Sikorsky S70C.

Over a period of eighteen months a contract was negotiated, and I was selected to remain in China as the Program Manager. The People's Liberation Army Air Force, PLAAF, was to operate and maintain the Sikorsky S70s. It was an odd feeling to be working with those guys who wore red stars on their caps.

Nancy and I lived most of our two-year tour in the People's Republic of China in one room at the Beijing Hotel near Tiananmen Square in Beijing. Those two years confirmed my belief that people are essentially the same the world over. Nancy taught English to doctors and nurses three days a week. I worked with my Chinese counterpart, the PLAAF Operations Manager, to deliver and introduce the Sikorsky S70 helicopters into the Chinese military.

Although I worked sporadically on the book while in China, the finishing touches were put on this manuscript after our return to the United States in the summer of 1986. With a new word processor on hand, Nancy typed all the old notes in, and I did the final editing.

Since finishing *A Code to Keep* in 1987 (it was originally published by St. Martins Press in 1988), many years have passed and my wife Nancy and I have had many new adventures.

In 1987 and early 1988 I assisted the Icelandic Coast Guard in their use of helicopters on small ships. When Israel tried to configure their CH-53D Sikorsky helicopters with long-range in-flight refueling capability, I was sent there to investigate.

In September 1988, Nancy and I returned to Beijing. The request for my return was made through General Alexander Haig during a reception for a visiting Chinese military staff at General Haig's home in Arlington, Virginia. Nancy and I left a large comfortable home in Connecticut to live in a small two-room suite in the Jianguo Hotel on Chang An boulevard in Beijing. We were about two miles east of Tiananmen Square.

From our balcony facing Chang An boulevard we watched as the riots and demonstrations built up over the month of May.

The Communist Central Committee's actions on the weekend of June 3-4, 1989, effectively ended our stay in China. Nancy and I watched the tracer bullets arcing over Tiananmen Square as tanks rolled by just below our balcony. We left with some difficulty the next Tuesday on a Thai Air flight to Bangkok.

Sikorsky told me to take some home leave so we went to Klamath Falls, Oregon to stay with Nancy's mother for a few weeks. Our home in Connecticut was leased for the next year.

While in Klamath Falls I was told that there was to be a reduction in middle management at Sikorsky and it was possible my position was to be eliminated. I flew to Connecticut and interviewed with a new Vice-President of Marketing, but the best I could get was a "golden handshake" retirement and a consulting contract to carry us over the next eighteen months. I retired from Sikorsky Aircraft in September 1989.

As a consultant for Sikorsky, I returned to China several times over the next months. Most of my efforts during that time were focused on explaining how the Tiananmen Massacre had affected business relationships for all of us. President Bush had cut off any military assistance to China and we could no longer offer product support. Before long, Nancy arranged to have the personal effects we had left behind shipped home to the States.

In December 1989 I joined an Evergreen International Aviation group on a business tour of Russia. Subsequent trips and negotiations resulted in several joint ventures being formed to provide landing rights, fuel contracts, and overflight rights for Evergreen's 747 freighters. I was designated as the American Director of these ventures and spent the next four years traveling to and from Russia from our home in Klamath Falls, Oregon. Some of our activities were to provide aircraft and crews for United Nations peace-keeping missions. I flew as an observer in a Mil-26 helicopter with a Russian crew to erect a power line transmission tower felled by guerillas on Mount Erlbus near Chechnya. I managed to get into Vladivostok and take pictures of the Naval Base before the city was open to foreigners. When Milhail Gorbechev visited the United States after Yeltsin took over, I accompanied him on his trip.

In March 1991, I was in Germany about to go to Russia when I received word to proceed to Dubai and obtain the first available transport into Kuwait City. My role was to establish contact with the U.S. military for support and housing of the soon-to-arrive helicopters and crews being sent to support the firefighters. Evergreen's Gulfstream jet picked me up in Dubai and I was at airport in Kuwait City two days after the cease-fire had been enacted. The sky was black with smoke from burning oil wells, inert bombs were being detonated, arms and ammunition lay strewn along the roads, and my teammate and I had no food or water except what we could beg from the scattered U.S. military units arriving. I stayed in Kuwait almost three weeks until a routine was established and I was eventually relieved by an Evergreen operations manager.

Russia continued to occupy most of my time until I finally felt it had been enough and quit my consulting role with Evergreen on December 31, 1993. Since then I have been fully retired and living in Klamath Falls where I have been working on a compilation of short stories covering my activities after Vietnam, some of which have been published as stand-alone articles in military trade magazines. Other than the occasional writing endeavor, much of my time is taken with speaking engagements and work on behalf of veterans within the community.

Ernest C. Brace

Klamath Falls, Oregon

August 2001

In 1993 when M. Gorbachev and his wife Raisa visited the U.S., I was asked to accompany them on a trip from Washington D.C. to San Francisco.

Welcome to
Hellgate Press

The Parrot's Beak
U.S. Operations in Cambodia
by Paul B. Morgan   ISBN: 1-55571-543-5
200 pages, Paperback: $14.95

By the author of *K-9 Soldiers: Vietnam and After,* Morgan's latest book divulges secret insertion techniques and information about Nixon's secret war that the government still refuses to acknowledge

How It Was
A Vietnam Story
by John Patrick O'Hara   ISBN: 1-55571-516-8
125 pages, Paperback: $12.95

How it Was is not a blow-by-blow record, but a shoebox of memories presented as they flashed inside the mind of a Vet trying to come to terms with what he had seen and done during his tour. It is a non-traditional, thought-provoking journey into a war-torn mind.

Honor & Sacrifice
The Montagnards of Ba Cat, Vietnam
by Anthony J. Blondell   ISBN: 1-55571-533-8
250 pages, Hardcover: $21.95

Special Forces (Green Beret) A-Team member, Anthony Blondell, tells an action-packed story of the exploitation of the Montagnards, and what happens when the South Vietnamese government not only backs out of a nearly completed, $5,000-per-day Special Forces mission, but tries to sabotage it to keep from paying.

1-800-228-2275   VISIT YOUR FAVORITE BOOKSTORE
OR ORDER DIRECT
Hellgate Press, P.O. Box 3727, Central Point, OR 97502

Coast Guard Action in Vietnam

Stories of Those Who Served

by Paul Scotti   ISBN: 1-55571-528-1

250 pages, Paperback: $17.95

Written by the author of *Seaports: Ships, Piers, and People* and *Police Divers,* this well-crafted lively and engaging history will rejuvenate one's pride in the American miliary with its little-known details of the Coast Guard's involvement in Vietnam. The fact that they were in Vietnam at all is a surprise to many. What they were doing there will be an even bigger surprise!

Regret to Inform You

Experiences of Families Who Lost A Family Member in Vietnam

by Norman Berg   ISBN: 1-55571-509-5

168 pages, Paperback: $16.95

How do you cope with the knowledge that a loved one is missing in action, remains not recovered? Thirty years later, real people still wait for the war in Vietnam to end—to know what happened to their loved ones. *Regret to Inform You* is a moving glimpse at the human strength and persistence it takes to survive the maze of government bureaucracy, miscommunication, and inconclusive evidence. Eight families relate their stories as only they can.

Rockets Like Rain

A Year in Vietnam

Dale Reich   ISBN: 1-55571-615-6

185 pages, Paperback, $15.95

Ten men from the little town of Oconomowoc, Wisconsin were killed in the Vietnam War; Dale Reich survived. He wants his hometown heroes and the war that took them to be remembered. This is the story of his year as an American infantryman in Vietnam—365 unforgettable days that took Dale 30 years to finally write about.